Throughout the entirety
interactions between huma
persistent legends are tales of Vikings gods. Expert seafarers, for centuries the Vikings dominated the northern seas and spread their narratives of beings that possessed extraordinary capabilities. Not bound by land or sea, sometimes they flew, either in craft or into battle as fierce female Valkyries on winged steeds did ride.

To simply write these wonderous and multifarious stories off as Norse mythology would be a disservice. Here, a most unique researcher, David Lovegrove, has emerged to illuminate long forgotten sagas that titillate the imagination. Who would have thought it would be an Aussie with arcane linguistic skills and who can read the Old Norse manuscripts in their original form who would update the world. But here you are, and this is the first in a series of books that will explore and bring to life Norse history as it once flourished.

Dr (Col) John B Alexander, Ph.D, Pioneering high-level US government paranormal researcher and author

Lovegrove's 'Viking Superpowers' brilliantly reinterprets Norse mythology through a paleocontact lens, revealing the Aesir 'gods' as advanced technological beings rather than supernatural deities. His analysis of artifacts like the Völund flying brooch - seemingly depicting an ancient jet-propulsion wingsuit - transforms our understanding of these ancient tales in ways that will resonate with anyone interested in the intersection of mythology and unexplained phenomena. By reviving his knowledge of Old Norse and meticulously retranslating original Icelandic texts, Lovegrove uncovers hidden technological meanings that conventional translations have obscured for centuries.

Michael Strange, Troubled Minds Radio (Las Vegas)

I've just finished reading 'Viking Superpowers' and David has managed to guide the reader from knowing very little about these things into a place where they must surely at least see it is possible for huge ships to be orbiting Earth and travelling beneath the waves, in the Edda's. Even the most diehard debunkers will have trouble getting around that.

I really look forward to the next instalment from David on the psi abilities they talk of, some of which I seem to have access to myself, though mostly uncontrolled and weaker than the Aesir, like a watered-down version, suggesting a genetic basis for them.

Ed William, author 'Over the Horizon: A Sailors Voyage Into The Unknown.

VIKING SUPERPOWERS WAY OF ASGARD

Do the Viking Myths Contain Suppressed Ancestral Memories of Ancient High Technology, and Powerful Spacefaring Humanoids Who Colonised the North of the World?

David Lovegrove

Barswin Books

Barswin Books

First published by Barswin Books, 2025

ISBN: 978-1-7640918-1-7

Dedication

Dedicated to my father, Neville, who taught me the old 'warriors way' and encouraged me to write about the Vikings, and to my mother, Freya, who loved hearing stories from the sagas, was very proud of our Norse - Scots ancestry, and loved me reading the sagas to her in Icelandic.

Acknowledgements

I have a lot of wonderful people to thank for helping me research and bring this book to print. Firstly, huge thanks to my wonderful wife Lizzy and my children Geordie, Rose, Declan and Terry, for encouraging me, helping me in many, many ways, and putting up with my enthusiastic raves about Vikings, flying saucers and ancient astronauts over the years, as well as tolerating my listening to Icelandic language saga audiobooks on long drives! I truly couldn't have done it without you guys.

I take my hat off to venerable author and visionary Erich Von Däniken, wishing him a very happy 90th birthday, and many more to come, you have greatly influenced my thinking since the early '70s mate!

Another '70's legend I must acknowledge is dear Mrs. Dodgson, the Head Librarian at Indooroopilly State High School, thanks for buying so many wonderful Viking Age books for the library to feed my passion. You lit a fire that is still burning bright!

Cheers to my friend, the brilliant Paul Wallis, author of the bestselling Eden series, firstly for doing me the honour of writing such a terrific foreword to my book, and secondly for his profound thinking, encouragement and generous help setting me on the path that saw this book become a reality. Collaborating with you through the intersections of our research, especially on The Eden Enigma, has not only been great fun, but has greatly informed my research for Viking Superpowers.

I would also like to thank Anthony Barrett, Paul's business partner, the creative genius behind The 5th Kind TV, for his great encouragement, and technical advice regarding video creation. Very much appreciated, mate!

My gratitude also to the marvellous Mauro Biglino, Italian author and world class Ancient Hebrew expert, whose Biblical retranslation work, and deep re-examination of the texts, greatly inspires me! Your recent answers to my questions, (through the 5th Kind), led me to some fascinating breakthroughs!

Thanks also to legendary researcher, author and explorer of the paranormal and the unusual, Col. (Dr) John B Alexander, for convincing me that my own paranormal experiences were indeed normal, and for setting me on the hunt for the paranormal in the ancient Nordic stories. It is an honour to call you a friend John!

My very warmest regards to amazing fellow Australian author and close contact experiencer Jane Pooley (Humalien Too), your friendship means a great deal to me and your brave testimony of your lifetime of contact experiences has changed the way I see everything. Chatting to you always leaves me feeling great and seeing my own experiences in a clearer light. Amongst other things, I am deeply in your debt for introducing me to Paul! Cheers dear lady!

In the study of the fascinating and challenging subject of Old Norse Language and literature, and the paranormal within it, my heartfelt thanks goes to Professor Ármann Jakobsson of the Háskoli Íslands (the University of Iceland), who has so generously given of his time and deep knowledge, in email exchanges over the last few years, and over our very pleasant lunch in Reykjavik last year. Your scholarship and encouragement means the world to me.

I must not forget to mention Professor Guðvarður Már Gunnlaugsson, Head of Research at the Árni Magnússon Institute. I will never forget your kindness in personally showing me those beautiful, priceless ancient manuscripts, Snorra Edda and the collection of Family Sagas. That will always be one of the most treasured experiences of my life.

My good friend, Swedish commando Asgeir, treated me like a brother in Sweden, generously looking after me, and driving me a long way to see the most incredible Viking 'gods'/paleocontact places he had discovered, all of which have ended up playing significant parts in this book. I secretly suspect that he might well be the god Thor, come to help out an old traveller. Skål min bror!

Then there's my Norwegian Viking mate, Johnny, who showed me all over the great recreated drakkar ship, the Saga Oseberg, drove me to see Midgard, the new Gokstad ship project, and the original great Oseberg Queen's mound. Cheers for your kindness and enthusiasm brother!

Also cheers to Tore Forsberg, Master Viking ship craftsman for 50 years, who went out of his way to introduce me to the crew of the Saga Oseberg in Norway, your dedication and awesome artistic skill greatly inspire me!

Thanks to talented young medieval bagpiper Aidrian Bausl, and his supportive Dad and Mum, who added greatly to the special Viking Age atmosphere at Roskilde Viking Ship Museum, Denmark.

And then there's my friend Robert Kvilhaug from Oslo, who never fails to point out valuable new Viking information to me, you are greatly valued mate.

A huge thanks to my Icelandic friends, especially to my dear penpal of 46 years, Guðrún, who treated me like family, put me up at her lovely family farm, and took me everywhere saga related and more, Þakk fyrir systír mín!

Very special thanks to Guðrún´s friend Inga, grand Icelandic lady, for the Icelandic conversations and your delicious grilled trout lunches and apple deserts!

And to Rúnabrúna, Gunnar and family for their great generosity, allowing me to stay in your beautiful sea-side home, for great saga and artistic conversations, and for giving me the chance to spend time with your lovely, cultured Mum and Dad.

Cheers to the magical poet priest Pétur, thanks for your hospitality mate, and to the big fella, Icelandic Viking Sigursteinn Snorrason for one of the best conversations I had on my trip. Also, to the Icelandic Viking and actor, Mikael Hannes Zontag, for another great conversation, and for the wonderful book sent by the Aesir (I really think so!).

A big shout out to my English mate, author Ed William, for his constant friendship and encouragement, and for including me in his riveting new book, 'Over the Horizon: A Sailors Voyage into the Unknown'. Your stories, very creative ways of thinking and enthusiasm really sparks me up mate!

Of course, I can't forget my new friends in the UFO, paranormal and spirituality podcasting scene who have so kindly invited me onto their very popular shows - Mike Strange from Troubled Minds Radio Network, Las Vegas, thanks for supporting me brother, and for the fantastic conversations. Love your pro style!

Nik Hunter, from the UFO Chronicles Podcast, a supercool English gent living in the Tropics with his finger on the pulse of Flying Saucer/UFO/UAP/USO latest, love the show and love the sticker for my car mate!

To another legendary Englishman, Marine Commando, Atlantic rower and great character Chris Thrall, cheers for having me on your cool 'Chris Thrall's Bought The T-Shirt Podcast', it was a blast and looking forward to more. Cheers!

Finally, to my good friends who always inspire me regarding this subject on Facebook and other platforms – author Dr Toula Gordillo, Joanne West, Åsa Edman, Ren Wagner, Andrew Musson, Rene Sonse, Alison McD, Eric Gottesman, Chance Michael, Patricia Webb, Maxine Ann Coe and Bala McLay.

Table of Contents

FOREWORD

Paul Wallis

Author of THE EDEN SERIES

Even on a first encounter, Norse lore holds such weight and resonance, that the most casual observer senses immediately that there is something important here. The Aesir are iconic, and their mythos is powerful and cinematic. But what is the nature of it? Have we read it right? The action of the Norse stories takes us well beyond the realm of fable and moral tale. Neither are they hortatory texts, impelling the reader to do or to believe certain things. What then is their purpose?

These questions interest me as a *"hermeneutics guy."* For thirty-three years I served as a priest and pastor in a wide range of churches, as a *"church-doctor,"* and a trainer of pastors in the fields of hermeneutics and the history of religious thought. *Hermeneutics* is the discipline of interpretation. It is a discipline which asks:

- *What kind of text is this and how do we know?*
- *What did the writer believe and what did they want us to know?*
- *Are we reading the original version of this narrative or is there an earlier, more primitive version, representing forgotten layers of context and meaning?*
- And most fundamentally, *"What do the words themselves actually mean?"*

When it comes to understanding the Aesir of the Norse people, the hermeneutics of Snorri Sturluson stand front and centre. How did this thirteenth century Norse leader interpret the traditional narratives of the Aesir? Moreover, how have scholars interpreted the writings of Sturluson in the centuries since? Sturluson regarded the legends of the Viking *"gods"* as a fusion of metaphor, myth and a deep cultural memory of real events in history. Was he right?
More contemporary commentators have often glossed over the subtle layers of Sturluson's own hermeneutics, framing all Norse lore as a canon of allegory and fiction, superseded through the irresistible expansion of mediaeval Christianity. Are they right? Who has the framing right and how can we know?
Of course, the moment we tell the story of another culture's mythology, we cannot help but distort it. The nuances of our own word-stock whitewash over the vivid colours of the original language. Our own vocabulary becomes a familiar veneer, obscuring the textures and detail of the original meanings. In this way, reports which once were concrete and earthy becomes something religious and ethereal. Ideas which once were material and technical become something magical and mystical, until finally the imaginary world we have constructed with this accretion of whitewash and veneers becomes the very lens through which we interpret the whole legacy of narratives and art left to us by the culture we have purported to understand. In this way, the academic mainstream has often interpreted Snorri Sturluson's writing as euhemeristic, suggesting that he is mistakenly deifying historic figures from the past. At other times, he is accused of the very opposite mistake, interpreting fictional and metaphoric figures as historic. These are not the only contradictions to be found in academic discussions of Snorri Sturluson.
Now, refreshingly, and in complete contrast, David Lovegrove presents a case for reading Sturluson's work, in particular his *Prose*

Edda and *Heimskringla*, with a deeper respect, and on the basis of translations more thoroughly grounded in the root meanings of his vocabulary. I applaud this approach as a way of clearing the fog of centuries of religious belief, assumptions and prejudice, a fog which has clouded our understanding of many ancient narrative traditions. To peel back centuries of distortions in this way takes a scholar who is deeply versed in the symbology and original language of the ancestors. It takes an eye as keen as that of a warrior like Gunnar, and an artist's heart to resonate with a storyteller like Snorri Sturluson. David Lovegrove is that scholar.

David is a friend of mine. A gentleman and a scholar, he is a former police officer, a martial arts master, a highly skilled, ambidextrous painter and a fellow Aussie to boot. A Viking by ancestry, and a descendant of the great Snorri Sturluson, David is an erudite scholar of ancient Norse language, symbology and mythology. What he writes about in this book is in his blood, and I am delighted to see my friend receiving widening recognition as a fresh and authoritative voice in this fascinating field. His work is undeniably at the leading edge of enquiry into the world of the Aesir and the sagas of Asgard.

Let me encourage you to enter the world of the Aesir and to let David show you what happens when we reacquaint ourselves with the ancestral mythos of Asgard, informed by the ancient texts themselves and the light of root meanings. But I must warn you to be ready, because you are likely to find many of your beliefs and assumptions surrounding the story of humanity challenged and changed along the way.

David's writing style is warm and easy, bringing us close as he shares his data, walks us through his logic and leads us to his conclusions, which are profound and far-reaching. What David finds in the treasure store of the Norse narratives echoes in ancestral story all around the world. Curious correlations in traditions as diverse as Nigerian, Filipino, Greek, Hebrew,

Babylonian, Ancient Armenian, South American, Mesoamerican and Native American, draw my attention to what appears to be widespread and diverse curations of very similar visual memories. And these correlations are not just in the form of overlapping stories. They can be found in petroglyphs, carvings and art, bequeathed to us by those who have gone before. So when, in the pages that follow, David shows me correlations, both in the ancestral stories of the North, and in the physical artefacts left behind by our northern ancestors, I have to sit up and take notice, and I think you will do the same.

My advice is to buckle up and prepare yourself for the pages ahead. They will stretch you and inform you. Set out on this epic journey in the company of David Lovegrove and I can guarantee that you will return home, awed, enriched and inspired.

Paul Wallis – Queensland, April 2025.

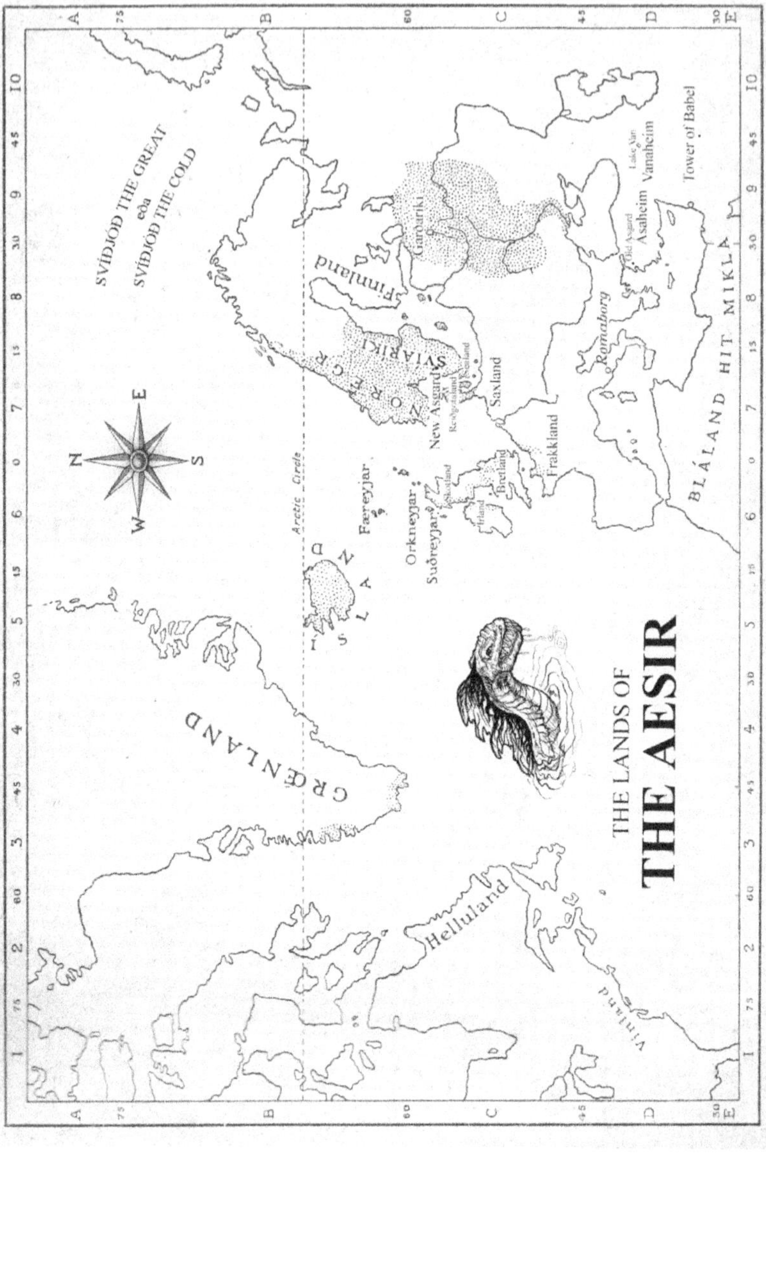
THE LANDS OF
THE AESIR
SVÍÐJÓÐ THE GREAT
eða
SVÍÐJÓÐ THE COLD
GRŒNLAND
ÍSLAND
Færeyjar
Orkneyjar
Suðreyjar
NOREGR
SVIARIKI
Finnland
Garðariki
New Asgard
Saxland
Frakkland
Bretland
Romaborg
Old Asgard
Asaheim
Vanaheim
Lake Van
Tower of Babel
BLÁLAND HIT MIKLA
Helluland
Vinland
Arctic Circle

LOST IN TRANSLATION

It seems that the whole world is crazy about the Vikings!

The phenomenal TV series of the same name is on everybody's lips, introducing new generations to a wild and adventurous time in human history and culture.
The Vikings are influencing music, hairstyles, tattoos, the growing of big gnarly beards, tribal jewelry and fashion. Many people are fascinated by their sagas (stories) and myths, and some folks attempt to recreate the Viking's philosophy and spirituality, based on what we can discover from archeological and written sources.

The other wildly popular vision of the Vikings is in the Marvel comics and films, based on the myths and exploits of the Viking Gods.
Here we are presented with high tech beings, humanoid, travelling in great flying ships, possessing awesome energy weapons, and inhabiting vast futuristic cities in space. These are super powerful and very long living people, and yet, like us, ultimately mortal.

In Viking Superpowers - Way of Asgard, I want to tell you the incredible story I have discovered through retranslating and reassessing the ancient texts, carvings and artefacts of Scandinavia. A story that seems to reveal that the tales of the Vikings, and their early ancestors, was a mixture of both these modern retellings, with the gleaming Marvel version being possibly as close to the truth as the heart pounding grimy adventures of Ragnar, Lagertha, and Floki et al!

So now…imagine, if you will…

In the deep past, a loose collection of advanced extraterrestrial beings, humanoid in appearance, settle on planet Earth and tweak the genetics of the anthropoid apes, the smartest native species.
Perhaps they use some of their own genetic materials, or perhaps they synthesize new genes. They breed the new beings in a safe enclosed environment, perhaps a beautiful garden, planted with all sorts of fruits and vegetables for the beings to browse on. Gradually the beings cultivate their creation's intelligence, teaching them new skills as they prove ready.

Perhaps these new beings prove to be smarter than expected, becoming self-aware, and realising that they are different to their creators. The creators look similar to them, yet they wear clothing to cover their bodies, seemingly in a display of status and superiority, and perhaps of insecurity. The new creatures are very intelligent and curious, and start to probe at the unnatural devices hidden within their environment.
An inadvertent security lapse leads to an exit opening, and some of the vulnerable new creatures escape, out into the wild world of tooth and claw.

A long time passes, perhaps the visitors leave, and much happens, including cataclysms caused by asteroids striking the Earth, and massive changes in the Sun's activity.
The collection of superior beings return and find that the creatures they created have advanced quite considerably.

The space farers divide the Earth into regions. Despite being very advanced, they are far from perfect, and begin fighting amongst themselves for power over resources, people groups, and land.
They are neither angels nor devils, but superpowered and extremely long living thanks to their technology.
Cruelly modifying the Earth creatures genetics dooms them to relatively short and brutish lives, restricting their ability to become too advanced.
The 'Powerful Ones' want to keep power to themselves.

We follow a group of these powerful beings, who have set up in the Middle East, in an area the Ancient Romans called Asia, and which is now called Anatolia, Türkiye. A very significant region, the land of Ancient Troy, thought to be the original home of the Sumerians.
This is also the mysterious 'Land of the Chaldean's' in the Hebrew Bible, the land from whence came the three Magi or 'Wise Men', who followed a great shining 'Star' which lead them to a very special child, born under mysterious circumstances.
A land close by the area of Mt. Ararat, where the Bible tells us the ark of Noah settled after floating above the vast, world destroying flood.
It is also here that the Sumerian Epic of Gilgamesh, beautifully written in cuneiform script on clay tablets, tells us of Utnapishtim's great 'ark', full of animals and humans, coming to rest, (an account written 2,500 years earlier than the Bible's Noah story!)

These particular 'Powerful Ones' had a name.
The Aesir.
The Gods of the Vikings!

The great medieval Icelandic Chieftain, historian and poet, Snorri Sturluson, calls them 'the men of Asia' and their land 'Ásaland' (Land of the Aesir) or 'Ásaheim '(Home/World of the Aesir). He tells us that they were some of the 'Regin', (the Rulers, the Powers), who met regularly in council, high up above the sky.

It seems to me that they were meeting not just with their own people, but with the representatives of many other advanced groups, part of what the Hebrew Bible calls the 'El-Bá Adat', The Council of Power, and which retired Israeli General and Professor, Haim Eshed, (for thirty years Head of Israeli Space Security), in 2022 called 'The Galactic Federation'.

My friend and fellow researcher, author Paul Wallis, writes in his book 'The Invasion of Eden' - 'A galactic federation may sound like something straight out of the fictional canons of Stargate, Star Wars or Star Trek, but Haim Eshed has simply applied fresh vocabulary to a concept repeated by ancestral narratives spanning the globe.

Whether we are reading about the Feathered Serpents of China or the Yucatan peninsula, the gods of Greek legend, the airborne kings of the Vedas, the Aesir of Norse mythology, the Apkallu of Babylonian and Sumerian texts, the Anunu of Hawaii, the Anunna of Sumerian cuneiform tablets, or the *El-Ba'adat,* the *Council of Power* in the Hebrew scriptures, we are essentially looking at the same thing, a committee of competing non-human factions, bound by some kind of accord to manage 'Project Earth' '.

Many thousands of years later some of these powerful beings, the Aesir, begin to migrate to the north of the world, drawn inexorably to set up dominion over that area. Much later they are finally forced to leave their Ásaland/Ásaheim bases completely, pushed out by the later incursion of another, seemingly more powerful group of beings, the 'Powerful Ones' who ruled over the Roman Empire.

Within the medieval Icelandic Sagas, (stories of Vikings, Poets and Icelandic family feuds), the Prose and the Poetic Edda's, (the great mythic stories and poetry about the 'Gods'), and the pictographic visual language of thousands of Bronze Age rock carvings and artifacts, scattered throughout Scandinavia, I have found a very unexpected, and seemingly hidden and/or suppressed history. A history that points to this ancient paleocontact, (contact between humans and intelligent beings in the ancient past), as well as the reality of human paranormal and physical superpowers!

Viking Superpowers!

The original stories are written in what is considered a 'dead' language, Old Norse, once the common language across Scandinavia (Denmark, Sweden, Norway and Iceland).
Due to it's isolation and uniquely preserved literature, the people of Iceland speak a modernized version of Old Norse, (often called Old Icelandic), and can read the original sagas with little trouble.
As a long-time student of this language my approach has been to respectfully put aside previous translations, interpretations, and the scholarly dogma of centuries, and seek to discover new meaning within the original language.
To look afresh at all possible meanings in the Old Norse words and sentences, keeping an open mind to unusual possibilities.

Many of the saga stories relate the adventures and interactions of groups of unusual beings, with names traditionally translated by words like Gods, Goddesses, Elves, Dwarves, Giants, Trolls etc.

Names that carry with them the baggage of long, (and often erroneous), association with imagined characters, species and creatures that derive from post medieval and modern 'fairy' stories and pop culture productions.

The standard translations of these 'Norse Myths and Sagas' tell us that the 'God's', and other strange beings, lived not only on the Earth, but also under and above it.

Sometimes they are said to reside in 'Heaven' or 'The Heavens', in vast glowing 'halls', perhaps connected to the incredibly massive 'World Tree', or to 'worlds' very far away indeed.

The beings ride 'chariots', 'horses', 'boars', 'eagles', 'hawks', even 'swans', and sometimes 'ships', above the clouds, over, (and under), the seas, and in the 'heavens'.

We hear of face to face interactions between humans and these powerful beings, stories of their interbreeding with us, tales of Elves, (including one who crafted a working flying machine), multiple stories of beings travelling on flying horses, (and even a huge bright bristled boar who can travel at great speed through the sky or deep under the water, the whole time lighting up the darkest night or the murkiest deep sea).

Sometimes these flying animals and devices carry single occupants, and sometimes they appear to be extremely massive, carrying thousands of beings.

There are even enormous 'halls' high in the sky, usually described as being metallic, bright, shining, containing hundreds of rooms, and sometimes located in powerful energy fields. In at least two of these 'halls' there is described a special attached viewing platform, allowing one to look down over the Earth, viewing the whole world, and even zooming in closely on places and people.

We are told that the most famous of these powerful 'gods', the mighty Thor, possessed a power belt, power gloves, and carried a fantastic weapon, (a short handled hammer named 'Mjölnir'), which can emit devastating thunderbolts. Mjölnir can also be cast to unerringly strike its target, and then return flying back to Thor's hand.
This is all well known to fans of the Marvel comics or films.

Less well known is the story of Thor, on a mission against the Giants, being caught without his power belt and gloves, and of a friendly giantess, Geirodd, lending him her own power belt, power gloves as well as a power spear!
It really sounds as if these power weapons, usually considered unique to Thor, were not all that uncommon at the time!

These ancient stories are of course regarded as myth, and in contemporary use, we tend to conflate the words 'myth' and 'mythology' with fiction and fantasy.
Thus have the so-called 'Myths of the Vikings' been treated for hundreds of years.
Merely colorful old stories, created and believed by simple, superstitious ancient peoples as they struggled to explain the mysteries of life and the world.
Good stories indeed to amuse children, (and adults), sitting by blazing fires during long cold Northern winters nights, the wind and wolf packs howling outside, with snow heaped outside to the windows.
In the Middle Ages, and even later, religious authorities painted these stories and spiritual beliefs as 'doctrines of devils', an evil memory of misguided spiritual beliefs, contrary to their own system of dogmatic belief.
Stories best forgotten.

The original word out of which 'myth' came is the Ancient Greek word 'mythos', which simply means 'an account of something that happened'.
However, in the world of academia something new is stirring.
There are voices speaking out about the possibility that these strange ancient 'mythic' tales could be relating real events, and describing actual technologies witnessed by humans, preserving these memories for the sake of those who would come after.

In their book 'When They Severed Earth from Sky: How the Human Mind Shapes Myth' (Princeton: Princeton University Press, 2004), Elizabeth Wayland Barber and Paul T. Barber write - 'We have argued that 'myths' were not intended as fiction in our sense, but as carriers of important information about real events and observations.
We have also given much evidence that contrary to prevailing belief today, this information can sometimes survive intact for thousands of years'.

What a remarkable statement!

People in the past, despite seeming remote from our modern way of life, were undoubtedly every bit as intelligent as us.
They certainly cared as much as we do about their families, their people, and about preserving extraordinary information.
My contention is that they experienced many, (perhaps very many), extraordinary events and interactions, which were carefully recorded in different ways, using poetry, song, oral stories and written sagas, as well as leaving us artifacts and artworks, and a large corpus of pictograph stories, painstakingly carved into stone.

In fact, it is somewhat miraculous how much has been preserved, despite the vicissitudes of time, and the persecution and purposeful destruction over centuries of these records, and of those who maintained them.

I like to think that all these brave devoted people preserved the accounts for us to solve, so that somewhere in the future, someone, maybe even you and I, might be able to discover what really happened to them.

In the overview to his fascinating book 'Lost Knowledge: The Concept of Vanished Technologies and Other Human Histories', Benjamin B. Olshin, Professor of Philosophy, the History and Philosophy of Science and Technology at the University of the Arts in Philadelphia, writes, (referring to his book) - 'It examines the idea of lost knowledge, reaching back to a period between myth and history. It investigates a peculiar idea found in a number of early texts: that there were civilizations with knowledge of sophisticated technologies, and that this knowledge was obscured or destroyed over time along with the civilization that had created it. This book presents critical studies of a series of early Chinese, South Asian, and other texts that look at the idea of specific "lost" technologies, such as mechanical flight and the transmission of images.

There is also an examination of why concepts of a vanished golden age were prevalent in so many cultures.'

Growing up accustomed to high tech science and having been gifted a complex language to describe previously inexplicable wonders, we are now in a position to reassess the ancient stories curated by tribal ancestors from all over the world.

We can seek to find other interpretations - that some/many of these collected and carefully passed down stories contain memories of events involving, (to us now), recognizable high technology, wielded by advanced races of beings.

Of course such thinking is still mainly viewed with skepticism by mainstream science and academia.
Scientist Carl Sagan, one of the founders of SETI (the Search for Extraterrestrial Intelligence), famously stated, (in 1979), that 'extraordinary claims require extraordinary evidence', (known as ECREE).
This quote is gleefully and regularly trotted out by the hard-core sceptics in the scientific community, who refuse to open their minds to the subject of UFO's, paleocontact and the paranormal abilities of humans.
Addressing this subject, Professor David Deming, of Harvard University, wrote - 'A claim or theory is not 'extraordinary' **solely because it is novel, unusual, or is in disagreement with human consensus** (my emphasis)**... an 'extraordinary' claim is one that is contradicted by a massive amount of existing evidence.** Science does not contemplate two types of evidence. The misuse of ECREE to suppress innovation and maintain orthodoxy should be avoided as it must inevitably retard the scientific goal of establishing reliable knowledge.'

There is certainly not a massive amount of evidence proving that UFOs, paleocontact and paranormal human superpowers are impossible. Up until recently very scant resources, (at least openly) have been devoted to investigating these claimed realities.
What happens instead is that sceptics and debunkers, unscientifically, maintain that it is up to people who experience these things to provide evidence over and above their sworn testimonies. In most cases this is impossible, as these experiences

tend to happen very randomly, and rarely when there is scientific equipment set up to capture them.

What I find incredible is that the apparent arch-skeptic, Sagan, with Russian scientist I.S. Shklovsky, wrote a book in 1966 titled 'Intelligent Life in The Universe', about the possibility of encounters with extraterrestrial civilisations by our distant ancestors, and how these ancestors might describe such encounters.

They wrote -

'Such an unusual occurrence would certainly be described in the legends and myths of the people who came into contact with space voyagers. The astronauts would probably be portrayed as having godlike characteristics and possessing supernatural powers. Special emphasis would be placed on their arrival from the sky, and their subsequent departure back into the sky. These beings may have taught the inhabitants of the Earth useful arts and basic sciences, which would also be reflected in their legends and myths. In 1959, the Soviet ethnologist M. M. Agrest postulated that representatives from an extraterrestrial civilization have indeed visited our planet. Despite the great dangers of confusion with legends generated in other ways, such hypotheses are entirely reasonable, and worthy of careful analysis. Agrest has boldly conjectured that perhaps a number of events described in the Bible were in reality based on the visit of extraterrestrial astronauts to the Earth. For example, the circumstances surrounding the destruction of Sodom and Gomorrah remind Agrest of a nuclear explosion as it might have been described by an observer living in ancient times. As another example, Agrest considers the incidents related in the apocryphal book, 'The Slavonic Enoch', to be in reality an account of the visitation of Earth by extraterrestrial cosmonauts, and the reciprocal visitation of galactic communities by a rather befuddled inhabitant of the Earth'.

This is the young Carl Sagan, pre-ECREE, stating what is so obvious to many of us.
It's hard not to come to the conclusion that he was later advised to muzzle his open-minded youthful candour if he wished to enjoy a successful future career.

Our pop culture, and the wonders of 21st-century CGI (Computer Generated Animation) in science fiction films, have accustomed us to the once very outlandish concepts of faster than light interstellar space flight, and of exotic alien races visiting Earth in ancient times. Consider the 'Stargate' films and TV series, which starts in ancient Egypt, leaps to distant worlds, and eventually even reveals an 'ancient astronaut' race called 'The Asgards'.
The online Fandom Wiki that is devoted to Stargate notes on their 'Asgard' page that - 'The Asgard are an ancient humanoid race, and had once assumed the personae of beneficent protective gods on many worlds and assumed the role of protectors of the Milky Way galaxy.'
The 'Asgards' commanded a fleet of huge spaceships, 'Bilskirnir class' vessels, shaped like ultra-high tech Thor's Hammers!
The series is obviously inspired by the stories from the saga's, and and shows that I'm not the only Viking obsessed thinker to imagine this connection!

Even the extremely high-tech world of Star Wars, one of the most famous 'myths' of our time, is set 'a long time ago in a galaxy far far away', making for the hypothetical possibility that an Empire or a Rebel ship could have made it here to the boondocks of the Milky Way galaxy, many thousands of years ago!

(I know it's not real, but it's a cool thought!)
A somewhat obscure, (but very entertaining) film, Outlander, (nothing to do with the Scottish Highlands TV series of the same name), starring Jim Caviezel, tells the story of a humanoid from a distant world who crash lands on Earth during the Vendel Age, just before the Viking Age. His onboard computer informs him that the Earth is an abandoned 'seed' colony, long forgotten, (an idea which many past sci fi writers have found appealing). He ditches his technology, (not before downloading Old Norse straight into his brain), and mingles with the natives, getting himself, (and them), into and out of big trouble. It's a story based on the epic Anglo-Saxon poem Beowulf.

We ourselves are on the cusp of extreme advancement involving space flight, artificial intelligence, synthetic lifeforms, humanoid robotics and cyborging transhumanism, (not to mention downloading Old Norse straight into our brains).
If we have the openness and imagination for it, we can look back into the records preserved from the depths of time, and start to see creatures and technology, and even human superpowers, that we can recognize.
We can start to see what amounts to ancient versions of who we are becoming right now!

Very recently the United States government has admitted the presence, for a very long time, of super advanced craft in our skies. These craft have been witnessed visually, and on every type of advanced radar and monitoring technology available to the world's most powerful military, with performance characteristics way outside the laws of physics known to our science. Many highly credible witnesses have testified under oath before the United States Congress of the existence of crashed and/or recovered craft,

technologies and even captured non-human entities, (or their remains), that bear strange resemblance to those told of in ancient myths and stories worldwide.
Others have testified that humanoid beings are walking amongst us, pursuing missions that, (hopefully), are to our benefit as well as theirs.

I recently made a video compilation on my Viking Superpowers YouTube channel featuring high profile people stating openly that, not only is there a non-human high-tech presence in our world today, possessing technology that is beyond our current abilities, but that the same entities have been here interacting with humans **for a very long time.**
I'd like to discuss a couple of the most important testimonies here, so that you can get a feeling for what a paradigm change we are experiencing.
Considering the last 80 years of official denial, ridicule, and even persecution of people coming forward with their stories, we are now in a situation where what is commonly called UFO Disclosure seems to be being trickle fed to us, allowing the people of the Earth time to get their heads around these absolutely earth-shattering revelations.

On the 21st of May 2024, Colonel Karl E. Nell, retired US Senior Military Officer, Aerospace Executive & Corporate Strategist, was asked a simple, but very profound question by Alex Klokus at the SALT iConnections Conference, New York City.
Alex - "Karl, here's the million-dollar question. Do you believe that a higher form of non-human intelligence has visited this planet?"
Karl - "Right, so non-human intelligence exists, non-human intelligence has been interacting with humanity, **this interaction**

is not new, and it's been ongoing, and there are unelected people in the government that are aware of that."
Alex - "And so Karl that is quite a bold statement… I'm wondering and I'm curious, how confident are you that that is true?"
Karl - " There's zero doubt."

Zero doubt!

A bold statement indeed, yet bold statements are being made daily, with more and more authority, and despite a worldwide distrust of governments, people like us are really sitting up and taking notice. Let's hear from another extraordinary witness.

This is the Right Honourable Paul Helyer, who was the Defence Minister of Canada from 1967 to 1969, interviewed on 'The Hannibal TV' YouTube channel in 2021.
Paul was an aeronautical engineer and served in the Canadian army during World War II from 1939 to 1946. He witnessed a UFO with a group of friends and became very interested in the subject.
He passed away in 2021, at the grand old age of 98.

'You know, talk about the Free Press, that's the biggest joke in the world, we don't have a free press. If we had a free press we'd have huge reports in the papers of all sorts of things, including the Armada that flew south over Europe in, I guess it was 1963, of about 50 UFOs, and the Supreme Commander of the Allied Forces in Europe was concerned, and about to press the panic button. Fortunately, they all turned around and went back over the North Pole, so he was satisfied they weren't Soviets, and that they were, in fact had to be, extraterrestrial.
So, he ordered a study to be done, and it took three years, and what the study concluded was, **there had been at least four**

species, at least four, visiting Earth for thousands of years. This is not a new phenomenon, this goes way way back, and it **predates what we call our modern history of the last 10 or 15,000 years.'**

10 - 15,000 years well and truly covers the period that we are studying in this book, from the end of the Viking Age (c1100 AD) back to the start of the Bronze Age (circa 2000 BC). In fact, many of the peoples and happenings that I will be telling you about, from the ancient stories, could well go back as far as that very long period of 10,000 to 15,000 years

The study that the Supreme Commander of the Allied Forces in Europe ordered to be created was called 'The Assessment'.
A U.S Army Sgt Major, Robert Dean, stationed at Supreme Headquarters Allied Powers Europe (SHAPE) in 1963, was allowed to read this secret document by an officer stationed with him.

Robert Dean states -

'The Defense Intelligence Agency, and every one of the, I think, maybe at least two dozen major security organizations in our government, concluded that, beyond the shadow of a doubt, this secret must be kept not only from the American people, but from the world population at large, and as a result of that decision they have created a worldwide conspiracy among governments, to keep the lid on this secret.
Now let me share with you what some of the four major conclusions of 'The Assessment' were in 1964 and consider those bits of information with what you've already learned in your own research and studies, and what's been brought out in films and

UFO conferences over the last 10 - 15 years (he was speaking in the 90's).
In 1964 they had determined (that), at least this is in the NATO study, and I know for a fact that these are the conclusions that had been reached by our own military as early as 1949.

Number One - the planet Earth is, and has, been the subject of an extensive, massive, very thorough and detailed study by several extraterrestrial civilizations. Now that's an attention getter in itself!
Number Two - these civilizations have demonstrated an extremely advanced technology, possibly hundreds or even thousands of years beyond our own.

Number Three - There seems to be a process or a plan of some kind unfolding, the studies indicated, and demonstrated that a development of some kind of program was underway, evidence collected indicated **that the program has been going on for a very long time, possibly hundreds or even thousands of years**, *and some of my associates and research fellows and I have concluded it's probably been going on longer than that.*

Number Four - the study concluded that there did not appear to be a major military threat involved in 1964, (and) that if they, whoever they are, were malevolent or hostile, there was absolutely nothing we could do.
The level of technology that had been demonstrated was so far beyond anything we had in 1964 that we felt that if they were hostile or malevolent, the game was up, it was all over with.'

I believe that Sgt. Major Dean was telling the truth, and these four points really made me sit up and take notice.

Another jaw dropping piece of the UFO puzzle was provided to us by retired Israeli General, and respected Professor, Haim Eshed.

In December 2020 he revealed to Israeli National Newspaper, Yediot Aharonot, that the UFO's are real, and that the US and Israel had been in contact with aliens for some considerable time. This after he had headed the Israeli Space Security program for 30 years, launched many satellites, and after receiving three Israeli Security Awards.

He further revealed that the US had signed a secret agreement with a 'Galactic Federation', allowing them to conduct experiments on Earth, and that humans and aliens were collaborating at an underground base on Mars.

Professor Eshed also explained that President Trump (in 2020) both knew about them, and was on the verge of disclosing their existence, only to be persuaded not to by the Galactic Federation.

Those who know the Professor say that he is neither senile or crazy, and that he still regularily lectures at University.

It's almost as though he is old enough to not really care what people think, and is just telling the straight truth whether we like it or not.

Once you get interested in this fascinating subject you will be amazed by the plethora of stories and data freely available in books, videos, magazines and online articles.

Stories told by hundreds of obviously credible and honest people.

The skeptics, and particularly the debunkers, will always tell you that anecdotal evidence is no evidence at all. They will tell you that you can't believe your fellow human beings when they sincerely relate something absolutely extraordinary that happened to them.

These superior intellects insist that they will not believe anyones word unless personally provided with concrete material evidence, such as part of a crashed craft, or an up close, super clear photograph of same, perhaps with untranslatable hieroglyphs engraved along its side.

(Of course, there have been many instances of this type of solid physical evidence being reported, however in the majority of cases it is said that mysterious officials rapidly turn up, take possession of said evidence, and warn the experiencers not to speak, often accompanied by dire threats.)

It doesn't seem to matter to the naysayers that, in many cases, unidentified and very mysterious craft and even strange living beings have been seen up close by many people at once.
A case in point is the very remarkable Westall UFO case in 1966, in Victoria, Australia.
Hundreds of children and one science teacher ran out from classes to watch the objects, and then when the craft appeared to land in a field nearby to the school, many of the children jumped the school fence and ran to where it was.
One witnesses even reported having touched the craft!

Or the case of Father William Gill, an ordained Anglican priest in Papua New Guinea, back in 1959, when he and thirty-seven of his parishioners watched a craft for hours, over two days, waved to the beings that they could see on the floating craft, and received waves back.
Or the case of the sixty-two children, (aged between 6 and 12), at the Ariel School near Ruwa, Zimbabwe, who saw two silvery craft land, and some children saw small beings dressed in black emerge. The beings, with long black hair and huge black eyes, walked up to some of the children, and communicated with them telepathically. When you watch the interviews taken at the time with these children, and the interviews they gave later as adults, you must be very entrenched in your dogmatic denial of the phenomena not to be affected by their obvious wonder, (and distress), at the power and strangeness of their experiences.

One of the laughable aspects of the outright dismissal of anecdotal evidence as 'having no evidentiary weight', is that this very type of evidence is a major source of data in both the medical and the legal field.
Severe illnesses are often treated based partly on the stories (anecdotes) that people provide to their doctors regarding their symptoms, and similarly in courts of law, both defence and prosecution argue their respective cases partly based on anecdotal evidence, provided by the witnesses in the case.
Yet, for some reason, this is not considered acceptable evidence when it comes to the extraordinary 'experiences of a lifetime' that people report.
Sober people, hard-working people, highly intelligent and accomplished people, often in positions of high authority.

Experiences of encounters with nonhuman beings, of people being abducted and taken into extraordinarily strange craft, sometimes challenge even the most convinced believers in the phenomena. And yet these accounts are told by thousands of people in all sincerity, who perhaps have hidden their stories for decades out of fear of the ostracization that they sometimes encounter.

I've talked to some of these witnesses personally, and as spine tingling as their stories may be, I choose to believe them.
I also choose to believe the ancient witnesses who experienced, remembered, curated, preserved and passed down similar experiences .
Associated with tales of unidentified flying objects and encounters with the occupants of same, we have stories of strong telepathic messages given to experiencers, of being levitated and moved without being touched, (perhaps a form of telekinesis à la Master

Yoda lifting Luke's X-Wing out of the swamp), and of other psychic paranormal events.

This phenomena of paranormal/psychic abilities is as debunked by the mainstream as is the subject of UFOs and visiting aliens.
In some way the two are treated as inextricable, and this may actually be the case. A recent whistleblower in the US stated that all technology that has been recovered from crashed and retrieved non-human craft seems to be intrinsically linked to the consciousness of the visitors, who often target humans with such abilities for visitation.

Within the compelling Old Norse stories we will venture into, extraordinary paranormal abilities appear to have been accepted as real by the writers and storytellers.
Those possessing them functioned in their societies as leaders, seers, spiritual guides, healers, remote viewers, weather changers, and protectors.
The great Icelandic Chieftain, historian and poet, Snorri Sturluson, (about whom you will hear a lot more), tells us, in his great masterwork, 'Heimskringla' (the Globe of the World) that - 'Þá er Ása-Óðinn kom á Norðrlönd ok með honum díar, er þat sagt með sannendum, at þeir hófu ok kenndu íþróttir þær, er menn hafa lengi síðan með farit.'
Which translated into literal English is - 'Then did Odin of the Aesir come to the Northlands, and with him the Díar (Spiritual leaders and Chieftains), and it is said with truthfulness that they initiated and taught their (paranormal) arts and skills, which people have long practiced ever since'.

Notice the wording - **it is said with truthfulness, that they initiated and taught their arts and skills, which people have long practiced ever since.**

Consider that this is from the supposedly devout Christian historian and Chieftain, Snorri Sturluson!

He states emphatically that it is 'said with truthfulness' that Odin, the Aesir, and the Díar are real, that they initiated and taught these paranormal and physical superpowers, and that people had been practising these superpowers ever since.

Right up to Snorri's time in the 13th Century, over 200 years after Iceland officially converted to Christianity!

(It's particularily noteworthy that these superior beings were not only the 'initiators' (the creators) of these powers but that they went out of their way to teach them to people. We have to assume from Snorri's statement that a continuous tradition of teaching these paranormal skills remained unbroken from perhaps the early Bronze Age (c.2000 BC) until Snorri's time (in the 1200's), and perhaps for a long time after. For at least 3000 years!).

So friends, follow me into the next chapter, and I will tell you a tale of the great Snorri Sturluson, and his single-handed preservation, against all odds, of this treasured knowledge.

I BELIEVE SNORRI!

It is high summer in Reykjavik and a balmy 10 degrees Celsius outside.
After a very enlightening time on my Viking Superpowers research tour of Scandinavia, including a couple of weeks driving and trekking the wild roads and mountains of southern Iceland, I am now set up in a bayside flat in Reykjavik.

Swapping my beloved 40-year-old knitted Icelandic jumper, (known as a Lopapeysa), for my more 'professorial' Harris Tweed jacket and collared shirt, I have walked several hundred metres to the University of Iceland, (Háskoli Íslands), campus.
At the entrance to the famous Stofnun Árni Magnusson building, ('The Árni Magnússon Institute for Icelandic Studies'), I am met by Professor Guðvarður Már Gunnlaugsson, Research Professor at the Institute.
There are tradesmen everywhere throughout the building, and we enter and walk past sheets of building plastic, hung up to prevent dust floating between rooms and floors.
At regular intervals there is the staccato grinding of heavy power tools.
I am visiting at the invitation of Professor Ármann Jakobsson, Senior Lecturer in Old Icelandic Literature at the University, who has organized a private viewing for me, to see some of the very oldest handwritten manuscripts of these 'Viking' sagas.

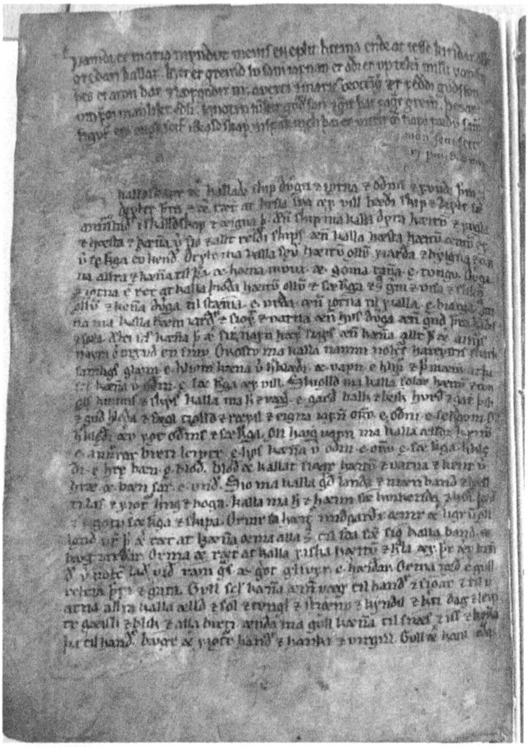

Professor Gunnlaugsson shows me to the Institute's reading room. He walks further down the corridor, and after a short while reenters the room carrying two white cardboard boxes. Lifting an unassuming, medium sized leather-bound volume from one, he slides it carefully towards me.

The unmistakable dark ancient calfskin parchment, covered in superfine and beautifully handwritten text, makes my heart skip a beat.
This is manuscript number AM 748 I b 4to, one of the very earliest handwritten copies of Snorri Sturluson's Prose Edda, aka Snorra Edda, from around 1300 AD.

I have dreamt of seeing an original Prose Edda manuscript since I was a teenage Viking enthusiast. It is from this 700-year-old manuscript, and a few others, that the famous stories of the Viking gods have come down to us, and it is also from this same book that so many of JRR Tolkien's wondrous characters and stories had their genesis.
Even the name of Gandalf the Wizard came from here!
A very magical moment.

Professor Gunnlaugsson tells me that it is a challenge for modern people, surrounded all our lives by mass produced goods, especially by books, magazines and our ubiquitous digital media, to truly comprehend what handmade manuscripts like this represent.
A novel sized book required the skins of hundreds of calves, each painstakingly tanned and scraped by Master craftsmen, just to create the parchment pages.
Add to that the hand ground inks, expertly made quills, and the hundreds of hours of calligraphic work by artists of sublime skill.

Creating this single manuscript would cost a very large sum of money indeed.
The stories and the information contained within were obviously considered to be vitally important and even priceless.

I recognize the name 'Óðinn' (Odin), written in the challenging antique script, and then further on the word 'Miðgarðsormr' (Midgard Serpent aka the World Serpent).
My years of studying the Icelandic language and Old Norse are standing me in good stead. This is the section of the Edda called Skáldskapamál, (literally 'Poet shaping words', usually translated as 'Poetic diction').
Reaching into my backpack I pull out my venerable Icelandic edition of 'Snorra Edda' from 1952, and quickly search up this page.
The Professor is pleased, and we read along together in the ancient manuscript, amazingly still possible for readers of modern Icelandic 700 years later.
I get the feeling that he is surprised to meet a foreigner who can read Icelandic, and who knows the stories, especially one faring from the far-off Antipodes (called 'Andfætlingur' in Icelandic).

After a very pleasant hour of saga viewing, I take my leave of Professor Gunnlaugsson.
He has devoted much of his life to the study and care of these priceless masterpieces, and I can't help but think what a wonder it is that a society like Iceland, with a population only just now approaching 400,000, should have preserved, cared for, and continuously funded the study of their cultural history with such love and dedication, for several hundred years.
These ancient books of bound skins, covered in stories scratched in handmade ink, are worth much more than gold to them.

I wander over to the recently completed Edda building, a beautiful and imposing building of curving glass sitting above a glittering shallow pool crossed by a bridge. It will now house the great collection of the Stofnan Árni Magnússon.
The original building I had just visited is being repurposed, and I could well have been the last guest to be received there.
Edda contains a magnificent library of Old Icelandic/Old Norse texts and related scholarship, and of course I spend a few very pleasant hours browsing their collection.
Edda is also the new homebase for Professor Jakobsson and the Faculty of Icelandic and Comparative Cultural Studies.

Just the day before he and I had met up for lunch at a famous Danish seafood restaurant Jómfrúin, beloved by the locals, at Lækjagata 4.
We have known each other for around two years, corresponding by email, and enjoying a very interesting exchange.
Ármann has the most remarkably open mind for a scholar at the pinnacle of his field, and his willingness to consider unusual ideas has never ceased to amaze me.
In fact, I came to know him through his superb book, 'The Troll inside you : Paranormal Activity in the Mediaeval North'.
It is an absolute tour de force.

His approach is to look at all the nuances of meanings for common words in the Old Icelandic stories, words that are usually translated simply as Troll, God, Elf, Witch, Giant etc., and to question the accuracy of these translations.
Being a native Icelander, and a renowned scholar in his field, his conclusions carry a lot of weight.
They certainly do with me.

Over lunch we chatted about Australia and Iceland, and of course Old Norse studies, and after a while I said to him - ' I expect that many academics in this field would think my theories, re-translations and investigations of the Old Norse stories to be perhaps a bit balmy, or even downright crackpot. I know it's very unorthodox to be investigating the paranormal and accepting that it could be real, and especially to be looking for Paleocontact, (ancient contact with off world, high tech civilizations), in these venerable texts'.

Ármann smiled and leaned slightly forward in his chair.
" On the contrary, I think you are the avant-garde, the cutting edge for new thought in this field ".
I, of course, was thrilled to receive such encouragement from him, and on my return from Iceland he happily gave his permission for me to use his statement in this book.
I had bought the two volume Íslenzk Fornrit edition of 'Morkinskinna' which he edited along with Þórður Ingi Guðjónsson. This is a history of the Norse Kings, one of the original sources for Snorri Sturluson's 'Heimskringla'.
I had also bought a copy of his first novel 'Vonarstræti'.
I asked if he would mind signing them, and jokingly suggested that he refer to me in his dedication as 'avant-garde'.
Taking the novel and he wrote –
'Til David avantgarde vinur minn, frá Ármann'
(To David my avantgarde friend, from Ármann).

He told me that his book - 'The Troll inside You', had been somewhat ignored by his fellow academics. The majority of people who had liked and bought the book were artist friend's like myself. People with creative open minds, habitually pushing against orthodoxies.

As we shook hands outside, Professor Jakobsson encouraged me once again.
"Keep going!".

So you might be wondering why I have titled this chapter 'I Believe Snorri'?

Snorri Sturluson's stories represent two thirds of the total information we have about the so-called mythical early history of Scandinavia.
He is universally accepted as the author of the great work 'Heimskringla' (The Round World or the Globe of the World), aka The History of the Norse Kings, and of the book that I'd just been viewing at the University of Iceland, variously called The Prose Edda, Snorra Edda, and in the past, the Younger Edda.
The other treasure is the anonymous manuscript called The Poetic Edda (aka The Elder Edda or Saemundar Edda).
This is a treasure house of preserved poetry from the Viking Age, and possibly earlier, relating some of the most fabulous stories from the ancient times.

Snorri's Prose Edda heavily references the poems in the Poetic Edda, and expands upon their meaning, adding many extra stories. The fascinating thing is that the Poetic Edda was written, despite containing the older poetry, in 1270, whereas the Prose Edda was written down 50 years earlier, in 1220. It seems that Snorri either had access to an unknown, earlier version of the Poetic Edda, or that he had collected still current oral poetry himself.
It seems reasonable to me that he could have accessed both of these sources.

So once again, why would I say 'I believe Snorri'?

I am obviously implying that there are people who don't believe Snorri, am I not?
And that, in fact, is the truth. There are many past and current academics, and students of the Viking Age, who don't believe that he was always truthful and sincere in what he records of the mythological stories.

They accuse him of 'euhemerism', which the Collins dictionary defines as - 'the theory that gods arose out of the deification of historical human heroes' and 'any interpretation of myths that derives the gods from outstanding men and seeks the source of mythology in history'.
Snorri's critics mainly make this accusation because, in his Edda particularly, he tells stories about the Norse gods that are often a confusing, and somewhat odd, mixture of characteristics. At times they appear to be 'all powerful', creating the world and humanity, as for example the leader of the 'Gods', Odin, being called the 'All Father', and with his two brothers creating 'Heaven, Earth and Man'.
At other times Odin is portrayed as being surprisingly mortal, even to the point where he has himself 'marked' with a spear as he was dying.
This so that he would be seen by his worshippers to be, after death, fit to enter his own hall, Valhalla, where only valiant warriors slain in battle may enter.

Snorri tells us that the famous trickster god, Loki, changes himself into a mare, mates with a Giant's stallion, and gives birth to Odin's eight legged flying horse, Sleipnir, 'the best of all horses'.
Loki is also said to be the father (mother?) of the Goddess of the Underworld, Hel, and more bizarrely, gives birth to the Midgard

Serpent (a dragon/snake so large that it encircles the world), and to the Fenris Wolf, a giant and fearsome wolf who will not only one day devour the Sun, but also devour Odin in the final battle Ragnarök!

Yet this is apparently the same Loki who gets caught out making a cowardly deal with the giant Thiazzi, purely to save his own skin, and thereby betraying and handing over the Goddess Idunn (Iðunn).
She is the immortality therapist of the Gods, daily dealing out her so-called apples, which have the power to turn back old age.
(A therapy that many scientists are predicting will be available to us in the near future!).
When the Gods find out that he has betrayed Idunn, and thereby them, they threaten him with torture and death. Loki quickly begs for mercy, borrows a flying craft from the goddess Freya, and heads off to fix the dilemma that he has created.

When Snorri was writing, Iceland had been officially Christian for 200 years, since the year 1000 AD, (although private practice of Heathen ceremonies and beliefs were legally tolerated for 100 years after that date).
These scholars and commentators I refer to accuse Snorri of having been a devout Christian, (and some have even called him a Monk or a Priest, though he was neither), who used euhemerism to attempt to defang the legitimate old traditional spiritual stories of the Norse/Old Germanic peoples, recasting them into stories of powerful men and women, who were not in fact gods.
The dominant and authoritarian Christian church of Snorri's time went even further, teaching that the 'Gods' were in fact false gods, evil spirits, and minions of the Devil, as were any who still might dare to venerate them.

In 'Viking Superpowers - Way of Asgard', I will be retranslating many important extracts from Snorri's Prose Edda, and from Heimskringla - The History of the Norse Kings, in a more literal way than is often done.
My aim will be to discover alternate possible meanings of many important Old Icelandic words which Snorri uses, words which I believe are often mistranslated, perhaps purposely, to give a pseudo-religious or mythical reading, thereby obscuring the literal meanings, which paint quite a different picture.

I will take the position that Snorri was not lying or obfuscating, and that he was very possibly not a Christian at all.
On the contrary I consider him most likely a secret heathen, doing his absolute best to preserve the cultural history, wisdom, spirituality and mysterious stories of his ancestors, so carefully collected by many generations before him.
In fact, as you will discover, I think that much of what Snorri, the anonymous saga writers, and the ancient poets preserved, far from being confusing and contradictory, can only make full sense to the children of the future, aka **us**.
We the children of this incredible new age of super science, artificial intelligence, aviation and space travel.
We who are finally witnesses to the very recent revelations concerning very long term visitation to our 'heimskringla', our 'round globular world', by advanced humanoids, and by other races from other heims (worlds).

I believe that the tales he preserves in his Edda, and in Heimskringla, are an honest, earnest compilation of everything that could be preserved, to be passed on and saved from the 'Inquisitors', and the flames of authoritarian religious intolerance.

Ancient and mysterious tales, pointing to deep, strange, psychic truths about the nature of existence, as well as being accounts of very advanced, high tech humanoid beings who came to earth and masqueraded as 'Gods'.
Beings who mated with many of our ancestors, purposely taking control over, and teaching, directing, and manipulating the peoples of Asia Minor, the great lands of Europe, and the Scandinavian lands of the North.

But first, the disbelievers!

In the modern echo chamber of YouTube and social media they are legion.
Information regarding the Eddas, Snorri's Prose Edda and the anonymous Poetic Edda are by far the most popular Viking related search subjects.
Many people, of all ages, are sincerely interested in the 'lost' pre-Christian spirituality of the Germanic and Northern peoples, and are seeking to find their own connection to it.
Because of this ease of sharing, and the isolated nature of online study, it helps to maintain a healthy scepticism around this subject, especially regarding stories originally written in an archaic language (Old Icelandic/Old Norse), a language read and understood by relatively few.

Anthony Faulkes, former Professor of Old Icelandic at Birmingham University, UK, was one of the greatest and most influential scholars in this field.
His translation of Snorri's Edda in the Everyman Library edition was first published in 1987, and has been a favourite of mine since I first bought it in 1995, as has been his translation of Heimskringla (with Alison Finlay).

I have the greatest admiration for his body of work and dedication to the subject.
His thinking on the subject of Old Norse mythology has obviously been profoundly influential on a great many people interested in this field, and so it is with some reluctance that I am forced to strongly disagree with him on the subject of who Snorri Sturluson really was, and upon how valuable his account of 'Viking mythology' is.

In the Introduction to his 'Edda - Prologue and Gylfaginning', first published 1982, and reissued 1988 and 2000 by The Viking Society for Northern Research', Professor Faulkes writes –
'Gylfaginning is the first part of Snorri Sturluson's Edda and contains the most extensive and coherent account of Scandinavian mythology that exists from the Middle Ages. The prologue that accompanies it develops a surprisingly rational theory about the origin of heathen religions, which is of great interest for the history of ideas in medieval Scandinavia.'

Sounds pretty great so far. 'The most extensive and coherent account of Scandinavian mythology that exists from the Middle Ages'.
A 'surprisingly rational theory about the origins of heathen religions'- now that's what we want to hear about!
Lead on McDuff!

'It is true that the value of the work for historians of religion is seriously impaired by the fact that the author was a Christian who lived at a time when the myths he describes had long since ceased to be believed in. His sources may have been unreliable, and his attitude to his material was clearly influenced both by his own

religious beliefs and by his education and reading, which were largely within the tradition of medieval European Christianity.
There is no reason to believe, however, that everything in Gylfaginning is derived from ancient tradition, whether oral or written.
Snorri was a Christian and had only a scholar's and an artist's interest in mythology; he was preserving it for antiquarian, not religious, reasons.'

Now this is where I have to politely disagree.

The Professor is unequivocally stating here that Snorri was a Christian, and that the myths he writes about 'had long since ceased to be believed in' in Snorri's time.
This of course would indicate that Snorri himself didn't believe in them.
'There is no reason to believe that everything in the first book of the Edda (and by extension everything in Skáldskaparmál and Háttatal, the second and third books), is derived from ancient tradition, either oral (declaimed by Skalds/Poets), or written (which means books written within living memory of Snorri and his elders).
Snorri's Christianity is then reiterated, and we are told that he had only had a scholar's interest, an artist's interest, (essentially a fiction writer's interest), in this ancient Scandinavian corpus of stories, reaching back over 2000 years from his time.
Regarding the other great source of this Viking mythology, the 'History of the Norse Kings', Heimskringla, Professor Faulkes writes –
'In Heimskringla he treated even his historical sources with a certain freedom, and clearly, he would not have felt it wrong to depart from or expand his sources in Gylfaginning too if artistic

or other considerations required it, and he would probably not have felt inhibited from inventing new stories or drastically altering old ones if he saw fit.
Moreover, it is unlikely that Snorri gives a very accurate picture of Norse mythology as a whole'.

As I stated earlier, I very respectfully have to disagree with this scholarly assessment.
I believe that Snorri Sturluson was a secret Heathen and a Norse hero, with the power, wit and courage to preserve the truth in the face of the very dangerous Church of that time.
I choose to believe Snorri.
Even just as a thought experiment, lets take what he writes at face value, and see if we can't just work out what he is really telling us, rather than dismissing what seems contradictory by our limited lights.

So in answer to Professor Faulkes and to those who would agree with him regarding this, I will simply allow Snorri, and other esteemed voices, to argue my case.

Let us first start with Snorri's own words regarding his historical project, a project that would become the 'most extensive and coherent account of Scandinavian mythology that exists from the Middle Ages'. Then we will briefly have a look at his remarkable life, education and historical mission. This paragraph is from his 'Prologus' (Prologue) to Heimskringla -

'In this book I have caused to be written ancient accounts about those chieftains who have held dominion in the Northern lands and who have spoken the Danish tongue, according to what I have heard wise men relate. Likewise, I have included some of their lineages, as they have been taught to me—some of it found in genealogies, wherein kings or other men of high birth have traced their descent. Some of it is written down from ancient poems or sagas which men have used for their own enjoyment. And though we do not know the full truth of these things, we do know this: that learned men of old have held such accounts to be true.'

Snorri states clearly here that he gets his information from 'wise men' who have personally related to him 'ancient accounts' regarding the genealogies of rulers and men of high rank in the mainland Scandinavian kingdoms.

He had personally spent two years at royal and noble courts in Norway and Sweden researching all this.

He was trained and given a very liberal education at home in Iceland as a lad, exposed to many 'old poems and narrative songs' (many of which are now lost to us). I will have much more to say about this soon.

'But when Harald Fairhair was king in Norway, Iceland was settled. With King Harald there were poets, and men still know their poems, and the poems of all the kings who have ruled in Norway since. We have taken the greatest example from what is said in those poems which were composed in the presence of the chieftains themselves or their sons. We accepted as true all that is found in those poems concerning their journeys or battles. For it is the custom of poets to praise most the one before whom they are performing, and no one would dare to recite to a king himself deeds of his which all who heard them knew to be lies or nonsense and the king himself as well. That would be mockery, not praise.'

Does this sound like the statement of a man who would make up stories of his revered ancient ancestors for the sake of a story, knowing that what he is writing will be heard by the Kings and nobility back in Norway, Sweden, Denmark, those who claim descent from those same 'Gods'? Wouldn't such invented and knowingly fictional stories be 'mockery, not praise'?

Something dramatic happened to Snorri as a little boy, which would greatly affect the course of his life.
His father was the Chieftain Sturla Þórðason the Elder, of Hvammur (in the Northwest of Iceland).
Sturla was also known as Hvamm-Sturla. His wife was Guðný Böðvarsdóttir. (In the Icelandic alphabet the letter ð is pronounced like 'th' in English. Personal names followed, (and still do), the patronymic system, where your surname is your father's name, plus son or daughter (dóttir).

Hvamm-Sturla was a famous warrior, and when the boy Snorri was three or four his father was involved in a major lawsuit against another Chieftain, (a prominent Christian Priest), Pál (Páll) Solvason.
During a very tense discussion between the opposing parties,
a dramatic and telling incident occurred.
This is from Chapter 71 of 'Sturlunga Saga', written c 1300, a history of the powerful Sturlung family, of which Snorri was a part.

'Þorbjörg, kona Páls, var grimmúðig í skapi ok líkaði stórilla þóf þetta. Hon hljóp fram milli manna ok hafði kníf í hendi ok lagði til Sturlu ok stefndi í augat ok mælti þetta við: „Hví skal ek eigi gera þik þeim líkastan er þú vill líkastr vera, en þar er Óðinn?" En lagit kom í kinnina, ok varð þat mikit sár. Síðan hljópu upp menn Sturlu ok reiddu vápnin. Þá mælti Sturla: „Vinnið ekki á mönnum fyrr en ek segi hvar niðr skal koma."'

'Þorbjörg (Thorbjorg), Pál's wife, was cruel in temper and greatly disliked this (what was being discussed). She ran from amongst the people and had a knife in her hand and rushed at (Hvamm) Sturla and stabbed at his eye and said this to him: "Why should I not give you the likeness of who you would like to be (most admire), and that is Odin is it not?
But the blow hit his cheek, and it hurt greatly. Then Sturla's men ran up and drew their weapons. Then Sturla said: "Do not attack anybody until I tell you where the blow shall fall".

When I first read this remarkable passage I was taken aback!

Here is the hot-headed wife of a powerful Icelandic Christian Priest, attempting to gouge out the eye of a Chieftain, and screaming in her furious attack that she intended to make Hvamm-Sturla resemble his hero, the one eyed 'Viking' God Odin!
Iceland had been officially Christian since the year 1000 AD, (officially, but under extreme duress from the infamously cruel and fanatical Norwegian King, Olaf Tryggvasson), and secret Heathen rituals had been legally tolerated for a further 100 years.
In fact, in the Kristni Saga, (from around 1200-1230, contemporary with Snorri's Edda), it is stated that 'although Christianity was established in the land, many sparks of heathendom remained. It had been a custom here that it was not forbidden to perform sacrifices in secret or to practice other ancient rituals'.
After that extra one hundred year period such worship had become a very serious offence.

Now here we find ourselves a further 80 years after that 100-year limit had expired, and one could be forgiven for wondering if what the savage Thorbjorg accused Hvamm-Sturla of could possibly be true?

This is not proof that he really was a secret Odin worshipper, but the fact that nothing is said about this accusation afterwards in the saga indicates to me that there was some truth in the matter.

Christianity was a foreign religion. It was literally forced onto this tiny, isolated, close-knit population, (as it was indeed forced on the other Scandinavian countries), making me think that the Church was tolerated out of necessity, and still resented in Snorri's time.
Indeed, according to a very informative modern Icelandic website – 'Mystic Iceland, True stories and Folk laws' (mysticiceland.com), 'many people continued to practice the old ways after the prohibition, and when the Protestant Reformation came and took over from the Catholics in the 1600s, so many people were still practising that witch hunting (and) incredibly vicious persecutions began happening.'

Mystic Iceland continues -
'For over 600 years the church left the heathen people in peace, but the idea of the island's original belief being satanic took hold.
In order to get everyone onboard, the age-old tactics of fearmongering and misrepresentation was planted in the hearts of the people. And so, the seeds of (the idea of) abominable deeds by the heathen people was planted.
As a result, their neighbors, the church and the authorities hunted them down.
During the 17th century the Icelandic population rose to about 50,000 inhabitants with an increasing membership in the Christian faith.

In the years between 1625 and 1683 about 170 Icelanders were accused of witchcraft. About 130 recorded court cases survive, which include the cases of 21 Icelanders burned at the stake.
Surprisingly, these were mostly men.
To date, we only know of ten cases against women.
However, only one woman was ever executed for witchcraft.'

Isn't that fiendish!
In a small, closely related population like that of Iceland at that time, such authoritarian fanatical viciousness would have taken a terrible toll on people's minds. Imagine seeing relatives burnt alive at the stake!
What feelings arise in your breast as you imagine this?
Certainly not a love for the burners. I would hazard a guess such an experience would engender a deep intergenerational hate.

It's very interesting that the majority of the so-called Witches were men.
One of the depraved realities of the churches persecution of heretics through the ages has been its targeting of the wealthy and powerful, ruining and excommunicating them so as to take their land and riches for themselves. Perhaps that was going on in Iceland, or it could be that these men were influential secret leaders of heathen faith groups following the old beliefs.
It reminds me of the fact that all the words in Old Norse related to the old faith, and its skilled practitioners, were usually translated to have negative connotations in English (e.g. sorcery, witchcraft, black magic etc.).

As Professor Jakobsson writes in his 'The Troll Inside You - Paranormal Activity in the Medieval North' - 'With their Greco-Roman roots, the terms "magic" and "sorcery" tend to carry connotations, having long been used pejoratively by Christian authorities, whereas "witchcraft" is a Germanic word, albeit one no less negative in the connotations it bears. None of these words are exact parallels for the terms describing the harnessing of the paranormal in the sagas, such as "fjölkynngi," "forneskja," "galdrar," and "trollskapr," all of which also bear connotations worthy of deeper exploration'.

Over many years of interactions with Icelandic friends I have noticed that they don't generally have a great love for organized religion, (not unlike my fellow countrymen here in Australia).
They seem to be agnostic or atheist, and yet at the same time more open to the paranormal than people in, say, continental Europe. (Yet they are not all believers in elves as they have been often painted by international media.)

So, getting back to little Snorri, born into a large, rich and powerful family, a family who potentially maintained a secret Heathen faith and tradition.
We have to consider that Thorbjorg must have had some very solid information about Hvamm-Sturla, enraging her to the point of taking such radical action!
Whatever the truth of the matter her attack could have brought ruin on herself, her husband and family.

As it turned out, Iceland's most powerful man at the time, Jon Loftsson, stepped in, and offered to foster and educate Snorri, at his own expense, on his estate in Oddi, southern Iceland. This was seen as a great honour to Hvamm-Sturla, and a tremendous start in life for young Snorri.
Jon Loftsson had royal blood. As Snorri would record years later in his collection of kings' sagas, Heimskringla, Jon's mother was an

illegitimate daughter of the warrior-king Magnus Bare-Legs, so-called for his fondness for Scottish kilts, (or a similar garment). Her brothers were King Sigurd Jerusalem-Farer, who ruled from 1103 to 1130, and his co-ruler, King Eystein, who died in 1122.
Jon Loftsson was born in Norway in 1124 and was raised for his first eleven years by the priest of Cross Church in Konungahella (a Norwegian royal city, now in Sweden).

In July 2024 I visited Jon's estate at Oddi, and despite there being only one building, a lovely little white painted timber church built in 1924, it is said that it was once a grand estate, and a major seat of learning in Iceland.
Excavations had been made into a grass covered hillside above and to one side of the church, and I was able to walk in a certain distance, carefully picking my way through mounds of fragrant sheep droppings, to see into an impressively large cave, thought to have once held large numbers of cattle and sheep.
Such a cave is called a Nautahellir, and this one had been in use since the Viking Age.
These caves and other evidence point to the people at Oddi being wealthier than the majority of Icelanders at the time.

It seems to me that many modern 'Viking enthusiasts' hold a bit of a grudge against Snorri, mainly for being a 'Christian', and supposedly muddying the old stories with his goody goody monotheistic fingers.
Part of the problem is that most of us are unaware what 'Christians' were like back then.
For one thing the majority couldn't read. Their understanding of 'Christian doctrine' depended solely on what had been told to them by the priests. They were not the gentle, high minded, Bible studying folks we often encounter nowadays.

The Christians of Snorri's time were a whole different type of beast.
They were pretty much rebranded Viking Age people, born into the rich and powerfully organized cult that their ancestors had tried for centuries to defeat, a cult that the Norse Kings, 200 years earlier, had decided was best to join up with, for the sake of their own continuing power.

Here's a telling insight from the excellent book, 'Song of the Vikings', by Nancy Marie Brown, about a typical Sunday at Oddi -
'The lovely Stave Church Homily might be read that morning from the great illuminated book of sermons resting on the lectern, since the priest 'knew that the congregation would take his words more seriously if they could see that he was reading from a book.' The four pillars of the church, this homily taught, were wisdom, righteousness, temperance, and fortitude, while its floor was paved with obedience, humility, and patience. It's clear Jon (Loftsson) aspired to be a pillar, not a paving stone. He had a beautiful singing voice, and as a deacon he had mastered the mysteries of Gregorian chant.
After church his men amused themselves with chess or dice, wrestling or ball games that resembled rugby, trials of strength like stone lifting, and horse races or horse fights in which two stallions were provoked to attack each other. Then came the feast at which both men and women could eat to bursting and get drunk on ale, beer, mead, or wine poured from a silver pitcher into a golden bowl. Stories were told, poems crafted and recited, songs sung to the thrumming of a harp, dances danced, and gifts liberally distributed, for the uncrowned king of Iceland lived like a king.'

Pretty much a good old day of heathen Viking fun with some preachy high-minded rituals to be endured before the fun starts!

This is the new world that little Snorri now entered at Oddi - a very aristocratic centre of traditional learning, overseen by his new foster father, who just happened to be closely related to the Royal family of Norway!

The school at Oddi had been set up around 1100, (80 years before), by Jon Loftsson's paternal Grandfather, Sæmund the Wise. He was considered to be a great Wizard, capable of magical feats of wonder, at least he was by a biographer of the time who also translated into Icelandic the 'Prophecies of Merlin' by Geoffrey of Monmouth, (who had a huge influence on the shaping of the 'Arthurian Legends' of King Arthur and the Knights of the Round Table).
Sæmund was also believed to have played a part in the creation of the Poetic Edda, the great collection of ancient poetry and related prose from which Snorri appears to have taken much of his inspiration. In fact, my venerable 1926 version of the Poetic Edda, (in Old Norse), is called by its traditional name, 'Sæmundar-Edda'. Tales of the Viking God's would have definitely been part of the curriculum for the young scholar!

In 1190 Snorri turned twelve, and a decision had to be made - would Snorri become a Priest or a Chieftain? Up until 1190, as we are told in 'Kristni Saga', 'most respectable men were educated and ordained as priests, even those who were Chieftain's'.
That year the archbishop of Trondheim decreed that from then on, no Icelandic Chieftain could be a Priest and vice versa'.
I like to think that Snorri made the decision himself, drawn as he was to the great tradition of the refined Norse Jarl, the Chieftain, the leader, the aristocrat, who could compose skaldic verse in its complex metres and kennings, based on deep knowledge of the old stories, compose love poetry, write runes, play chess, sail a ship,

fight with skill using both hands and various weapons and shoot fast and straight with a bow.

At the age of 16, to celebrate Jon Loftsson's 70th birthday, an eighty-three verse poem was composed and written down, and it is possible that Snorri wrote it.
Nancy Marie Brown tells us 'whether he was a poet on this occasion or not, Snorri became a very skillful one. Skaldic poetry was a game of puzzles and Snorri mastered all its metres and rhetorical tricks. Few poems had been written down, so Snorri learned the way Icelandic skalds had for hundreds of years: by ear'.

The education he received, in contrast to most continental ecclesiastic schools, was in the vernacular. Students overseas were trained in Latin, but Snorri shows little signs of having ever learnt Latin or read it. He never shows off Latin in his writings as others of his generation did.
His Icelandic is in his own style, and is not influenced by the classical writers.
Snorri was unique.
He was his own man.

When he turned forty, he set off on a research tour of Norway and Sweden, undoubtedly thinking about his great historical projects to come, Heimskringla (a huge work), and the Edda (not a small project!). There was no internet, no library of maps from which he could research all the nuances of geography for his stories.
He must go and see the lands for himself.
We can imagine him seeking out the elders, the poets and storytellers who remembered the old stories, and possibly, if my theory is right, he would be seeking out the old 'hidden' heathens.

(In fact, Sweden is known to have been solidly heathen in some areas well into the 17th century).

Nancy Marie Brown tells us, (pg. 83 of 'Song of the Vikings') that 'when Snorri sailed to Norway in 1218, he was, by most calculations, the uncrowned King of Iceland'.
Like his foster father Jon Loftsson, he was fascinated by royalty and kingship, and the ancient history of the Norse people. He seems to have set off on his own volition, with the hope of winning the affection and acclaim of the young King of Norway, Hakon (14 years old at that time).
In this he no doubt dreamed of following in the footsteps of the great Icelandic Skalds of the Viking Age.
Icelanders were famous for their poetic gifts and cultivation in the traditional knowledge of the ancient stories, and Icelandic Skalds served at the courts of the Royal houses of Scandinavia.
Snorri was taking himself to the Viking homelands, the great forested, fjorded, snow covered lands of the North, where royalty and the nobles claimed and curated the memories of their long, long family lines, (an interest still very much alive in Iceland to this day).
These family lines explicitly linked them to their god-like forefathers and mothers, the Aesir (and numerous Giants (Jötun's) and Elves (Álfs)).
We will be meeting these forefathers, mothers and fabulous beings up close in the next chapters.

Over two years Snorri was guided through the Northlands, making copious notes and sketches undoubtedly, as evidenced in his incredibly detailed and realistic stories, reaching back into the mists of time.

He eventually spent time in the company and court of young King Hakon, and despite the fact that relations turned sour for him in the end, he undoubtedly gleaned a tremendous amount of knowledge, both open and secret from that group of families related to Norwegian royalty. Who knows what sources were still available in that now remote time 800 years ago?

In 1219 he came to Skara, Sweden, and met a fellow law speaker, Eskil Magnusson, and Kristina Nilsdotter Blake, his wife.
Eskil and Kristina were related to Swedish royalty, and I don't have any trouble imagining them on many pleasant days and nights, sitting by a fire over a meal, or traveling through the lovely countryside, discussing the ancient history of Sweden.
I imagine that these royal relatives imparted much to Snorri that was not common knowledge, and which, but for his Edda and Heimskringla, would have been lost forever.

Having said that, and not to let the cat out of the bag just yet, in my travels in Denmark, Sweden, Norway and Iceland on my Viking Superpowers Research Tour 2024, I concluded that much of this secret paleocontact and paranormal history is still surprisingly close to the surface, preserved in memory if one just knows where to look.
Much is also still hidden from English speakers behind the language barriers, in old books, folk tales, special local knowledge and custom.

Let's hear from some modern scholars and authorities who have made statements about or hinted at my contention - that the writer of the Prose Edda and the voluminous Heimskringla, Icelandic Chieftain, Historian and Poet Snorri Sturlusson, was not a Christian. That in fact he could well have been a secret Heathen, someone who researched and gathered and collated the stories about the ancient spirituality and strange happenings in the North, no matter how at times odd and confusing, for the sake of later generations better equipped to solve the puzzle.

Us!

We will start with a powerful statement, an extract from an interview in the online journal Norsemyth.org, with Jóhanna.G.Harðadóttir, an Icelandic journalist, author and artist. She was (at the time of the interview in 2011), Deputy High Priestess of the Aesir Faith Fellowship, (Ásatrúarfélagið), the pagan Church founded in 1972, and officially recognised by the Icelandic government.
(KS below refers to the interviewer, Dr Karl E.H.Seigfried, a prominent American Professor and Pagan scholar. JH refers to Jóhanna Harðadóttir).

KS - Ásatrú doesn't really have 'holy books' in the way that other religions do. The main texts of Ásatrú are the two *Eddas*, which were both written down by Christian scholars after the conversion of Iceland. Jews, Christians, and Muslims have books written by the prophets of their faith; Ásatrú has a collection of poems written down by monks and a manual on how to write archaic poetry. How do you think that the use of these "filtered" sources affects the psychology and practice of Ásatrú today?

JH - I really don't know how to answer that question. Of course, we know that Snorri Sturluson was writing this in a Christian age, but why did he do it? **He must have been pagan. He must have. Why do you write these things down?** (my emphasis).

He wrote this prologue to excuse himself, really, because you're not supposed to write things like that, but he does it anyway. He would not have written it, unless he cared.
Just like today, we don't have this dogma. Snorri Sturluson is a scholar. He knows stories; he gets them. Storytelling in Iceland was very much alive at that time. People were telling stories, and they were not written down. They were something that you told your children, and your children told *their* children. That's what he's taking.

KS - So, Snorri collected folk tales like the Brothers Grimm did in 19th-century Germany.

JH - Yes. You're getting bits and pieces. For me, it doesn't *matter* all that much. I'm very thankful for Snorri Sturluson - who was my twenty-seventh grandfather - for writing this down, because now we have *something*. But even if he didn't, I'm still myself, and I would still believe in the same things'.

Isn't that incredible!
Professor Seigfried is obviously a true authority on the subject of Old Norse culture, and yet he begins his interview with that very strong statement.
He categorizes the Edda's and Heimskringla as not being 'holy books', because of this perceived fanatical Christian bias that many believe Snorri to have had.
Yet one could just as easily ask why other religions so-called holy books are any more or less believable than what this Icelandic Chieftain and scholar preserved for us?

Professor Seigfried considers Snorri's Edda, (and by extension Heimskringla), to be 'filtered' through a Priest and Monk-ridden lens.
However, Jóhanna, the Deputy Chief Priest of the official heathen religious group of Iceland, leaps to Snorri's defence, with obvious passion developed from long consideration.

"He must have been pagan" she counters.

Jóhanna goes on further in the interview to back up my contention that contemporary Icelanders don't really care much for religion, and still hold some fairly understandable bitterness against the authoritarian enforcement of Christianity upon them since the year 1000.

Maria Kvilhaug, Norwegian artist and scholar, in her superb and thorough book 'The Seed of Yggdrasil'(2020), writes
'Sturluson wrote his Prose Edda in an attempt to explain the real meaning behind the poetical metaphors - this was in fact his stated intent. And without his work we would have understood nothing at all of the Edda poems.
The problem with using Snorri is that his work, too, was biased. He was probably a devout Christian who loved his ancestry and thus desperately tried to make it more acceptable to the Church. **Or he was a secret pagan who desperately tried to preserve the myths in a fashion that would hide pagan messages in plain sight.** Snorri's way of making the pagan ancestry acceptable was by explaining away the gods as actual ancestors that were misjudged by their descendants and turned into false gods. The Church would not look kindly upon pagan gods (demons, idols), but it would not mind ancestors. The Church would not accept pagan doctrines of salvation and resurrection, but it would accept

ancestral history. There is a reason why Snorri's work on the pagan myths was known and accepted throughout the Middle Ages, while the Poetic Edda manuscript was hidden away.'

This is an excellent assessment of the truth in my view.
I have to disagree however with the idea that Snorri was 'explaining away' the Gods as ancestors. The Royal Houses of Scandinavia and Anglo-Saxon England all remembered their Æsir ancestors as actual men and women, albeit very exceptional people capable of flying, unbelievable technical feats, paranormal powers, and able to live very long lives by artificial means.
In the next chapter we will delve into the exciting world of those Royal ancestors.
I get the sense that the Church authorities thought that these strange ancestral stories had some basis in fact.
They just refused to countenance any worship of these remarkable ancestors, or the idea that they could still be present and operating in the affairs of humans.

In her masterpiece, 'Scandinavian Mythology', the great Norse scholar H.R (Hilda) Ellis Davidson writes of the difference between the two medieval scholars who set down the old stories of Gods and Goddesses 'still current' in their time. The first is a Danish ecclesiastical historian of the twelfth century, Saxo Grammaticus, who wrote a lengthy history of Denmark in Latin. She states that Saxo often shows disapproval of the characters in the legends, and evidently found some of the doings of the gods and early heroes improper and distasteful, but nevertheless he tells the stories.

'He has preserved many tales and traditions which would otherwise have been lost. Very different was the second writer, Snorri

Sturluson, a brilliant poet and historian as well as an active politician, who wrote in his native Icelandic. About the year 1220, he produced a handbook for poets, so that they would recognise allusions to the myths, and use them correctly. Possibly he felt some indignation at his predecessor's disparagement of the Gods, for he recorded the old myths with love and enthusiasm.

He wrote in controlled ironic prose far ahead of most of his European contemporaries, with a full appreciation of the imaginative beauty and the dry humour of the tales he told. His Prose Edda was so successful that our knowledge of the northern myths is largely derived from it, and **where we have been able to check his information from surviving poetry, it is surprisingly accurate.**'

Very interesting indeed!

Snorri 'felt indignation at his predecessor's disparagement of the gods'! Doesn't sound like someone who had no actual belief in the reality of these same 'gods' does it.

One also gathers from Hilda's statement that a lot of people have spent a lot of time checking Snorri's information, and this renowned scholar attests that Snorri has not been found fibbing or making things up.

I'd also like to share some correspondence I had with my friend Ármann Jakobsson, Professor of Old Icelandic. It was Ármann who pointed out to me that remarkable passage in the Icelandic 'Sturlunga Saga', concerning Snorri's father Hvamm-Sturla, and the attack on him provoked by his alleged admiration, and even hero worship, of the heathen God Odin.

This is what I wrote to him on the 22nd of October 2024 -
'Hæ Ármann,
I am thinking a lot about Snorri's Dad and wondering whether he might have been a closet worshipper of Odin? It seems to me that the incident with Þorbjörg indicates as much.

Which leads me of course to wonder how much influence Hvamm-Sturla had on young Snorri's thinking?
You are the only scholar or layman who has mentioned this incident to my knowledge.'

He replied to me that evening in his careful, yet deeply informed and scholarly manner.
'I'd say she is certainly implying that, although that does not mean she is right.
I am quite sure though that young Snorri would have heard all about the incident and would definitely have thought 'Who is this Óðinn?''.

In a previous conversation Professor Jakobsson had also said to me something along the lines of 'I really wonder why Snorri would have bothered collecting and writing down all these legends if he actually was a devoted Christian.'
Ármann was not making any firm statement one way or the other, yet personally I detect a change in attitude amongst scholars since the time that I first engaged with this subject in the mid 70s.
At that time the church was still a force to be reckoned with, both socially and politically. Younger scholars are now free to empathize with pagan and non-Christian mindsets, which can only be a benefit to real academic inquiry into this subject, so long hampered by dogmatic attitudes to the culture of the Vikings.

I like to think that Snorri's father, Hvamm Sturla, (though Snorri was a mere 5 years old when Sturla died at the age of 68), could well have encouraged him, as a well born Northern lad, to stick to the old faith as he, (and perhaps his family), had done, yet to keep that faith quiet, and to himself.

Undoubtedly the intelligent little boy would have asked his father about Odin and the dramatic accusation, made before many witnesses, by the Priest's knife wielding wife.

I also like to think that perhaps other members of his family were on the same wavelength as his father, and may well have secretly tutored him as he grew up.

Now to end this chapter sticking up for Snorri, I'd like to address one other important matter concerning his honour.

Those who are well read in the literature of this subject will know that there is a low bit of gossip that gets bandied around, gossip concerning the manner of his death.

This is the accusation that Snorri died a coward, failing to live up to the high standard of courage and manly honour that he so esteemed in his heroic writings.

On the rear cover of one of the otherwise excellent books about the Vikings in my library, I found this statement.

'He died a coward, cringing in his cellar, his Viking ideals abandoned. But his books live on.'

There is indeed a cowardly story related to his death, but it was not Snorri who was the coward!

It is a matter of history that his deadly enemy, Gissur, attacked his stronghold with 70 men one night. Snorri had, despite his situation being precarious, left the drawbridge of his fortification down, and hadn't even placed guards on the walls.

He had been asleep, and at the alarm had leapt out of bed, dressed only in his nightshirt, and tried to seek the shelter of his writing studio, where a secret spiral staircase led to an escape tunnel.
Snorri is 62, overweight, but not necessarily lacking in fighting strength. He doesn't make it to his writing studio, but instead one of his household priests locks him into another cellar, one that unfortunately does not have an escape route. The priest is questioned, and either gives him away to save his own life, or Gissur's men find the cellar.
We are then told Gissur ordered five of his most thuggish retainers down into the cellar. The head thug perhaps shouted to one of his underlings -
"Strike him down!"
"Don't strike," said Snorri
"Strike!"
"Don't strike!" commanded Snorri.
The first man struck as did another.'

Snorri's execution had been ordered by the Norwegian King, Hakon, because he had failed to allow the King to take control of proud, independent Iceland. Snorri has earned the King´s deadly ire because of his courage in resisting the tyrant.
Now I ask you, is it fair to besmirch Snorri's name and honour with the label of 'coward'?
He was unarmed and confronted by five killers with swords (or axes).
Snorri is not reported to have blubbered for mercy, offering to give the killers anything they wanted, is he?
He merely says, 'don't strike!'
That seems exceptionally reasonable, and indeed courageous to me. The only witnesses to the scene are the five killers, and so we only have their word for what was said. He could have actually

said 'at least give me a weapon you lowlife scum, and come at me one by one, like real men!'.

It is the very definition of cowardice for five armed men, obviously hardened killers, to strike dead a trapped, unarmed older man in a nightshirt. It is Gissur and his men who are the cowards! It is they who should have been maligned for 800 years!

I don't suppose the majority of people who have accused Snorri of cowardice over the years have ever faced so much as an angry pensioner armed with a pocketknife, let alone five hardened armed killers.
Personally I think Snorri lived up to the heroic Viking ideal.
I think Snorri had 'guts'!

So now you know why I believe, (and admire), Snorri, and why I think that it's very important to take this new attitude to his work. If we can just try to simply believe him, to relax and put previous judgements aside, and say to ourselves - 'I'm going to choose to believe what he writes, take it at face value, and see where that leads me', then I think we'll be surprised by the story that emerges.

WILL THE REAL GODS PLEASE STAND UP

The stories of the gods have come down to us in a form that at times can seem confusing. In Snorri's book, Gylfaginning, from his Prose Edda, there are stories that seem purely mythical, in that large, magical, unscientific fantasy sense, such as the story of a giant cow, Audhumla, who appears out of ice and 'rime', and gave out four rivers of milk from her teats, specifically to feed the ancient frost giant Ymir.
This cow licked a man out of a block of salt, a big, handsome, strong man named Buri, who then somehow had a son called Bor. Bor married Bestla, who then gave birth to three sons named Odin (yes that Odin), Vili and Ve.

We are later told that Odin and his two brothers found two logs by the seashore, and created people out of them, a man and a woman, whose names, Ask (Ash tree) and Embla (Elm tree or Vine), rather resemble those of the biblical first pair, Adam and Eve.
From the great 'Poetic Edda' story, Völuspá, some scholars have made the educated guess that, before this transforming of logs into living beings, they may have first been carved into human shapes by dwarves.
The three brothers then gifted the figures with breath and life, secondly consciousness and movement, and thirdly with faces, speech, hearing, and sight.

From these two humans descended mankind, who were given a place to live called Midgard (Miðgarð), meaning the Middle Enclosure/Fortress. 'Middle Earth', as JRR Tolkien called it.
We are also told that the three brothers created and were the rulers of all that exists, and that Odin, the chief brother, was also called the Allfather, and that 'this is the name of the one who is the greatest and most glorious that we know, and you would do well to agree to call him that too'.

So we would seem to be talking 'God's of the whole Universe' level God's here. Undoubtedly immortal, omniscient, omnipotent, and surely not human, let alone Earthly.
Yet in other places we are told a very different story about these three immortal world creators.
For instance we learn that one time Odin had been away on one of his long, world travelling missions, and had in fact been away so long that people decided that he must have died.
His two brothers, Víli and Ve, then chose to not only divide up his belongings, but also to start sharing his beautiful wife!
Odin, being a real party pooper, arrives back shortly thereafter, and takes back his stuff and his wife!

We are later told that he eventually dies of sickness.
As he is about to 'shuffle off his mortal coil' Odin asks to be marked (stabbed) with a spear, so that his followers would believe that he went to Valhalla, the after-death warrior's paradise, the high and holy place that he himself was said to rule!
As you probably know, dear reader, only warriors killed in battle are said to be worthy to enter that holy place, and all others are consigned to the Underworld.
So remember Odin's workaround warriors if you inconveniently find yourself dying a cow's death!

Of course it is obvious to us that these are descriptions of two very different types of beings having the same name.
It is all rather odd isn't it.

In this chapter we will discuss these two different streams.
One stream appears to be a mystical ancient set of beliefs, reaching back a very long time, and pointing us, however obscurely, in the direction of spiritual practices of the wild Bronze Age and probably Stone Age peoples. The other stream relates stories that are very hard not to see as accounts of paleocontact, that is, of human ancestors encountering advanced humanoid, high-tech, yet spiritually powerful beings, beings who appear to have usurped the older stories for their own ends.
Ends that include the reasonably peaceful takeover of the vast rich lands and the virile warlike peoples of the North.

At this juncture I would like to introduce you to two quite exceptional ancient humans.
According to the stories these two men were the original sources of the stories of the Gods, and a significant proportion of the whole mythology of the North, at least as passed down to us by Snorri Sturluson in his Edda and Heimskringla.
They are said to have been told all these stories face to face, up close and personal, by the 'Gods' themselves.
Both were then sent back to their peoples, charged with the mission of recounting everything they had been told, and everything that they had personally seen whilst visiting the home of the Gods!

One was named Gylfi, and the other Aegir. Gylfi was a human as we consider ourselves to be human. Aegir was a Jötun, a mysterious human type often translated as 'giant'. Gylfi lived in Sweden near the great lake Vänern. Aegir lived on the island of Hlésey, (now named Læsø), off the Jutland Peninsula, Denmark.

Gylfi's story is related in the first book of Snorri's Prose Edda - 'Gylfaginning'. This title is usually translated as 'The Deluding of Gylfi', yet it could just as well be translated 'The Scamming of Gylfi'. You will find out why soon.

Aegir's story is told in the second book of the Prose Edda - 'Skáldskapamál', a title usually translated as 'Poetic Diction', but which more literally means 'Performing Poets Shaping Words').

Gylfi is introduced to us in Old Norse like this -

Gylfi konungr réð þar löndum, er nú heitir Svíþjóð.

(Gylfi the King ruled there the land, (which) is now called Sweden)

And again - Gylfi konungr var maðr vitr ok fjölkunnigr.

(Gylfi King was a wise man, and a practitioner of great knowledge.)

He was a Wizard! A man steeped in the ancient knowledge of paranormal and normal powers available to humans, as passed down by his ancestors and fellow practitioners.

A Wizard King.

He was the most powerful person in Sweden.

(The word 'fjölkunnigr´is often translated as Sorcerer or even Witch, however I avoid these words in most cases, they having become weighted with very negative connotations over the years. The word Wizard, however, thanks to Gandalf and Radagast, has a dignity and goodness to it, (though we won't mention Saruman will we!).

Aegir, the Jötun from Hlésey, is described in the Old Norse in this way - 'Einn maðr er nefndr Ægir eða Hlér. Hann bjó í eyju þeiri, er nú kölluð Hlésey. Hann var mjök fjölkunnigr.'

(A man is named Aegir or Hlér (his a.k.a name). He lived on an island there, that is now called Hlé's island. He was a very great wise man of knowledge).
A great Wizard.
In essence (probably) the most powerful person in Jutland/Denmark. We have no account indicating that these two gentlemen Wizards ever met, but we do know that they were connected together by a unique common thread – they both seem to have been abducted, in very unusual circumstances, without their knowledge, whilst on self-motivated missions to meet the fabulous Powerful Ones of the East, the 'Aesir' (the Gods of the Vikings!).
They were both targeted, it seems, to act as the perfect future spokespeople, two men carrying the greatest respect and authority in Sweden and Denmark, to spread what would appear to be a manufactured theology, a carefully considered version of various (even disparate) native beliefs and customs and folklore.

But first they needed to be impressed big time!

In this chapter we will focus on the Swedish Wizard King Gylfi, and in the next chapter we will again meet Aegir the Jötun (Giant).
Gylfaginning begins by introducing Gylfi as the king who rules the land that is now known as Sweden.
We are told that 'it is said of him that he gave a 'travelling woman', (a 'farandi kona' in Old Norse), as a reward for giving pleasure to him, one plow land in his kingdom, promising that she could have as much land as four oxen could drag up in a day and a night'.
Rewarding beautiful ladies who give one pleasure with 'plow land' is somewhat out of fashion these days, but it was indeed a generous and practical gift at that time.

Young King Gylfi must have been very taken with this woman, and we might guess that he gave her plough land rather than gold and jewels because he wanted to keep her close to him. Unbeknownst to him, she is one of the Ása family, the family collectively known as the Aesir, and her name is Gefjun (aka Gefion aka Freyja…yes, that Freyja.)

The King is about to find out, in an extremely dramatic way, exactly what this means.

The next thing we know, the lovely Gefjun heads off to Jötunheim, the world, (or even the home world), of the Jötun, the often beautiful, humanoid and dangerous beings of whom Aegir is a part. We are not informed of her means of transport to Jötunheim, but we assume that it is some distance off, and she appears to get there pretty quickly.

The Edda tells us that she had previously bred with a certain Jötun there and given birth to four oxen. Ouch!

This of course is a pretty weird piece of information, possible in a fairy story, but I have reason to believe that these four 'sons' are something different, perhaps some form of enormous and completely anachronistic terraforming machines.

In Heimskringla we learn that Gefjon not only 'had four oxen with a certain Jötun' but that 'hon brá þeim í yxnalíki' - 'she shaped them into ox likenesses'.

Which sounds as if she had four little human babies and then somehow shaped them into gigantic earthmoving oxen. If we are going to take the naturalistic paleocontact approach then this doesn't seem likely does it.

As we will learn in a later chapter, the ancient language seems to use terms that would be normal for a non-high-tech people to try and describe things that are for them almost indescribable. The classic example is that of Native American's describing the steam locomotive as an 'iron horse'. It's obvious that a locomotive doesn't look like a horse in the slightest, but what it does do is move fast and carry heavy loads, which is exactly what a horse does. So, the word 'horse' really becomes a code, meaning 'something that moves by itself and carries things'. This talk of oxen, (very strong creatures that pull heavy loads and big ploughs), is to me using a code to describe Gefjun literally shaping (designing and building) very large earthmoving and terraforming equipment!

She returns to Sweden with these 'oxen', and proceeds to plough wide and deep, and dredge a massive chunk out of the land.
Using another mysterious technology, Gefjun takes all that land and terraforms an island out in 'The Sound', between Sweden and Denmark.
We are told that this terraformed island is called Selund (Sealand), which just happens to be the island where the capital city of Denmark, Copenhagen, now lies.

It's hardly worth noting that King Gylfi would have been absolutely stunned, feeling greatly ripped off, and asking himself who on Earth this 'farandi kona', this travelling woman, really was!
Imagine what it was like to be a witness to this event!
The massive chunk of land that Gefjun had taken in a day and a night, with her four so-called oxen, has now filled with water to form a huge lake, almost a sea, which Snorri tells us becomes known as Lögrinn (The Lake).
A very creative name!

Most commentators consider that this refers to Lake Vanërn, the largest lake in Sweden, which also bears an uncanny resemblance to the outline of the island of Selund/Sealand (modern Zealand).

The thing about this story is that it could be just considered a wild mythic fantasy, (even by Snorri), when he was writing it into his Edda, an old story good for poetic training and worthy of preservation.
My question is, why would he go ahead and repeat it in his 'History of the Norse Kings', Heimskringla, which is obviously written to be a straightforward book of history?
Snorri must have believed that it was actually true!

When we read the account of the meeting of the Wizard King and the beautiful Aesir woman in Heimskringla, we discover some very interesting extra information!
It is as if we zoom out a bit and start to see the bigger picture.
The saga, Ynglinga saga, (within Heimskringla), informs us that it was Odin himself who sent Gefjun on this wild mission to grab a huge chunk of King Gylfi's land!
Odin and many of these mysterious people, the Aesir, have recently moved into the area from a long way away (much more about this soon).
In Old Norse we are told - 'Þá sendi hann Gefjun norðr yfir sundit í landaleitan' which translates as
'Then sent he Gefjun north over the Sound in land search'

So we return to the young King, Gylfi.
As a Wizard he is steeped in the great ancient knowledge of human superpowers!
Yet here, in what appeared to be a young and gorgeous woman, he had more than met his match.
At some point in this adventure he had learnt that she was of the people called the Aesir. Obviously human and yet… 'he was very surprised that the Aesir people were so knowledgeable, (more knowledgeable than him)'.

He wondered whether this was to do with their very nature as beings, or whether it was to do with the gods that they worshipped? Gylfi had also learnt that these beings came from a place called Asgard, which literally means 'the city/the enclosure/the fortress of the Aesir people'.
In Gylfaginning, (in Snorri's Edda), we are told that the original Asgard is called 'Old Asgard', which of course indicates that somewhere there is a 'New Asgard'.
It would seem that the new version of Asgard is only in the planning stage at the time of these events.

King Gylfi determines to head off to Asgard and meet these very powerful people face-to-face, a bold thing to do, but one would expect no less from a young Wizard King, who more than anything else valued deep knowledge.
I believe that he was heading for Old Asgard, and my reason for this is that very soon we are going to meet the three rulers of Asgard, one of them Odin, and his two brothers, (who he had put in charge of Old Asgard after he and many of his people had left to go North).
(I also assume here that Odin flew back, (in some type of flying craft), to the old capital, specifically for this meeting. You'll soon see that it was all part of a plan).

Gylfi is a smart guy, so he decides to disguise himself as an old man for the journey, undoubtedly thinking that Gefjun must have some way of communicating to her leaders that he was coming.
He would assume that she would provide them with a detailed physical description. This in itself is interesting, because as I'm about to tell you, it's a long way to Old Asgard and he had seen enough to believe that she surely must have some magical way of long-distance communication.

He didn't know the half of it.

Gylfi even changed his name to Gangleri, which is probably not the trickiest pseudonym, a little too close to the sound of Gylfi if truth be told.
Interestingly, 'Gangleri' is considered by the best Old Norse - English dictionary, Cleasby and Vigfusson, as related to the (still current) Scot's word 'gangrel', which means 'stroller, vagabond'.
To my eye it also hints at a possible meaning of 'gang'- to walk, and 'leery'- to wish to avoid something, wary of, even sick of.
Sick of walking!
Theres no doubt that, on foot or on horseback, it's a long way from Sweden to Old Asgard!

So, let's get to the nitty-gritty about what sort of place Gylfi can expect to find when he gets to Asgard.

The Prose Edda (Gylfaginning Ch.9) states - 'There next they (Odin and his brothers) built a fortress in the middle of the world, that is called Asgard. That we call Troy. There lived the Gods and their families, and there happened many events and tales, both on the Earth and up in the sky'. Isn't that strange!
'both on the Earth and up in the sky'.
This statement indicates pretty clearly that the three brothers built Old Asgard both on the ground, and up high in the sky!

With my paleocontact hat on, I can imagine a great city on the ground, somehow connected to a city up in space, perhaps in geostationary orbit, perhaps tethered to the ground?
Massive theoretical devices like this have been seriously proposed by many physicists over the years, seeking to solve the problem of

efficiently moving large masses up into space, without the prohibitive costs and problems of rockets.
A natural thought that might occur to you is, *'Dave, that's a nice, neat science-fiction way to think about this, but is there any basis in the old stories for such an idea?*
Well, I'm glad you asked!

There are in fact two concepts in the stories that appear to represent a physical attachment between the Earth and sky.
The first concept sounds very like what is referred to as a 'space needle', a 'space elevator' or a 'star bridge', a literal bridge between outer space and the ground.
In Gylfaginning it is written that -
'goðin gerðu brú af jörðu til **himins**, er heitir Bifröst'.
'The 'gods' built a bridge from Earth to **above the sky, to the stars, to outer space**, it is called Bifrost (trembling or shimmering bridge).
(Note - I always translate the word **'himin/himins'**, etc, with its literal meaning - 'the sky or above the sky or space or outer space', rather than the incredibly archaic, and disingenuous translation, 'heaven', that previous translators have almost always used.
'Heaven' was certainly the correct translation for himin five hundred years ago. For centuries however, 'heaven' has been almost solely selected as a translation to add a pseudo-religious, supernatural, 'mythical' cast to these stories, rather than the obvious straightforward translation. More about this later.)

The text continues - 'Hon er með iii litum ok mjök sterk ok gör með list ok kunnátu meiri en aðrar smíðir'
'It has three colours and is very strong and made with art and skill more than other smithing (highly skilled construction)'.

So obviously 'Bifrost' was enormous, reaching from the ground up into space, having (only) three colours, an engineering marvel beyond anything we could achieve today. In popular translations of the Viking myths, it is often called the Rainbow Bridge, but we are not supposed to believe that it is really a rainbow, the storyteller is just suggesting it looked something like a rainbow. The last time I looked at a rainbow it had more than three colours!

The second concept that appears to represent that connection between Earth and the sky is the 'World Tree', or the 'World Ash', as it is sometimes called.
In Old Norse this unimaginably vast tree is called 'Yggdrasil'.
In Gylfaginning this 'tree' is described -
'Hvar er höfuðstaðrinn eða helgistaðrinn goðanna?'
(Where is the temple place or the holy place of the gods?)
'Þat er at aski Yggdrasils, þar skulu goðin eiga dóma sína hvern dag'. (That is at the Ash (tree) Yggdrasil, there shall the gods give their judgements every day').

A little later we read -
'Áskrinn er allra trjá meztr ok beztr. Limar hans dreifask um heim allan ok standa yfir himni', that is -
(The Ash is of all trees most (greatest/largest) and best. It's limbs drape (spread out over) the whole globe/world and stand over the upper sky.)
Then we are told that when the 'gods' hold their court, to make their judgements and decisions, basically having a group meeting, they ride there '**up over Bifrost**, (aka the Ás (Aesir) Bridge).

Thus, we learn that the 'gods' have their daily meetings at the great tree, (at a place called Weird's Well, which we shall talk about soon), and they ascend **up** Bifrost to get there.

We have a pretty far out story developing here!

The name of this gigantic tree, Yggdrasil, literally means 'Odin's Horse'!
'Ygg' is one of Odin's many, many names, and 'Drasil' means horse. So once again, applying my thinking about symbolic words being used to represent difficult to explain high technologies, I believe that 'horse' here refers to the fact that Odin the Aesir used this means of transport, this 'horse', to get quickly up into space for meetings and on other missions.

Let's look again at what the description says.
'It's limbs drape (spread out over) the whole globe/world and stand over the upper sky'.
Now we know that, contrary to popular belief, the people of the Viking Age had a pretty good idea that the Earth was a globe, and not a flat disc.

At least the people in Snorri's time knew this, because that's what the name Heimskringla means – the globe or the orb of the world. So let us imagine this 60 km (35 mile) long trunk, reaching the edge of space, firmly planted in the ground, and spreading out its branches circling over all the world and extending above the whole earth. If these branches were all actual tree branches and covered in leaves, then this would obviously throw a great shadow on the earth, because the sunlight wouldn't get through. Surely this effect would be noted in somebodies old stories?
So, I'm discounting the mythic idea here for a moment, and thinking outside the square, my paleocontact hat firmly on my head.
What if Snorri is describing a great network of connected satellites, covering the sky right around the whole globe!

I find this profound concept quite exciting, and it fits in with a lot of the other stories we will be looking at in the next chapter, stories about all the huge, glittering, light filled 'halls', belonging to the Aesir, and floating up in the sky and in space.

Further proof for this idea of an Asgard in the sky/space is revealed in the next statement, speaking of at least one of the activities for which Odin would 'ride up' his 'horse', Yggdrasil, or would ride 'up over' the Bifrost bridge.
'There is a place, Hliðskjálf (meaning 'on the side or sloping shelf') it is called. Odin sits there in a high seat, then see's he over all the world, and every man's deeds, and he knew (understands) all that he saw'. Whenever I read these sentences, I get goosebumps.

I see Odin sitting in a seat, (or floating), in an area that is like a shelf, jutting out from the edge of a part of this great city, Asgard, in space. He is looking down from orbit, observing the doings of men, (and others), consulting an array of very high-tech instruments, (viewing devices, recording devices, communication devices, etc.), and gathering information.
Information including that gathered from the network of spy satellites described as the branches of the great tree.

So now let's consider who Snorri believed these Aesir people to be?

We learn that Odin's wife, (one of many), is named Frigg Fjörginsdottir (Fjorgin´s daughter), and that from them are descended all the 'Aesir', and those that are descended from them, which we will discover includes many many families and family lines, throughout Europe and Scandinavia, especially the Royal families.

The text sometimes refers to the Aesir as gods, which can be a bit confusing, as in English it tends to refer to all-powerful, omnipotent and omnipresent divine beings. In the old Germanic languages, however, the word god originally meant 'one who is invoked, and called upon for help, one to whom offerings and sacrifices are made'.

This is what Snorri writes in Chapter 2 of Ynglinga Saga (at the start of Heimskringla) -'To the east of Tanakvísl, (the great river Don), in Asia, it was called Ásaland (Aesir Land) or Ásaheimr (the Æsir World), and the capital city, that was in the land, called they Asgard (Ásgarðr).
In that town was the Temple Lord (Chieftain) who was called Odin (Óðinn).
There (in Asgard) was a great worship place (a great Temple).
That was there the custom, that (there were) twelve Temple Chieftains (knowers of God).'

The Aesir were 'the people of Asia'.
I remember quite clearly, when I first read this description in the Edda, thinking 'What the heck, the Aesir came from Asia?!' To an Australian like me, Asia means the great lands of the Far East.
Upon doing some research, I learnt that Asia, according to the ancient Romans and others, begins in the area of Turkey (modern Türkiye), and that it is marked as Asia on the old maps. Even today it is still sometimes called Asia Minor.

In Snorri's 'Prologue' to his 'Prose Edda' he writes - (my translation)-
'From the north and down the eastern half, all the way to the south, that is called Asia (Ásíá). In that half of the world is all exceptional

beauty and splendour found, and all of the Earth's fruits, gold and gemstones. There is located the middle of the world.
Just as the land there is shiningly beautiful, and better in all qualities than other places, so too the people there were exalted for their almost magical abilities and powers - profound wisdom, physical strength and paranormal power, and great physical beauty.
Near the middle of the world was built that (hús) house and (herbergi) room , the greatest that has ever been, that is called Troy, there where we call Turkey (O.N.Tyrkland) (modern Türkiye).'

Writing about a great city like Asgard, and calling it a 'house and a room' seems decidedly odd. This is where a translator can dig deeper, looking for hidden meaning.
That last sentence, in Old Norse, is-
'Nær miðri veröldinni var gört þat **hús ok herbergi**, er ágætast hefir verit, er kallat er Trója, þar sem vér köllum Tyrkland.'
The word 'hús' simply means a house, and one generally thinks of a house being perhaps small, or perhaps quite large, but generally being one unit. In this context, however, as we are talking about these very unusual people, perhaps the use of this word is pointing towards the city being one gigantic unit? A house, but a house like no other?
The next word, 'herbergi', is still used commonly in modern Icelandic, and just means a room in a house. However, when you break the word apart, you get two significant clues to a forgotten ancient meaning - the word 'her', (sounds like 'hair'), meaning 'army', and 'bergi', meaning shelter/protection or mountain.
A place of protection for an army, or an army mountain. For me, this conjures up the idea of a military base buried under a mountain!

Is it possible that Asgard, on the ground, could have been both a single very large city, in effect like a massive landed mothership, as well as containing a deeply buried military base, covered by a mountain of rock? A 'herbergi' protecting the inhabitants from potential massively powerful attacks, from weapons such as those we are able to deploy in our own time?
A concept that really makes sense, if we remember that the powerful beings visiting and ruling over earth seem to have gone to war with each other at times.

The Prologue continues -
'This city was built far larger than any before it, and with great technical skill in many ways, with no expense or materials spared from the available resources. There were twelve kingdoms and one High King, and many nations were subject to each kingdom. There were in the great city twelve Chieftains/Kings. **These twelve Chieftains/Kings were above even the greatest men (of the past) in all manly virtues.**'
Thinking about my previous idea, that Asgard could've been one great single unit, a 'hús', then this description of it being divided into 12 brings to mind the divisions of the hours on a clock. The number 12 of course is significant in many ways, but this clock concept suggests something round. Perhaps a great mothership, an enormous round craft filled with thousands of rooms?
A gigantic 'city' that could move location if necessary?

All told, these people, the Aesir, their lands in the middle of the world, and their great city, (on the ground and in space), are really pretty awesome!
They seem almost too good to be true, and I think that this is one of the telling aspects of these descriptions.

There was something about these people, and the way they lived, that just blew the minds of ordinary humans who encountered them at the time.
One can image the wonder that someone might experience, growing up knowing only sunlight, moonlight and firelight, surrounded by wild beasts and wild people, living in the survival manner of all creatures of nature, and then suddenly being confronted by one of our massive shopping complexes, full of thousands of squeaky clean sci fi city people, with every kind of light and music, with shining surfaces and great panels of glass, incredible clothes and exotic foods on offer.
This is the type of wonder that these stories are expressing.

In this passage Snorri calls the city Troy, yet in the previous Heimskringla passage, we were told that it was called Asgard. This is not as conflicting as it may seem, because Troy is the name that the great city was known by in the Ancient Greek stories, and by the mediaeval scholars of Iceland, yet the word 'Asgard' has more of the nature of a description, meaning as it does 'an Aesir fortress/city, or enclosure', an 'Ás Garð' (our word 'garden' comes that word Garð).
We have already heard that there was an Asgard on the ground, and an Asgard up in space, above the sky. It strikes me that this word could be simply a generic term describing any such fortress belonging to these powerful people. In some cases, it might be literally a 'flying fortress' (and isn't that how Marvel portrays it?).

Now let's check back in with our young Wizard Gylfi.

He has set out from his kingdom in Sweden, probably both on foot and on horseback, and passes through innumerable wild, wolf, bear, bandit and cannibal ridden forests, crossing innumerable

rushing streams and roiling rivers, living off the land, against all odds staying alive.
What a story this would be just on its own!
The journey undoubtedly takes months, and maybe he is injured, bitten, speared, whatever along the way, and has to get aid and shelter at times.
When questioned later by the Aesir, amazed that he made it all the way to Asgard, he answers that he had travelled through 'trackless ways'.
This tough, determined, gnarly dude is someone who never gives up!

I suspect that his 'old man' disguise wasn't worn the whole time, but probably became his persona once he was into easier country, down in the south, closer to Turkey.
He guessed that the Aesir would be looking out for a young Wizard King, and thus wouldn't expect a fragile old man.
His disguise would let him get up close, allowing him to inspect their fabled realm for a while, before he had to confront the Aesir personally.
This is where something very unusual happens.
The Edda tells us 'En æsir váru því vísari, at þeir höfðu spádóm, ok sá þeir ferð hans, fyrr en hann kom, ok gerðu í moti honum sjónhverfingar'.
(But the Aesir were wiser, as they had the gift of seeing visions/the second sight/prophecy, (in Old Norse 'spádom'), and saw they his journey, before he came, and **put in front of him visions (O.N sjónhverfingar)**).

Now lets just imagine Gylfi, posing as footsore Gangleri, limping along a dusty road, over rolling hills and farmland, perhaps wondering what on earth that enormous thing was that he could see in the far distance. It seemed to reach right up into the sky, above the clouds, like a gigantic tree.

He starts to suspect that that impossible tree might well be the location of Asgard.

Next thing, Gylfi has a vision put in front of him, such as, oh I don't know, maybe a great glowing craft coming down from the sky, a beam of strange light dropping from its underside and surrounding him.

He finds himself levitating, helplessly lifted up into the air, floated up through a tunnel of light into the underside of the glowing craft.

Next minute he is standing in front of the biggest building he's ever seen, it's roof covered with something that looks like glittering shields. He realizes that the strange building is one single great house, a vast hall, the biggest thing he can imagine, a gigantic glittering construction.

A sight pretty much beyond his imagination.

Gylfi realizes that he can't remember how he got here.

The last thing he remembers is standing on top of a small hill, looking towards the enormous tree.

He remembers what his mission is however, and he feels sure that his old man disguise is solid. Once inside this hall he should be able to check things out unnoticed.

(The joke here of course is that, as we will learn later in the next chapter, there are no old people amongst the Aesir, making him and his tricky Gangleri disguise stand out absurdly).

Gylfi notices that there is a man standing beside a doorway that must open into this great building.

Oddly, the man is amusing himself by juggling several hand axes at the same time. (An ancient astronaut busker perhaps? Or are they in Zero G and the man is demonstrating it's effects?)

Gylfi has seen people do this sort of thing before, mostly entertainers at feasts, but he has never seen a performer with such high skill.
He asks if he can get a night's lodging here, and who this great hall belongs to.
The juggler tells him that the great building belongs to their King, and he suggests that he lead the way to the King's chamber, where the inquisitive visitor could ask the King his name, face to face.

The Aesir Juggler and Gangleri enter the doorway, and then the Edda tell us that, 'the door closes immediately on his heels'. Maybe the door just swung quickly closed, but for me this description sounds for all the world like one of those original series Star Trek spaceship doors, the ones that zip in and out of the walls behind people, automatically opening and shutting ' immediately on their heels'.
Self-opening doors, set off by sensors, that slide in and out of walls, are pretty standard tech for us now, but for people before the 1970's, this was not a thing.
Seeing those doors on the Starship Enterprise automatically sliding open and shut on people's heels was a real 'gee whiz, space age' experience for most of us. That's why such doors became a cliche in science-fiction films.

Gylfi follows the juggler into the great building. We are not told how far they walk or where they go, but we are given a very interesting description of the activities he sees on the way.
The Old Norse says 'Þar sá hann **mörg gólfs** ok margt fólk, sumt með leikum, sumir drukku, sumir með vápnum ok börðusk. Þá litaðisk hann umb ok þótti margir hlutir **ótrúligir**, þeir er hann sá'. ('There he saw **many floors** and many people, some playing (games or sports), some drinking , some with weapons who are

fighting. Then he had a (good) look around, and thought many things **incredible**, those that he saw').

Some English translations say that 'he saw many apartments', yet the Old Norse specifically says 'many floors' (mörg gólfs).

I read this as meaning floors, in the sense that we use the word, e.g. a large shopping centre or a skyscraper having many floors.

He doesn't see everything, he just reports what he saw, and those things he saw seemed to him **ótrúligir** - incredible, unbelievable, inexplicable.

We can assume, staying with our paleocontact approach to the stories, that he was seeing some seriously far-out, high-tech machines, objects and lifestyles going on.

He's brought before three men sitting on 'thrones' (Old Norse 'Hásæti'- literally High Seats, where the leader/s sit), and he is introduced to them.

These three, like Wizard Gylfi, are being tricky, and instead of calling themselves Odin, Vili and Vé, (Odin and his two identical brothers), they call themselves High, Just as high, and Also High. The high seats are said to be arranged one above the other, and I imagine them set out like the flightdeck of the Starship Enterprise, in command centre fashion, on different tiers.

Gylfi asks who their ruler is, and High responds that it is he. He asks the visitor if he has any further mission, and if not, he is welcome to food and drink, like everyone else in that incredibly tall building.

I like to imagine at this point that Gylfi is looking out and down at the bright green and blue orb of the Earth, through a gigantic viewing window, and perhaps starting to wonder whether he should've stayed home after all.

Yet he courageously stands a little taller, perhaps takes off his old man grey wig, grey beard, and baggy clothes, and reveals his true self, the muscular, lithe Bronze Age warrior Wizard King.

Arrogantly, hiding his deepening fear of the obviously god-like power of these beings, he replies 'I wish to find out if there is any wise man inside this place.'
He uses the term 'fróðr maðr´, 'wise man', which in the ancient way of thinking would be a word combination easily translated as Wizard, a practitioner of paranormal skills and abilities, which in Christian times translated as a practitioner of magic.
In effect, he is challenging these three kings to prove to him that their magic and wisdom is greater than his.
High puts him in his place, and replies that Gylfi will not get away unharmed unless he can prove that he is indeed wiser, that is, a greater Wizard!
(We learn in Heimskringla that, later on, back in Sweden, Gylfi can be quite a handful, wizard-wise, even for the King of the Wizards, the mighty Odin).

A long conversation of questions and answers ensues.
Disappointingly, there are no magical telekinetic or lightning casting duels described, yet we get to listen in as a very solid corpus of stories and myths are laid before the young Wizard. It also seems possible that during this rather long conversation Gylfi may have been taken on a further tour of this vast and mysterious 'house'.
Not only are his questions answered, but much more information is offered, explaining the sorts of things any thinking person of the time might ask themselves -
Who am I, where am I, who created me, who created this world? What's happening out there above the clouds, what sort of

creatures and gods exist up there, and also down on the Earth in other places?
How should I behave, and who can I look to for help and aid?
What does the future hold for Gods and men?
As a Wizard, who can train me to the next levels, when I have already reached the highest levels as a human?
Gylfi was, undoubtedly, also wondering what his future relationship would be with these super-powerful Aesir people.

Despite the initial threat from High, (Odin), it's obvious that the three wise kings wanted to feed him a lot of information, and would seem to be relying on him having a fantastic oral memory. This, of course, is one of the defining qualities of pre-literate cultures, when it is said that, for example, the Celtic Druids memorized vast amounts of knowledge.
The Old Norse poets (the Skálds) did the same. In fact, that's how we know so many of these stories, because that tradition of long elaborate memorization was still alive in Snorri's time. A similar tradition survives to this day in Iceland, in the form of Rímur, very long songs based on the sagas, sung for hours on end around the fire at night during the endless winters.

In the next chapter, 'The Elohim of the North', we will look closely at many of these stories and see that, as I suggested at the start of the book, they fall into two fairly distinct categories – pure ancient spiritual myth, and then surprisingly futuristic science fiction-like stories that are, I believe, solid records of paleocontact with high tech races in the ancient past.
We, along with Gylfi, will discover what his relationship, and that of his people, would be.

Now Odin wraps up this remarkable interview.

He says to Gylfi something mysterious and quite telling.
'And now if you know any more questions to ask further into the future, I do not know where you will find answers, I have heard no one relate the history of the world any further on in time. And may the knowledge you have gained do you good!'
Odin is here explicitly revealing that he is not omniscient, (an all-knowing god), and that he also doesn't know who one could ask to find out about the far future (which is where you and I live!).

Suddenly…'Gangleri heard a great roar coming from all around about him, and he looked out to his side. And then when he looked again, he was standing out on a flat plain and saw no hall and no fortress.'
Just as happened on his way to Asgard, one minute walking over rolling hills, and next minute in front of the massive building and the great city, here Gylfi is one minute receiving a farewell from the three Aesir leaders and then...blank…next thing he's on his back, looking out to his side (through a porthole?), a great roaring all around him, then…blank…he's standing on a great empty plain, no city, no building.

Does this description bring anything modern to mind?

As I read this in the Norse, I was struck be how much this sounds like the experience of an astronaut, lying on an acceleration couch, in a capsule re-entering the Earth's atmosphere. The roar of the furnace of re-entry plasma surrounds the craft, he looks sideways through the porthole (a spacefarers head being pinned to the couch on re-entry, and only able to turn).
It doesn't sound too farfetched to me.
Perhaps the poor guy then lost consciousness under the massive G forces, comes to after safely landing, the hatch automatically pops,

and he finds himself on a great open plane. Exactly the sort of landing place that modern re-entry vehicles aim for, avoiding smashing into uneven landforms, forests or manmade objects!

Next Snorri writes -
'Gengr hann þá leið sína braut ok kemr heim í ríki sitt ok segir þau tíðendi, er hann hefir sét ok heyrt, ok eptir honum sagði hverr maðr öðrum þessar sögur'.
('Goes he then on his way abroad and comes home to his kingdom and tells the story, of all that he has seen and heard, and after him each man told others these stories'.

Let's pause here for a bit of a debrief. What exactly has gone on?

Simply put, the most powerful man in Sweden was approached by an agent of the powerful people, the Aesir, the Elohim of the North, who gave him a demonstration of their personal beauty and attractiveness, and of their awesome technological abilities.
This demonstration of power and knowledge completely hooked the young Wizard, who set off on a very long, dangerous and arduous journey to get to the bottom of who these people were.
When he came near to where Asgard lay, he was once again shown how powerless he was against them.
These Aesir somehow spirited him away from the country road, and into a vast futuristic city, quite possibly in orbit. He got to ask every question he wanted, and he was answered fully, and also undoubtedly shown much that is not mentioned in the story.

Having been thoroughly indoctrinated and impressed, he is then told that he needs to go back and tell everyone what he has seen and learnt. That is exactly what he does.

He became essentially the founder of a new belief system, one that appears to have been put together from a foundation of the genuine but disparate ancient stories and beliefs of peoples all over the North.

A lot of extra information would have been included to set up these Áss and Ásynjur (Gods and Goddesses) as the true holy ones, worthy to be worshipped and obeyed, (and not to mention, feared). The Wizard King Gylfi was undoubtedly very famous in Sweden, hero worshipped by many people, and his word would've been taken as the absolute truth.

We can imagine that he told these stories for the rest of his life, with passionate certainty, because he really was there, and he really was told the stories and shown the wonders. These stories became legend, and as Snorri says - 'after him each man told others these stories'.

It is in the very next paragraph, at the end of Gylfaginning, that I found something so unexpected that, when I first read it, I gasped out loud.

I was incredulous!

This information appeared to perfectly confirm my suspicion that these stories, these myths, were actually (in the main) about paleocontact.

Gylfi has literally just 'left the building', by the sounds of it strapped into an escape pod similar to the one R2D2 and C3PO used in 'Star Wars', as the pair escaped from Darth Vader, making a blazing re-entry down to the surface of the desert planet of Tatooine.

This is what I read –

'But (the) Æsir then sat down to talk and discuss together, and remembered all these stories that had been told to him (Gylfi), and gave these same names that had been mentioned before to the people and places that were there (at the meeting), so that when a long time had passed, people would not doubt that they were all one, those Æsir, (as in mythic God's), about whom he had just been told, and those there now given the same names.'

What an incredible revelation!

I can see the Aesir now, those high-tech space-faring Asgardians, all relaxing, perhaps taking off costumes, or strange headdresses used to impress the visiting Earth man. They stand chatting in groups and the Commander calls them to order, suggesting that they gather in 15 minutes time in the main meeting room. Soon they wander in there and take their seats. On the wall is a large high-tech whiteboard style affair, and the crew start to excitedly call out the names of which ancient mythical characters part they would like to play.
It's a given that the Commander and his two cloned brothers, (more about this later), will take on the names of Odin, Vili and Vé.
Odin's chief pilot takes the name of Forseti (in Old Norse - 'The Front Seater', the man up front), a name still used in Iceland to this day, the title for their President).
Methodically, all the many names and roles in the stories told to Gylfi are assigned to crew members.
The beautiful second-in-charge has joined the meeting from Sealand, Denmark, via 'Aesir Zoom', and indicates that she would like to continue playing the role of the love Goddess Freya/Gefjun.
Odin agrees, and asks for a show of hands, Já or Nei?
The Já's have it.

What happens to the Wizard King of Sweden next?
How will he react to the newly named Aesir's upcoming sneaky move?
Find out next exciting chapter, here at Viking Superpowers!

THE ELOHIM OF THE NORTH.

It is summer in Sweden, and there's a heat wave, 28°C every day, but we, (the Swedes and I), are loving it.

It is the most perfect weather, with blue skies and cool breezes.

I have tracked down the location of an incredible and anachronistic artifact, a Viking Age brooch, (c1000 AD), recently discovered by archaeologists in a great heathen Temple courtyard in Uppäkra, Sweden, and I'm heading to the Library Museum of the University of Lund to see it.

This brooch backs up two very remarkable saga stories about an Elf, Völund, who builds himself a flying machine to escape from a cruel King and his Queen, in a time long long ago.

The most well-known of these sagas is called 'Volundakvitha' (Volundakviða), (The Escape of Völund the Elf), which is recorded in the Poetic Edda, and the second is 'Velent the Smith's story' (Velents þáttr smiðs), from Þiðreks saga af Bern, (Thithrek of Bern's saga).

We will take a deep dive into these two great stories soon.

Climbing to the second floor of the museum I first enter the room where the fabulous brooch is housed, along with numerous other strange bird-like artefacts. After some time filming and photographing there, I head to the next room, which happens to be devoted to the Swedish Bronze Age (c.2000 - 500 BC).

My prime historical interest on this Scandinavian trip has been researching the belief systems, archeology and artifacts of the Viking Age (793 AD - 1066 or thereabouts), and somewhat the previous Vendel Age, (550 - 750 AD).

Little did I know that I was about to make the most sensational discovery connecting the Bronze Age to the Viking Age, leading to an ongoing series of related revelations and artifacts in Denmark, Norway and eventually Iceland.
These finds opened up a whole new world of understanding and possible paleocontact stories and mysteries for me.

The first object I saw in that second room (and it was hard to miss), was quite a large rock, mounted on a shallow rectangular box.
I instantly recognised the two 'sun crosses' carved into this rock, one on the front side as I entered the room, and the other on the face to its right.
The sun cross is a symbol found all over ancient Scandinavia, and much further afield, and consists of a symmetrical cross surrounded by a circle.
Scholars in the field uniformly recognize it as a symbol of the sun, and yet at the same time cannot be sure that this interpretation is always correct.

The sun cross is believed to be the symbol of the 'Sky People', beings the ancients tell us came down from the sky, mated with humans, and established dynasties and ruling elites/families.
This is also an accepted mainstream interpretation, though treated as a religious fable created by those ruling dynasties to give themselves the credibility, cache and kudos that comes from being descended from 'gods'.

I have my own interpretation.

I consider that there is good reason to view the sun crosses as representing great glowing, sun-like craft, in which these Sky

People came to the Earth, abducted, tweaked and experimented with chosen humans, sometimes mating with them, and making advantageous partnerships allowing the Sky People to rule silently behind the scenes.

This of course is not a mainstream view, (though it is steadily growing in acceptance), but it has been very convincingly argued by other scholars, including Paul Wallis, a Church of England Minister and translator of Biblical texts in his excellent Eden series of books, and Mauro Biglino, the highly regarded Italian scholar and translator of Ancient Hebrew.

Mauro's books are similarly excellent and convincing.

Both scholars argue that interactions between these beings and humans, in cultures all around the world, have happened since the dawn of time, and are ongoing.

It's still happening!

I initially recognised the sun cross symbol from a book I had bought in the mid 1980's titled 'The Mound People', by Professor Peter (P.V) Glob, a pioneer in the field.

It was written in 1970 about the Bronze Age cultures of Denmark and Sweden.

The cover had always stuck in my mind.

It is a striking image of a rock carving from Sweden, depicting in a pictographic way a man and a woman, the woman having long hair and the male perhaps bald, and having an erect penis. The male figure also carries what at first glance looks like a shield, but which is in fact a sun cross.

I say that it's a pictographic drawing because I believe that the key to these mysterious Bronze Age works, (which number in the many thousands, and more are being discovered all the time), is to realise that different parts of the drawings represent different words.

This is a brilliant way to send a message across time, because one's language doesn't matter. A language of visual symbols should be potentially recognisable to people from any language, or any time. This particular pictographic message says simply, 'one of the powerful Sky People mated with one of our women'.
The standard interpretation is that this is pure superstition, because we scientific moderns know that the gods don't exist, do they?
My position however is that these gods did exist, though however wonderful they were, and perhaps worthy of some worship, they were not supernatural, but very natural indeed.

One of the most well-known of these pictographic ancient carvings is displayed on a broad area of smooth rock in Tanum, Bohuslän, Sweden, showing what appear to be several Sky People, each with a sun cross symbol, standing tall, holding up above their heads hammers or axes.
A touch of extra mystery is that beneath each hammer / axe there appears to be a lightning bolt.
Surrounding these figures, on both sides, and stretching off into the distance, is a virtual fleet of Bronze Age ships.
For all the world it looks like a meeting between a group of Sky People showing off their power, and a mass of Earth people watching on in awe. But I'm getting ahead of myself.

Returning to the rock in the Lund Museum, the second thing I noticed, besides the two sun wheels, was that the whole rock surface was covered in what archaeologists call 'cup marks'.
These are deeply incised hemispheres, in a range of sizes, and on this rock they are laid out very randomly over three dimensions.

Mainstream archaeology insists they have no idea what cup marks mean, even though they are found in their thousands, from Great Britain right across Scandinavia.
One of the skills I bring to this study is that I am a classically trained visual artist, and as I surveyed the 'cup marks' on this extraordinary rock I instantly saw stars represented, and not just stars, but a really effective sculptural representation of a starfield in three dimensions!

'Didn't primitive people's think that the stars were just holes in the curtain of night?'.
Looking at this awesome rock sculpture I felt that I was in space travelling through a great field of stars! I could see large stars and a variety of smaller stars (suns) laid out like a 3D map.
Surely only somebody who had actually been out there, either in reality or in virtual reality, could come up with such an effective visual concept?

Upon my return to Australia, whilst I was looking at my photographs of this carved rock, I was taken by something that I had noticed in other carvings and artefacts.
Beneath one of the sun crosses, with the deeply incised stars as a background, I saw the faintest cone-like shape descending from the bottom of a sun cross.
This cone began at the base of the cross, where the incised sun cross circle was flattened slightly, as if to visually say - 'something came out of here'.
I noticed that the base of the cone shape rounds, in a surprisingly realistic way, as would a light from above hitting the ground.
This looked to me to be a representation of what has become a classic sci fi trope - 'a bright light coming down from a flying saucer, lifting up a person being abducted'.

Exactly the imagined scenario that occurred on the road to Asgard when the Aesir abducted the brave Gylfi!

I wrote to the museum in Lund, and asked if I was perhaps seeing things when I discerned this faint conical shape beneath the Sun Wheel. I didn't let the cat out of the bag and tell them what I thought I was seeing.
(My feeling in Scandinavia was that people generally were very open minded, but that institutions were more wary of anything smacking of 'Ancient Aliens').
Understandable I suppose. These ideas, even in the 2020's, are still very orthodox.

I received a kind response and was told that these cone or 'ladder' shapes underneath some Sun Crosses are seen all over Scandinavia. Academics believe them to represent the timber stand that would hold up a representation of the Sun Wheel during religious ceremonies.
Whilst I can see the reasoning, I personally doubt that an ancient artist would bother carving a simple stand into super hard rock, just to represent how their Sun ceremony literally looked.
All told, this carved rock was one of the most amazing and convincing proofs of paleocontact I encountered in Scandinavia.
It appears to be an eyewitness account carved with great skill and effort.
I can't really see this artistic masterpiece saying anything other than something like this - 'there were two great shining Sun Wheel craft that appeared in our skies, a great and terrifying light dropped from one craft and somehow lifted me up into it. I was taken away from my people, (and incidentally I saw that we live on a great blue, green, brown ball), we sped away into the night and to my surprise I saw that the planets and stars are also like balls, in three

dimensions, some extremely large and bright and others, smaller, lit by their light.
They are NOT just lights on a flat field of black!'

I continued my journey north, along the west coast of Sweden, and caught up with a good friend, Asgeir, who looks for all the world like the god Thor! We had met in the comments section of my YouTube channel, and hit it off right away, as he is a very dedicated and enthusiastic researcher into exactly the same areas that I am researching.
We have shared some quite uncanny experiences together, including my making a video about Valhalla, uploading it, and then him writing to me almost instantaneously, saying that he had just driven to an airfield called Valhalla that morning, and that he was standing there as he wrote his comment.

I stayed over at his fine Swedish country house that night, and of course we talked about paleocontact mysteries into the small hours. The next day we went for a long drive, (in a Volvo of course), and first he took me to a 3000-year-old national park area of standing stones. We stopped beside a particularly interesting group called Hagbards Galge (Hagbard's Gallows). These tall and massive stones are named after a grim, but romantic Romeo and Juliet style story, well known in the Viking Age.
The stones are much older than that however, and the first thing I noticed was a carving on one of them, a pattern of concentric circles.
Asgeir told me that this area was famous for UFO sightings, and also unusual crop circles, and that a lot of discussion had been had about this place on Swedish TV at times.
Paul Wallis has written in his latest book, 'The Eden Enigma' - 'As I show in 'The Eden Conspiracy', standing stones have been used

through the ages, all around the world, to mark places of first contact. They tell us, 'This is where our ancestors met the 'gods'.'

There was a definite energy about this place. Perhaps it was because Asgeir had told me that it had been a place of human

sacrifice (shudder) in the Bronze Age, or perhaps it was because when he had tested these standing stones, with a special instrument from the US that measures levels of static electricity, he got extremely high readings.
So here was another circular shape, concentric circles, carved on an ancient stone, different to the sun wheels, yet still seeming to be related.
This design has a similarity to other important Danish Bronze Age artifacts, particularly the bronze 'belly disc' found in the young Egtved girl's grave, and on the famous horse drawn bronze and gold sun disc from Trundholm.
Perhaps these were representing Bronze Age experiences of crop circles (and perhaps related craft), that modern Swedes are still scratching their heads about.

I could sense a pattern appearing, and had the sense that there would be more clues coming up soon. I was not wrong.
We headed off again towards a 'secret' spot that Asgeir wanted to show me, saying that he didn't want to spoil the surprise by telling me too much.
On the way there, we dropped in on a huge, picturesque castle in Vastergotland, Bohus Fortress, a place with a long, (and frankly, really horrible), yet storied history. Nearby lay a famous meeting place, Kungahälla (ON Kongungahella), where Snorri Sturluson, in Heimskringla, tells us that the three kings of Denmark, Norway, and Sweden had met in 1101.
These were King Inge 1 of Sweden, King Magnus Barefoot of Norway and King Erik Evergood of Denmark.
This was at the very end of the Viking Age, and where a significant peace treaty between the three warring countries had been agreed upon.

We stood high on the ramparts of the castle, looking in one direction up the river to where it flowed into the great lake, Vänern, which the powerful Aesir woman, Gefjun/Freyja, had caused to form by artificially scooping out up the 'plough land' from under king Gylfi's nose, creating the island of Zealand as an Aesir base.
In the other direction lay the fabled final resting place of the great hero Beowulf, slayer of the monster Grendel, (and his terrifying Mum), and of a dragon that came to lay waste to this area when Beowulf was an aging King.
King Beowulf died fighting evil, unrelenting, like the great man he was.

Proceeding on, we finally came to a stop beside a long curving road. Asgeir directed my attention to what at first seemed to be a great strip of forest, approximately 500 metres from us across grassy fields.
As I surveyed this 'forest' I was amazed to see that it was in fact three huge mesa-like landforms, edged by tall cliffs, rising straight up from the surrounding plain. Each landform was topped by thick forests of great Scandinavian trees and brush.
I looked up the area on a satellite map and saw that each landform had a distinctive shape. The largest one was roughly circular, the one beside it triangular and touching the edge of the great Lake Vanërn, and between them and to one side a significantly smaller tear drop shaped landform.

Asgeir informed me that these three landforms are the property of the Swedish Royal family, and have been their royal hunting grounds since the Viking Age, and probably for a lot longer.
He grinned.
"Believe it or not, these three are called Asgard, Valhalla and Odin's lookout!".

I said, “You have got to be kidding!”.
Asgeir replied, “I’m not kidding, these are the original names. The modern names for the two large landforms are Hunneberg (Asgard) and Halleberg (Vallhalla), and just behind Halleberg is the great lake, Vänern (Gefjuns lake!). Odin’s Lookout is called Häcklan”.

As we learnt earlier, there was the original Asgard in Anatolia, Asia Minor, which was known as Old Asgard, and it seems logical that this amazing place was the best candidate for the fortress we might call ‘New Asgard’.
Up in the forest of Asgard, (modern Hunneberg), there is an old-fashioned Hunting Museum also belonging to the royal family.
It showcases a huge collection of taxidermy, as well as exhibits showcasing ancient legends about these mountains.
We were a little late to visit this particular day, but Asgeir had visited on other occasions, and had taken photos of these historical exhibits.
Below is a translation from modern Swedish confirming that at least the historians of the Swedish Royal family think the same way as I do.

‘Odin searched for a long time for a place where he could live and live well, together with the other Aesir gods.
After a long journey, he finally found excellent land and plains at Hall, the mythical mountain we call Halleberg today. There he had Asgard and Midgard built, as well as one of the largest ancient cities in the whole of Svitjod (Svíþjóð - the ancient name for Sweden).
From Häcklan - ‘Odin's Lookout’, indeed from the whole Halleberg, he and his Aesir had a good view of the surrounding lands and over the small magical lake ‘Odin's dam’.

He looked from his high seat, over all the worlds. Just next to the foot of the mountain he saw a large burial ground and in the center of this burial ground was the mighty judgment ring "Hästevadet stenar"- a holy place surrounded by a beautiful temple grove'.

Straight from the horse's mouth.
In my 50 years of interest in the Viking Age, and having read many scholarly books on the subject, I have never come across this story before.
Asgeir and I had been let into a very special, very ancient secret.

Halleberg (Valhalla) is considered to be Scandinavia's largest hillfort (about 20 sq kms or 7.7 sq mi), being almost completely naturally fortified by the large surrounding cliffs and very steep slopes. There are large ancient ramparts and fortifications up there, some of which we saw hidden amongst the trees.
I looked again at my satellite map, and looking down from outer space, the image of Asgard, (Hunneberg), revealed a definite circular shape, and possibly other circular shapes within it.
The first thing that came to mind was the satellite photograph of Ancient Troy, which I had seen as I was researching the location of Old Asgard, the original homebase of the Aesir.
Troy looked very similar, like looking at what was left after a gigantic circular structure had been removed thousands of years before, leaving only vague traces of the foundation.
Once again I felt goosebumps.

This great circular shape, the sun crosses on the carved rock in Lund, the circles on the stone at Hagbards Galg, the sun crosses as part of depictions of the Sky People/ Sky Father all over the ancient rock carvings in Scandinavia, and now this.

So totally unexpected, here next to the very lake where it is said the Aesir had begun carrying out their plans for the conquest of Scandinavia.

We drove up and parked, heading off on foot down the steep track to where the forest of Valhalla meets the great lake. I had to pinch myself, thinking that I was here where the story of paleocontact in Scandinavia began. Maybe this was where Gylfi had his royal fortress? Maybe this is the place where he took the beautiful woman Gefjun for a night of feasting and love?
Along the track we saw large stone walls covered in moss, and I could just imagine the whole area being fortified in the ancient days.
Asgeir was very tuned in, having visited the mountains many times, and as we walked he picked up chunks of silvery heavy metals to show me.
I was surprised to see that they were just sitting on the surface, along with all sorts of other unusual geological bits and pieces.
The trail got wilder and steeper, and there were spectacular small waterfalls and vertiginous drops, and great tree roots tangled together everywhere.
I had to really keep my wits about me.
There was something very reminiscent of Tolkein's novel 'The Hobbit' in this landscape, at least to my romantic mind.

It certainly felt like we were in an old and sacred place, rediscovering forgotten history that had been very important in the Viking Age and well before.

As we neared Lake Vänern I noticed a tumble of very large squared off stones, covered in thick moss, leaves and sticks, which appeared to be the remains of a building. Rounding the corner of

the precipitous trail I saw that there were a number of these buildings, and that these were in somewhat better shape.
They were tall, perhaps 14 feet high, massively built and mysterious.
We were able to enter one of them, and saw that the walls were close to eight foot thick.

A very small official sign nearby stated that these structures were thought to have been lime burning kilns, but that this was not absolutely certain.
I didn't get that vibe from them.
Asgeir told me that the structures were called the Lost City by some people, and that their age was unknown. He believed they were thousands of years old.
They really felt like places where ancient peoples could have lived, or maybe they were storehouses for a port where ships unloaded supplies and visitors bound for the great fortress.
Asgeir considered that these structures could well guard the entrances to great tunnels, running deep down underneath Valhalla and Asgard, and now filled in and blocked off.
I think that's a pretty reasonable thought.
His theory also put me in mind of those mysterious 'herbergi' mentioned earlier, 'army mountains', shelters deep underground protecting the Aesir from attacks by other advanced enemies.
There is even a story in the Prose Edda that the Aesir had what sound like anti-aircraft weapons installed in tunnels under Asgard. We shall visit that story soon.

Now let's rewind to the very beginning for a bit, to the stories passed on from the Viking Age to Snorri, and thereby to us. We'll find out more about who these Aesir were and why these god-like 'people of Asia' came to leave their original home in Anatolia, coming all the way up to the far north to settle in many places, including this 'new' Asgard by the lake.

This is the story that Snorri tells us in Ynglinga Saga, (about the Swedish royal dynasty, the Ynglings), at the beginning of Heimskringla, the 'History of the Norse Kings'.
These Ynglings are the first dynasty of Swedish Kings, (also later to be Kings of Norway), many of whom, as we will discover, were descended from Odin and the Aesir people. Keep in mind that Snorri believes that this was actual history, writing in exactly the same pragmatic way in which he writes all the later stories of the Norse Kings, who are generally considered historically real.
He doesn't say at any point that this is a fantasy history of primitive ancient people, made up to entertain children. He writes it as straight fact.

Chapter 2 of Ynglinga Saga tells us, (as we learnt earlier), that there was a place in the east called Ásaland, (land of the Aesir), or Ásaheimr, (home or home world of the Aesir), and that the capital city of that land was called Asgard (Ásgarð).
Odin was the ruler, there was a great temple there, and there were twelve Goði, (Chieftain Priests), who were in charge of the worship rituals and legal judgements over the people of the land.
These twelve were referred to as **'Díar'**, and as 'Lords'.
'Díar' is an obscure and very interesting word. It only occurs twice in the ancient literature.
This is what the excellent Old Norse/English dictionary, by Cleasby and Vigfusson, says about this passage - ' where díar means not *the gods* themselves but *the priests;* and by the old poet Kormak in an obscure periphrasis, in a poem addressed to the staunch heathen earl Sigurd; Snorri (Edda 96), in quoting Kormak, takes the word to mean *gods;* but the version given in Ynglinga

Saga seems more likely; the díar of the Ynglinga Saga were probably analogous to the Icelandic 'goði', from goð (*deus*). The age of Kormak shows that the word was probably not borrowed from the Latin'.
(Note - The Icelandic old Norse word Goði is pronounced something like 'go thee', the letter ð having a th sound.)

So here it seems we have found the first instance of this institution of Díar / Góði.
Chieftains/Lords, ruling over humans, and being in charge of the ceremonies that humans are participating in, to honour and invoke the gods. Remember that the word god (goð) simply means ' one who is invoked'.
In the later sagas set in the Viking Age we assume, generally, that these Goði are invoking 'gods' who are not physically and obviously present, (though we can't really say that with accuracy. We don't really know what was going on, and who was appearing to who in those days).
Yet here, in this historical account from Heimskringla, seemingly set in the early Bronze Age or even earlier, are Díar/Goði serving the actual 'gods', the Aesir.

This to me seems remarkably similar to the situation in the Hebrew Bible, where you have human priests and chieftains/tribal leaders ministering to the 'holy one or ones', 'The Powerful Ones', and acting as intermediaries between them and the ordinary humans.
One would thus suppose that the same situation was present in Old Asgard, as in the Bible, and in the ancient Mesopotanian stories - the Elohim/ Annunaki appeared to be immortal, or at least extremely long living, and yet their human servants live normal human (relatively short) lives.

This is a very exciting piece of knowledge, and I'll explain why. One of my contentions is that these so-called 'Gods of the Vikings', the Aesir, are part of the large group of beings that the Bible's Old Testament Hebrew language calls the 'Elohim', and which the earlier civilizations of the Sumerians, Akkadians, Assyrians and Babylonians called the 'Annunaki'.

The Annunaki were believed to be powerful Sky People who had descended to Earth, and both created/tweaked human genetics, and taken control of them through guided instruction and training. This included training in literacy, and the handing down of laws of behaviour and punishments for infractions.

Interestingly the Encyclopedia Britannica says of them that the name Annunaki means 'Princely seed'.

Jeremy Black and Anthony Green, in 'Gods, Demons and Symbols of Ancient Mesopotamia: An Illustrated Dictionary', The British Museum Press(1992) write -

'The Anunnaki were believed to be the offspring of An (the Sumerian God of the Sky) and the Earth Goddess Ki'.

Surely this translation points to that Spring Wedding that we have talked about, depicted on the Bronze Age stone carvings?

The royal marriage between a Sky Father and an Earth Mother, which really means a male from the Sky People and a female from the Earth.

This also puts me in mind of that old paleocontact chestnut - Genesis 6:1-2

'And it came to pass, when men began to multiply on the face of the earth, and daughters were born unto them, that the sons of God saw the daughters of men, that they were fair; and they took them wives of all which they chose'.

All this of course leads to hybrid babies, half 'god/ half human'.

Could it be that the Díar are just these sorts of beings?

Which leads me to question, as I write this, were the Aesir themselves products of these unions?
Were they half 'God' and half man?
This is getting really interesting isn't it!
More about this coming up in the chapter entitled 'Chariots of the (Norse) Gods'.

The word **Elohim** in the Bible is normally translated as singular 'God' (the Almighty, Lord of Lords etc.), but the word is definitely plural in the original.
In the book of Genesis, it is explicitly stated that the Elohim said to each other, 'let **us** create man in **our** own image'.
(For a deeper dive into the subject of Biblical and ancient Mesopotamia paleocontact, make sure you check out Paul Wallis's 'Eden' series of books, and his fascinating videos on YouTube at The 5th Kind TV, and the Paul Wallis channel.
'The Naked Bible', and other books by Mauro Biglino, are another must read on this subject, (and his videos are also superb)).
Both scholars are profoundly versed in this subject, and have decades of professional linguistic and theological training.
I believe them, as I believe Snorri!

An accurate translation of the Hebrew word Elohim is 'the Powerful Ones'. These beings are said to be part of a Sky Council, groups of powerful beings, secretly and not so secretly ruling over different areas of the Earth's lands, peoples and cultures, and who meet at a neutral place up above the sky (Outer Space).
Sure enough, we are told in Gylfaginning, (from the Prose Edda), Ch 15 - 'Þá mælti Gangleri: (our old friend Gylfi, disguised as an old geezer) Hvar er höfuðstaðrinn eða helgistarðrinn goðanna? (Then said Gangleri: where is the temple place or the holy place of the Gods?)

Hárr svarar: Þat er at aski Yggdrasils; þar skulu goðin eiga dóma sína hvern dag.
(High answered: That is at (the) ash tree Yggdrasil (Odin's Horse): there shall the gods hold their judgements / courts each day).
Later in the same chapter High, (Odin), tells Gangleri/Gylfi, 'the third root of the ash tree stands above the clouds/in outer space, and under that root is that well which very much is holy, called 'Weird's Well' (Urðarbrunnr).There the gods have their court. Every day the Aesir ride there up over Bifrost. It is also called Aesir's bridge (Ásbru).'

So here we have our friends the Aesir riding up to what would appear to be the Biblical Sky Council.
I have no trouble imagining that they meet there with other Sky People/Elohim/Powerful Ones ruling over other areas of the Earth.
You will note that in standard English translations both in books and online, regarding the third root of the ash tree, you will find the standard English translations say that 'the root extends to heaven'. Obviously, because of the word 'heaven', this doesn't really necessarily indicate that the root is going into the sky. It could just as well read 'the root goes into some other mystical or fairy tale realm'.
I would personally like to 'root' out the use of 'heaven' as a valid word in translations from Old Norse to English!

The word 'heaven' is an archaic English word that is no longer used to indicate the sky, or up where the stars are, except in most Bibles, Shakespearian plays and very sappy poetry for greeting cards etc. It comes from the Old English word 'heofon', which originally meant 'sky' or 'firmament', (another very archaic word which

literally means 'up there where the stars are'). It later came to refer to the Christian concept of the 'place where God dwells'.
And that's the problem!

The Old Norse word used is 'himni', in this instance - 'Þriðja rót asksins stendr á himni'.
'The third root of the Ash stands in himni'.
Which unequivocally means above the sky, where the stars and planets are, in our modern English - 'outer space'.
Simple as that.
Heaven is a theologically fraught Christian word for a supernatural place where God lives. A place outside of time and our natural world. By translating this word as 'heaven' when dealing with the old stories, what is actually going on? It is my opinion that the translator is saying, consciously or unconsciously, that these stories didn't really happen, but that the deluded pagans/heathens thought they happened in a supernatural realm. Basically like 'our' Christian heaven, (though undoubtedly run by the devil and his nefarious offsiders).
So why have secular scholars continued to use this word when translating the Old Norse stories?

It seems to be quite simple. It's just a bad habit, a bit like chewing your fingernails. It's unconscious, and it's following the guys who went before you, without really thinking about what you're doing. When I look into my Old Norse dictionary by Geir T. Zoëga, I am horrified by the translations under the word 'himinn'.
Every word containing 'himinn', and it's grammatical derivations, is defined as 'heaven' this and 'heaven' that, even in the absurd case of 'himintungl', which simply means the moon or a planet or even a star and yet is defined as 'heavenly body'.
I mean, give us a break!

When you look at the definition for this root word 'himinn' in Zoëga's influential dictionary, it states that is a masculine word, and that it means 'heaven', and then, helpfully, as dictionaries do, it gives us an example phrase - 'undir berum himni'.
What does that mean in English I wonder?
Well thankfully we are given it – 'in the open air'.
No 'heaven' in sight!
Cognitive dissonance anyone?

Essentially the word changes according to how the translator wants people to perceive it. My Zoëga's dictionary is from 1910, a very different, and much more religious time than now, and it has been a mainstay of translators since that time.

My point in making this digression is that as soon as you change the word 'heaven' to 'the sky/outer space', you get a whole different meaning. A huge difference.
This 'sky/outer space = heaven' mistranslation is one of the great breakthroughs that the paleocontact pioneer, Erich Von Däniken, made, when he realised how this mistranslation corrupted the meanings of the ancient texts, which the ancestors so diligently wrote and preserved for us.
Paul Wallis has spoken at length about this problem that plagues the translation of the English Bible, and no doubt the Bible of many other languages.
A theological interpretation is laid on top of the ancient words, which are literally saying, 'they came down from the sky'.

So now let's compare my translation of Gylfaginning Ch 15 a few pages back, to these verses from the Poetic Edda, (the book of collected ancient poetry that helped inform Snorri Sturluson's Prose Edda).

This from the poem Voluspa (Völuspá) verse 26 -
'Þá gengu **regin** öll á rökstóla, ginnheilug goð'
(Then went '**the ruling powers**' all to their judgement chairs, the very holy Gods').
That's the word 'Regin', which means the 'Ruling Powers', the 'Powerful Ones'.
In context with Gylfaginning Ch 15 it is obviously synonymous with the word Aesir!
As you will remember, Elohim means 'the Powerful Ones', and that is why I have titled this chapter 'The Elohim of the North'.
We are looking at a very big picture indeed.
As I mentioned in the first chapter, 'Lost in Translation', Professor Haim Eshed told the world that meetings with the Galactic Federation aka The Sky Council are current and ongoing. It looks like this current collaboration with the Sky Council is only the latest iteration in something that has been going on for a very long time indeed.

Speaking of a long time, a couple of years ago, when I first started thinking about this book, I was pondering the Hebrew word Elohim, and wondering whether there were any similar words in Old Norse that might somehow have a similar meaning. It didn't take me long to find the word 'Élhöll', an old poetic word for 'himinn', the sky/outer space.
I was genuinely excited when I discovered that this word also means 'hail hall', and is suggestive of storms and the power of storms, and the place way up in the sky where these phenomena 'live'.
This Old Norse word Él is perhaps an unexpected survival, an ancient echo of that Hebrew word El that literally means a god, and Elohim, meaning 'gods/powerful ones'.

Perhaps it was brought from the place where they originally lived, in that area not too far from where the Semitic languages developed?
There many mysteries to be uncovered!

For now, let's move on to the next chapter and find out how these awesome Powerful Ones happened to come to the North, and how they set themselves up to rule there.

SUPER CLONES, SUPER ROBOTS AND THE BEST OF ENEMIES!

Odin was a great warrior, and we are told that he travelled very widely, and took over many kingdoms. These two things seemed to have been his main priorities in life.
He sometimes travelled so far that he went away for months.
I believe that it is possible that he travelled all over the Earth, and from the stories, it would appear that he may have been travelling outside of the Earth's atmosphere, and perhaps outside of our solar system. But we will get to that.

You will remember back in Chapter 3, 'Will the Real Gods Please Stand Up', that Odin lived in an extremely beautiful place, and we might really wonder why he would ever want to leave home.
It would seem that he was a very inquisitive person, genuinely fascinated by the myriad peoples and cultures of the world, our Earth, of Heimskringla, our globe shaped blue green jewel.
His great city of Asgard sounds like a true, working multicultural society, such as we are working towards in our own time, and Odin was the King, the Chief of all twelve divisions of it. We know that he had two brothers, and it appears that they oversaw Old Asgard whenever he was off on his long journeys.
Which brings us to a mysterious (and somewhat raunchy) story.

This is from Chapter Three of Ynglinga Saga -
'Odin had two brothers. One was called Vé (sounds like Veeyay), and the other Vílir (Veetleer).
These brothers steered the kingdom when he was abroad.
There was one time, when Óðinn had been away somewhere for a very long time, and had long dwelt there, that the Æsir lost hope that he would return. Then his brothers began to divide up 'the inheritance' between themselves, and his wife, Frigg, they shared between them both. But a little later Odin came back. Then he took back his wife'.
(One assumes that he took back his property as well, but it seems obvious that his wife was the most important to him).

I have always felt that there was more to this story than meets the eye. If we think back to the meeting up in Old Asgard in the sky, Wizard King Gylfi meets three men who are apparently the same guy, somehow identical.
The wizard is initially told that he was going to meet 'the' commander and yet is presented with three.
So now we have these three brothers, one of whom seems to be the dominant one, Odin, and he is away a very long time, and so the other two grab his stuff AND start sharing his wife.
We can assume they did this with the beautiful Frigg's consent (no one dares mistreat these powerful goddesses!).
We may ask why this powerful woman, officially married to Odin, was so open to this arrangement? Obviously, we don't know what the moral code might have been amongst these advanced people, able to live for a very long time compared to us.
They well might have had very different ideas about marriage and faithfulness than we do.

My question is, were these three guys identical? Could it be that Vili and Vé were actually clones of Odin, clones created to look after things while the boss was away?
Were they so interchangeable in looks, physique, voice and personality that they were absolutely identical?
It's an interesting thought isn't it.
Extreme biological high-tech always seems to be a characteristic of these ancient Sky People groups.

In the next chapter of Ynglinga Saga we read -
'Odin went with his army to come to grips with the Vanir, but they stood up well to the attack, and defended their land, and both had victories. They raided each other's lands and did much damage, injury to each other. When both sides had grown weary of this, they arranged a truce meeting, made peace and exchanged hostages'.

This is our dramatic introduction to the mysterious people called the Vanir.
As a long-time student of the Viking Age and their stories, I feel that I have always known of these people the Vanir, but I have never found any good explanation of who they were and where they came from.
Paul Wallis and I were talking a while ago, and I mentioned that the Gods of the Vikings had originally come from the area of modern-day Turkey/Anatolia.
Asia Minor.
He was very surprised and interested, and told me about his proposed research trip, along with fellow author and researcher Matt Le Croix, Swedish archeologist Hasse Oreheim, and a crew of experienced cameramen, into an area called Lake Van, in the Kef Kalesi region of Türkiye.

In 2017 archeologists had been engaged to investigate findings at a site called Adilcevaz, and this had led to a team of divers investigating the deep waters of Lake Van, where sophisticated megalithic remains were found.

The exciting thing about these discoveries was that the time when the water level of the lake had been low enough for these structures to have been above water was over 6500 years ago, and could be up to 10,000 years ago!

Making them amongst the very oldest man-made structures in the world.

The thing that puzzled Paul and his team was that these very ancient remains were more sophisticated than later structures in the area.

(Something I find very cool is that this is also in the area of Mount Ararat, the legendary location where, so the Bible tells us, Noah's Ark came to rest after the Great Flood subsided). A very important place for human history.

In our exchanges I filled Paul in as much as possible on the history and legends preserved by Snorri Sturluson, especially regarding the Aesir and their origins in 'Tyrkland', in this area which the Romans called Asia, and where Paul was making investigations.

We spoke about the possibility that the group of people in the old Norse stories called the Vanir, people just as sophisticated it appears as the Aesir, could well have been the people who inhabited this area around Lake Van.

The Vanir play a very important in the stories of the 'Viking Gods', and from them, we are told, came many of the most famous figures in the stories.

We will meet them again soon.

In 2024 Paul and his team set off on his research trip, and he and I caught up via Facetime one day, during what he calls 'beer o'clock'.
He writes of our conversation in his newly released book 'The Eden Enigma'-
'It's beer o' clock and I am back in Van at the Doubletree Hilton, enjoying an online conversation with David Lovegrove. He has just returned from a research trip to his ancestral home of Iceland and is overflowing with scholarly excitement as we chew over the implications of what he saw there. David is the author of Viking Superpowers. A gentleman and a scholar, he looks entirely the part as a Viking by descent. He also happens to be the person who first switched me onto Snorri Sturluson and the ancient Norse stories of the Aesir from Asaland, the neighbours and rivals of the Vanir from Van… I ask David about the prevalence of the four-armed Sun Cross across the North.
I want to know if it means in Iceland what it does at Ayanis (an important ancient castle/fortress above Lake Van) . How does he interpret the symbol?

This was my reply –
Most archaeologists see this fascination with the Sun Discs as indicating primitives worshipping the sun. But I am coming to believe that these images are visual recollections of the Aesir coming to the North. I interpret it as paleocontact. I think, to the best of their ability, they were recording exactly what they were seeing and experiencing.
So, yes, I think the ancient people were seeing suns, but some of them were artificial suns. I think that is what caught their attention. These artificial Sun Discs are references to things in the sky which visited and interacted with them. Let me show you some objects, which I think you will find support that view.'

I sent Paul images of many different rock carvings from the Bronze Age in Scandinavia, particularly from an area called Bohuslan, where there are literally thousands of wonderfully artistic and mysterious examples.

Bohuslan is rather close to where Asgeir and I stopped to walk around the massive Swedish Bohus castle, where the three great Kings made a truce in the Viking Age.

I also sent him the image of a beautiful ornate Sun Cross found in Alacahöyük, 13 hours North-West of where Paul, Matt and their team were based in Van City.

A Bronze Age object excavated from a Hittite royal tomb at the site.

This masterpiece takes the form of a complex lattice of crosses, framed within squares. Around its perimeter are eleven unusual sinuous protrusions in bronze, which suggest flames or conceptions of energy, and hanging on the front of the object are three sun wheels/discs, exactly as I had found in Scandinavia and Iceland on my research tour.

Paul notes later in his new book, 'The Eden Enigma', that the energetic flame-like protrusions mimic quite remarkably a similarly ancient rock carving at Bohuslan, in Southwest Sweden, where we see a round object surrounded by flame-like shapes.

To one side of this carved, round (hovering, glowing?) object, there are two female figures touching it (with the same head shape and long ponytailed hair we see in the 'Spring Wedding' carving).

To my eye these women appear to be floating!

They are also touching the object with their hands.

We shall return to this mysterious tableau!

Now let's return to our story in Ynglinga Saga (Heimskringla)- 'Odin was a great 'warman' and very 'far travelling' and took over many kingdoms. He was so victorious that in every battle, he won, and so it came about that his men believed that he could give them victory in every battle. There was this custom of his, that if he sent his men to battle, or on other missions, then he would lay his hands on their heads and give them **bjannak**. They believed then things would go well. So it was with his men, when they were in trouble on the sea or land, that they called out his name, and it was always thought that they received assistance from that calling.'

So here, once again, is something extremely interesting!
If you search for the meaning of this word, 'bjannak', you will generally find that it is considered mysterious, that it is not a Norse word, but that scholars make an educated guess that it derives from the old Irish word meaning 'blessing'.
However, if you go to The Old Norse/English dictionary by Cleasby and Vigfusson, we find a very intriguing clue.
They write - 'It (bjannak) is commonly interpreted as *benedictio* (blessing), but it is no doubt the Scottish. *bannock,* from Gaelic, *banagh, an oatcake;* cp.Latin. *panis.* The whole passage in the Heimskringla points to Christian rites and ideas brought into the pagan North, but which are here attributed to Odin, (cp. the breaking of bread and the Eucharist.)'

This is a very surprising, yet authoritative take on 'bjannak', but personally, I don't consider that it's an inserted Christian idea being attributed to Odin.
My interpretation is a bit more far out, but I think it has legs (as they say in the barista world).
When I was in Uppåkra in Sweden, looking for the fabulous Völund, (the flying Elf) broach, I saw a half size reconstruction of

a Viking Age 'heathen' Temple, a Höf, and beside it was a white statue of Odin.

This statue was based on a metal artifact from the time, and depicts Odin wearing a helmet with very two long horns reaching up above his head. There are other instances of Odin with a helmet like this on his head, (easily found in books and online), and very interestingly indeed, the horns are often depicted as two ravens.

As anybody who knows even a little of Norse mythology will recognise, these represent the two ravens Hugin and Munin, (Thought and Memory), who are spoken of in Snorri's stories as Odin's constant companions and worldwide gatherers of information.

So, what does this have to do with a Scottish bannock cake?

Being a Scots Australian, part of the great Scottish diaspora, I was very interested in learning more about these old staple foods.

It turns out that bannock cakes are not the size of a scone, (as I imagined), but were rather large, about the size of the top of your head.

They have been cooked and eaten since at least the eighth century in the North (at the start of the Viking Age).

So then I thought about a photo I took of the most incredible Bronze Age artifact in the National Museum in Denmark.

It is part of a bronze horse harness that was plowed up on a Danish farm. On the top of the harness are two small heads, and the faces have a distinctly alien quality to them. They have no noses, big round eyes, open mouths, a small owl-like beak on their foreheads, and on top of their heads are mysterious flat caps.

Proportionally the size of a bannock cake.

On the top of the bannock-like caps are two horn-like curved shapes, somewhat reminiscent of tiny, flattened versions of the bronze 'Lur' horns of the time.

They are not like the horns on the statue of Odin, yet I believe they represent the same concept that Huginn and Muninn represent. (Researching this online after I came back to Australia, I found two almost identical female heads that were found in the same place, also bronze and mounted on a horse collar. The incredible thing is these heads, the same size as the two other 'alien' heads, are obviously human females, and they have that swept back hair as we see in the rock carvings. The contrast between the two pairs speaks volumes - one pair are obviously human females, and the other are surely humanoids from the sky (hence the tiny bird beaks on the brows - a pictographic symbol for the power of flight)

I was then naturally drawn to two other treasures that I had photographed in Denmark.
These are the Veksø helmets, found in a Danish bog and dated pre 900 BC.
They are considered to be helmets worn by human leaders or priests, invoking powers who they believed wore something similar on their heads. Helmets with horns are not practical fighting helmets, and so they have always been considered ritual objects. These helmets were also found as a pair (which is a significant connection).
I realised that these large helmets, which were obviously worn by men by their size, could well be exaggerated and simplified versions of what had been seen on the heads of, for want of a better word, gods.

Mainstream archeology considers that these twinned beings and their helmets are related to a mythic legend of 'Divine Twins', youthful horsemen, either gods or demigods, who served as rescuers and healers in Proto-Indo-European mythology. They

appear to be the same as the 'Ashvin's', found in the Vedic (ancient Indian) stories.
In that literature these Ashvin's are characterized as **'sons of the Sky God'**(!)
In the Rigveda (a very ancient collection of Vedic Sanskrit hymns) it is written - 'Your chariot, O Aśvíns, swifter than mind, drawn by good horses, comes to the clans.'
They were always considered to be dedicated to helping and saving people. How interesting that they are said to be swifter than mind!
Once again, we're hearing about horses, and these are surely not just horses, but symbols for a means of transport. An incredibly swift means of transport!
Could it be possible that, in these two small bronze twin heads, we are looking at actual portraits of the Sky People, as they really were? Could these be the faces of the Aesir? Of the Vanir? Even of the Jötun!

So putting all this together, thinking about our bjannak story, my reasoning is this -
When Odin lays hands on his men's heads, sending them off on dangerous missions, or to fight (and lead) battles, he was putting something on their heads that looked to observers like a bannock cake. He was 'giving them bjannak'.
I think that these 'bjannaks' were a form of very advanced telepathic communication devices, (perhaps with multiple functions, interfacing with the human brain).
Obviously I'm thinking in a very 21st-century, science-fiction sort of way, but honestly, I don't see why not.
If these people were more advanced than we are now, and were visiting the Earth thousands of years ago, then witnesses / experiencers would have not the slightest way of knowing what they were seeing.

They could only try to describe these things using objects and creatures familiar to them.

It says it clearly in the bjannak paragraph - 'They believed then things would go well. So it was with his men, when they were in trouble on the sea or land, that they called out his name, and it was always thought that they received assistance from that calling.'
This really sounds like our 21st-century rescue communication devices and networks, doesn't it? The only difference is that I'm thinking about what the next level up for us now might be.
Faster than light quantum entangled communication devices, tapping into PSI (the so-called psychic abilities, which those of us who have experienced them know to be absolutely real), biometric monitoring, GPS style pinpoint positioning, and related 'assistance'?
(Ancient astronaut drone strikes anyone?).

Modern experiencers, (including children), especially those who have had close encounters with beings, seem to always report very strong telepathic interfacing with the beings. It is basically a given in UFO lore.

In chapter 6 of Heimskringla we are told that - ' Odin possessed knowledge such that he could cause his enemies in battle to become blind, or deaf, or full of fear. His enemies weapons however did not bite any more than thin sticks may. His men went without armor plated war clothes, and were frenzied like dogs or wolves, biting their own shields, and were strong like bears or bulls. They dropped other warriors, but neither fire nor iron could hurt them. That is called going berserk'.

There are many modern theories about what this fury could have been, some to do with unusual and aberrant states of human psychology, others to do with a combination of certain drugs and trance-like states, and to tell the truth, I can see the rationale behind both.

Connecting this remarkable passage with the previous passage, it would seem that two different very advanced battle tactics were used.

Firstly, Odin has weapons that intensely affected the minds of his enemies, causing blindness, deafness, and overwhelming fear. It would also seem that these weapons could make your opponent lose physical strength, making their strikes feeble.

Once upon a time such weapons would have seemed impossible, or just pure science-fiction, yet our military scientists have already developed weapons just like this!

Colonel (Dr.) John B Alexander, in his influential book 'Future War - Non-Lethal Weapons in Twenty-First-Century Warfare', explains how 'non-lethal electromagnetic and pulsed-power weapons, the laser and tazer, chemical systems, computer viruses, ultrasound and infrasound, and even biological entities will be used to stop enemies. These are the weapons of the future.'

Weapons of the future and apparently weapons of the distant past! John was a Special Forces soldier during the Vietnam War, and a key player in the very remarkable Project Stargate, run by the US Army in the early 1980's. He has been at the cutting edge of official and unofficial studies into both the paranormal, the UAP reality, and the development of non-lethal weapons, with the purpose of de-escalating and controlling violent situations without excess injuries or death.

It would appear that this was also Odin's approach.

Secondly, laying 'his hands on their heads and (giving) them bjannak', suggests the possibility that these bannock sized head caps were connected directly to their brains, allowing Odin to switch on certain extremely powerful non-human mind states as needed, primal states where they became as dangerous and powerful as animals.

I have some experience of this as an internal kung fu practitioner, as in this traditional kung fu we practice accessing our subconscious mind, releasing what can only really be described as mind force. We learn to access this mind state unemotionally, yet it can also sometimes be accessed by somebody in a state of extreme anger, (or extreme desperation, as in the old stories about mothers lifting cars from off their trapped children).

There is more to be said about this, and I will revisit it again later. For now, let's take up with the saga story again, when the truce is made between the Aesir and the Vanir. I think you will find this is pretty mind blowing.

Heimskringla Ch 4 continues with the treaty between the Aesir and the Vanir, and how they exchanged hostages -

'Sent then the Vanir their best men, Njörðr the Rich and his son Freyr, and the Æsir in return the one called Hænir, who they claimed to be was very suitable to be a ruler. He was a large and very handsome man. With him the Æsir sent the one called Mímir, their wisest man, and in return the Vanir gave them the wisest amongst their people. He was called Kvasir.

But when Hænir came to Vanaheim, he was straightaway made a chieftain. Mímir was there to teach and counsel him. But when Hænir was present at 'Thing's' (legal assemblies) or meetings, when Mímir was not near, and there came some difficult matter before him, he always answered the same: 'others may decide'.

Then the Vanir suspected that the Æsir might have deceived them in the exchange of hostages. They took Mímir and 'neck struck' (beheaded) him and sent his head to the Æsir. Odin took the head, smeared it with herbs so that it would not decay, and chanted over the head formulaic incantations, powering it up so that it spoke to him and revealed many hidden things.'

There are a lot of things going on in his story. Firstly, exchange of hostages was a typical ancient way of keeping peace between two sides, each side handing over important people, usually from the leaders' families, people who they really cared about.
If one side broke the truce the hostages were in danger of being killed.
The Vanir gave over two of their most notable men, a father and son, and the Aesir handed over a very large and handsome man who they claimed would be a great leader (which is a little odd. Why would the Vanir be lacking in leaders from amongst their own people?).
The Aesir also sent a very clever man called Mímir, who is a mysterious being indeed. His wisdom appears to be beyond the wisdom of a normal human, and in the Poetic Edda, Mímir is spoken of a number of times, and he is said to dwell beside a well, connected to the great Ash tree Yggdrasil (aka The World Tree). In this well Odin apparently deposited one of his eyes in exchange for wisdom, and it is also here that, before the final battle of Ragnarok, Odin will come to consult with Mímir, presumably on battle tactics or to get some morale boosting advice.
You will also note that another very wise and mysterious man was handed over by the Vanir as a hostage, a man who, like Mímir, appears to have wisdom way beyond the normal human scope. His name was Kvasir.

When the big handsome Aesir airhead Hænir is caught out, because he can't say anything intelligent unless Mímir is beside him, the Vanir chop off the head of poor old Mímir and send it back in a parcel marked 'return to sender'.

I find it rather odd that they didn't keep the smart guy, but that's what happens, even the ancients didn't like 'know it all's' it appears. As it is, the Vanir really shot themselves in the foot with this one, as you will find out.

The Aesir still had the Vanir man, Kvasir, the super wise hostage, and now they had the head of their own super wise guy, Mímir.

A severed head, however, doesn't seem of much use, does it?

Luckily Odin had some tricks up his sleeve.

The Old Norse original tells us 'Óðinn tók höfuðit ok smurði urtum þeim' (Odin took the head, anointed it with herbs) 'er eigi mátti fúna' (so that it would not decay).

Now let me put on my fully operational paleocontact hat, (the one with the long tin foil tip that looks a bit 'wizardy') and read between the lines here.

I think that Mímir was a robot.

A perfectly humanoid robot, with high-level self-aware AI onboard, manufactured with realistic functioning synthetic skin, bones, organs, hair etc.

The most probable etymology of the name Mímir is that is derives from an Indo-European word 'mer', meaning 'to think, recall, reflect, worry over', thus linking it to the English word memory, which derives from Latin 'Memoria' (memory and recall). Famous Old Norse scholar Rudolph Simek translates his name as 'the rememberer, the wise one'.

" How much memory does your computer have?" was once a very common thing for us computer nerds from the Stone Age to ask each other. It was a bit of a status symbol to have a lot of memory.

I remember clearly when 128 Mb of RAM was considered to be a massive amount of memory. Snicker.

Mímir´s name also appears to be related to the Ancient Greek word 'Mimesis', from which comes words like mime and mimetic. Part of my thesis for my Masters degree in Visual Art, back in 2002, was looking into this concept, and its potential meaning in the near future. I considered the idea that the ultimate mimesis would be when the artificial child of the human, the self-aware artificially intelligent robot, would sit drawing pictures of us, the ultimate mirror of ourselves drawing ourselves.

I suspect that the reason Odin sent Mímir as a hostage was so that he could spy on his enemies the Vanir, gathering and sending intelligence back to the Aesir.
The Vanir somehow twigged that he wasn't human, (of the Aesir variety), and realised that they'd been tricked. Maybe they caught him spying in areas he wasn't authorised to go? Whatever happened, they decided to take his head, either crudely and barbarically with a sword, or clinically with a tool kit.
Because the Vanir could hold their own against the Aesir militarily, we have to assume that their technology was at a similar level, so they sent his head back as a mark of their displeasure, and probably because he was an artificial life form.
They were letting Odin know that they were onto his little game, and betting on the fact that the Aesir probably wouldn't retaliate, as they would have over the killing of an organic being. Odin undoubtedly signs for the package at the front door, and then gets to work in his lab, applying advanced medical therapies to the head, perhaps refilling it with whatever artificial blood such a robot uses.
The text tells us that Odin 'kvað þar yfir galdra'.

This is usually translated 'and spoke then over it magical chants'. With my pointy silver tipped hat still on, I would say that this means he did some profound re-coding of Mímirs operating system. (Don't you think that very advanced computer coding seems akin to magic and repetitious chanting?).

Lastly, we read - 'og magnaði svá, at þat mælti við hann ok sagði honum marga leynda hluti' – And powered it up so that it spoke with him many secret / hidden things. Powered it up!
There's a whirr and a ding, lights start to flash, and then 'it spoke to him and told him many secret / hidden things'.
This gives me chills.
I can just see the great scientist, Odin, sitting in his chair, looking at the head of his robot friend, rebooting him, and asking him to report on exactly what happened in the fortress beside Lake Van, (perhaps even at the great mountain-top temple and fortification at Haykeberd (Çavuştepe) in the Kef Kalesi region, which Paul Wallis tells us about in his two most recent books, 'The Invasion Of Eden', and the newly released 'The Eden Enigma').
Mímir begins a monotone debrief at first, and gradually starts to regain his normal personality. I like to think that Odin could have given him a new body, or perhaps Mímir decided after this experience that having a body was a bit overrated.

What we do know for sure is that, in Chapter Seven of Ynglinga Saga, we are told that 'Odin kept Mímir's head near him, and it told him 'much news (updates) from other worlds'.
Isn't that rather far out? It's not terribly hard to conceive of this advanced AI companion being constantly in contact with information, streaming in from other inhabited worlds, perhaps from space stations, moon bases and motherships within the solar system, and perhaps from interstellar outposts all over our Galaxy.

Snorri writes in the same clear, down to Earth manner as the other, mostly anonymous saga writers, telling the stories of the Viking Age. Their writings have an eerily modern style, a way of thinking and style of writing more akin to modern novels than to the works produced by medieval authors in the rest of Europe.
They state things as they are/were, in a very relaxed, pragmatic and down to Earth manner. Which makes the strange and the paranormal stuff really stand out, as it is treated in the same 'business as usual' way.
I believe that Snorri wrote these stories down verbatim, exactly as he received them from people 'in the know', and from authoritative, and perhaps now lost, ancient sources.

Regarding the Aesir's hostage, the Vanir´s own super-intelligent being, Kvasir, he is as mysterious as Mímir!
There is absolutely the same humanoid robotic AI powered vibe about him as with Mímir. To learn about the creation of Kvasir we finally return to the second Wizard who was mentioned in the last chapter, Aegir.
You will remember that this Wizard was not a human, but a Jötun (a 'giant'). He lived in Jutland, (literally Jötun land, or perhaps Jötunheim), in what is now northern Denmark. His relationship with these Aesir 'Sky People' was a bit different to that of our friend, the Wizard King Gylfi of Sweden.
For one, Aegir was spared having great chunks of his land usurped. He seemed to be in special favour with them. We can guess that he must've been very influential amongst his own people, making him another excellent mouthpiece to spread the stories that the Aesir wanted people to believe.

We also learn that eventually the Aesir started coming to his island, Hlésey, to party, because apparently he was a legendary homebrewer!
He also had nine beautiful daughters and a beautiful wife, whose name was Ran. Perhaps he was more fun to be around than Gylfi?

The Aesir, however, still treated him as an inferior, and as with Gylfi/Gangleri, he appears to have been abducted and taken to Asgard.
The opening chapter of Skaldskapamál (the second book in Snorri Sturluson's 'Prose Edda') tells us -
'There was a man named Ægir, also called Hlér. He lived on the island that is now called Hlésey. He was very much a 'man of great knowledge'(a great Wizard) . He made a journey to Ásgarðr (Asgard). But the Æsir knew of his journey beforehand and (though they) welcomed him warmly, many things were done through illusions (optical illusions?).
Here we find the same scenario as in the account of King Gylfi's experience.
The Aesir knew of Aegir's journey beforehand, they literally seemed to be able to look into his mind and see what his intention was, which, if you remember, was what happened with Gylfi. In that story it was said that the Aesir had 'spádom', (the sight, clairvoyance, a telepathic/psychic ability to connect across space and time to another person).

The difference between the two tales, it seems to me, is that Gylfi was a more powerful, sharper man, a brighter man, because it appears that he was shown the full reality of the Aesir's world. Maybe as a Jötun, Aegir was a bit simpler, a little more brutish?
He wasn't required to ask smart questions and match wits, under considerable duress, as Gylfi was, but rather was spirited straight

into what seems to have been a fairly relatable feasting place. Essentially a grand party, with all the gods and goddesses present, and as a special guest plied with drink and food and told endless stories.

Near the end of that Old Norse passage above we find the word 'sjónhverfingum'.

This is the word that I have translated as 'illusion', or even 'optical illusion', but this word even carries with it the sense of altering reality. Translators in the past would have been tempted to translate it as 'magical illusions'.

Quite possibly, instead of seeing the huge inside of a space station and the vast vista of the Earth, the moon, and the stars outside the wide windows, (as Gylfi probably did), Aegir is shown what he expects to see, the great feast hall of the handsome bearded Gods and gorgeous sexy Goddesses!

One of the coolest details for me is that Skaldskaparmal tells us - '…and in the evening when the drinking was about to begin, then ordered Odin to be brought into the hall swords, which were so bright that no other lights were needed while they were drinking'. As soon as I read this sentence, Jedi light sabers came to mind. But less dramatically, they could've just been some kind of fluorescent tubes?

Yet they still, to the Jötun, Aegir, looked like something relatable - swords in this case.

They were certainly unlike anything he has ever seen before, and therefore worthy of note. (I think that it's these odd little touches in the stories that make us feel as if we are listening to a real first-hand account, passed down over millennia).

I also like to think that they were drinking 'magical' Aesir beer, something like the magical brew that has often been promised us for many years, one that doesn't give you a hangover!

So Aegir sits beside someone called Bragi, who seems to be a very friendly guy, (he is eventually revealed to be the God of poetry, so he's a great storyteller).

Bragi starts 'bragging', telling a whole series of entertaining and amazing stories about the exploits of the Aesir, the Jötun, the Álf's (Elves), the Dverga (dwarves), and filling Aegir's head with the same sort of lore that Gylfi received.

Stories that appear partly based on very ancient mythic shamanic constructions, to do with visions and traditional spiritual quests, and other stories that appear to be based on the actual exploits of these high-tech people (air battles and longevity therapy et al).

A carefully curated and created 'religion' is presented, one that suits the purposes of these powerful people, whilst still generally benefiting humans with their simple understanding.

Dare I say it, pretty much like most established religions have always done!

Which brings us back to Kvasir, the super-wise man who was sent by the Vanir as a hostage to the Aesir.

In Skaldskaparmal, Aegir hears about Kvasir during the great feast, and how he was created.

Bragi, (the 'God' of poetry), had been asked by Aegir where the art of poetry originated. A very reasonable question to ask such an expert. Bragi tells him the story of what must have been a previous great war between the Aesir and the Vanir, where the two sides agreed to a truce. This time, rather than their later hostage swap deal, they had decided to swear to keep the peace by spitting into a special vat.

This seems a rather odd thing to do for the sake of keeping a truce, doesn't it?
What happens next makes a bit more sense of this.
As we modern people know, our saliva contains our DNA, and it's the main source of DNA used to discover your ancestry, and ancestral places based on it.
So the Aesir and the Vanir set out to create a man from this great vat full of spit!
A record of genetic engineering at a very advanced level.
If you took the DNA from all the leaders on two opposing sides, and with that created one individual, somehow based on that mixed DNA, then this being becomes a very special child of all the people involved.
I'm not pretending that I know how this would be done, but it seems, based on the story of Mímir, that he was initially indistinguishable from a human, or at least these mysterious humanoids.
Perhaps they used their combined DNA to create organic yet super durable bones, organs, muscles, sinews (flesh) etc., creating a humanoid biological 'robot' with a biological AI brain.
Once again, totally science-fiction, but as in the rest of this book, I am bringing a fresh eye to what we could be being told in these carefully preserved ancient stories and secrets.
The name given to this strange child thus created, Kvasir, appears to be related to the idea of something crushed, squeezed and made into a fermented alcoholic drink.
It is a poetic way of portraying the feeling of inspired intoxication, that somewhat blissful feeling of poetic inspiration.

In Gylfaginning we are told the story of the Aesir hunting the trickster god Loki, who as usual had done some horrendous

misdeed, this time surpassing himself by arranging the killing of the most beloved and beautiful God, Odin's son, Baldur.
Loki was sitting, hiding, in a high mountain hall, knitting together fishnets from linen.
He saw the Aesir coming, and threw the fishnets into the fire, somehow changed himself into a salmon, and leapt into the stream nearby to hide. Kvasir was the first to walk into the hideout, and 'High' (Odin), who is telling this story to Gylfi, says that Kvasir was 'the wisest of all'. Kvasir scans the fire and makes out the faintest pattern of the burnt nets, and he reproduces that exact net for the Aesir (presumably at an outrageous speed, his knitting needles ablur!) The Aesir instantly realise that it's a salmon net, and they take it out into the stream, and use it as they always would for catching this strong leaping fish.

The story backs up my AI/robotic conjecture, as one of the strong suits of artificial intelligence is pattern recognition. Which is exactly what Kvasir demonstrates here.
So, coming back to Aegir's question of Bragi, we learned that Kvasir was so wise that no man could ask him any question that he could not answer.
You will have to admit this is a pretty wonderful trait, and doesn't that sound exactly like our currently emerging AI friends.
Then we learn that 'Hann for víða um heim at kenna mönnum fræði' (he travelled widely around the world to teach men wisdom/learning/scholarship/lore).

There is a world within this short statement! What exactly are we being told here?
We know for sure that Odin, the Commander and father figure/leader of the Aesir, was an inveterate traveler, often

travelling very far indeed, and being away sometimes for a very long time.
Now we learn that he possibly had two advanced beings, (Kvasir and Mímir), as companions, (Mímir certainly was), both extremely advanced artificially intelligent entities.
Both of them are remembered as having unmatched knowledge, the limits of which couldn't be reached. Now we learn that Kvasir was specifically a profound teacher, who travelled far and wide around the world, on an altruistic mission to teach humans his limitless wisdom/learning/scholarship/lore!
This is exactly the story that we hear from so many ancient cultures, that people came from the sky, people described us being distinct and unusual, who then proceeded to teach folks these exact things for the benefit of mankind, including but not limited to knowledge of medicine, astronomy, architecture, mathematics, agronomy, art, literacy and much more.

Few would suspect that such sophisticated knowledge is hidden within the stories of the supposedly barbaric, bearded, wild people of the Viking Age!
And in no small measure we have two Bronze Age human Wizards to thank for these stories being preserved!

OLD ASGARD THE AWESOME

Throughout my research for this book, and especially during my month-long Viking Superpowers Research Tour 2024 in Scandinavia and Iceland, I felt a strong sense of being assisted and led, with that kind of luck happening that seems to be more than luck. Coincidental meetings and conversations, 'accidental' happenings, that then led me to meet just the right people, who often took me to the coolest places.

I discovered things that, honestly, would have eluded me normally. On my very first day in Denmark, where I began my tour, I went to the Viking ship museum in Roskilde, a town just next to Copenhagen. Roskilde has been a very long time dream destination for me. A Danish friend and fellow Viking enthusiast told me about it when I lived in Byron Bay in the early 90s, and had insisted that I absolutely mustn't miss it.

That's why I made it my first port of call.

I met a young German Piper, Aidrian Bausl, who was playing his mediaeval bagpipes at the front of the museum. I'd spent a couple of enjoyable hours taking in the six restored Viking Age ships recovered from the harbour, and carefully preserved since the early 1960s.

Aidrian and his father had sailed into Roskilde in an authentic handmade ship, after sailing and rowing all the way up from Germany. Adrian had played his pipes as they rowed into port.

He's going to create some special mediaeval bagpipe tracks for my Viking superpowers channel on YouTube, which I'm very pleased about!

Down beside the Viking Ship Museum is the large workshop complex, where for many decades Danish shipbuilders have been relearning the art of building Viking ships, using only original tools hand forged in the old way. Carving the long curving strakes, and myriad smaller parts of the ships is pure art, inspired sculpture that is also intensely practical. Creating seaworthy ships, yet carved and decorated in the unique Old Norse style, often painted in a rainbow of colours including gold leaf.
This long term project is a great credit to the people of Scandinavia!

One of the gentlemen using an axe to plane a long strake was Tore (Thor) Forsberg. He is a Master Viking ship builder with 50 years' experience, and we both noticed that we looked like doppelgängers!
We had a great conversation, and Tore taught me much about practical tool use and the ship building process, and about the new ships that were coming along.
It turned out he was down from Oslo, capital of Norway, where he is one of the Masters directing the recreation of the famous Gokstad ship, the original of which is in the Viking Ship Museum there. We found that we had a surprising amount in common and vowed to keep in contact.
After I had visited a couple of very special places in Denmark and Sweden, I headed up to Oslo. I discovered to my dismay that the museum that housed the original Oseberg and Gokstad ships was closed for major renovation until 2027.
I sent a text to Tore and he wrote back saying that he had radio/telephoned the great reconstructed ship, the 'Saga Oseberg',

at sea and got permission for me to meet them after they sailed into harbour, a few hours south of Oslo.

A couple of trains, buses and a taxi later I arrived at the harbour at Tønsberg, and walking down the long jetty towards the beautiful Viking ship I felt that I had entered a time slip.

Saga Oseberg, all rigged up, bobbed gently where it was tied to the large mooring posts. I felt somewhat glad that I could speak enough Old Norse to get by, just in case I'd actually slipped back 1000 years!

Fortunately, the crew and I were still here in the 21st Century, and they were exceptionally kind, greeting me as a friend. I ended up dressed in Viking sea gear, sitting in the Skipper's seat holding the steer board, (the Starboard, O.N. Starborð), in the stern of the vessel for an impromptu photoshoot.

I then sat down on the jetty for dinner with the crew, and course we talked about Viking ships, and I told them a bit about my Viking Superpowers project. I must say here that, as in other places I went in Scandinavia, I was surprised by how open people were to my ideas about the 'gods' being advanced visitors from somewhere else in the deep past. I truly expected more resistance, (and I got a little at times), but also a surprising amount of 'Yes, I have sometimes wondered that myself'.

The next day I caught up again with my friend Johnny, a certain 'Viking' sort of character, with a great bushy beard, long hair, and a very friendly and humorous personality. He had shown me all over the ship, and on this day we met again at the special harbour at Vikingodden, Tonsberg. I had the chance to inspect the ship totally cleared of cargo, and tread the bare hand carved deck timbers. It was a real blast. (Viking ships have a wonderful fragrance of timber and tar by the way!)

Johnny asked if I would like to visit the mound where the original Oseberg ship had been found in 1904, and of course my answer was an enthusiastic yes!

Driving through the Norwegian countryside we stopped at Midgard, a recreated Viking Age fortress complex, complete with a number of great halls, all hand carved and authentic, and surrounded by a large timber palisade.

It absolutely felt like the real thing.

Finally, we came to the great mound, where the Viking Queen, (and a second woman), had been buried in state, along with much treasure and ornately carved wooden furniture and objects. I felt a bit of a shiver to think that this woman could have been one of my grandmothers many many times over!

We then drove to a forest whose trees the Norwegian government had set aside for the Oseberg Viking Heritage Foundation, specifically for shipbuilding. Walking through the forest we came to the place where the latest large tree had been felled, and Johnny, (a carpenter), told me how they had gone about the project, in the same way that the ancestors had, thousands of years before. There were still timber and bark chips all over the ground, and the stump of the tree, and he explained how they had also split the great log on the spot.
Standing in that forest with Johnny, surrounded by those tall trees, and thinking of all the ships I'd seen in the previous week, I reflected on how central trees were to the people of the Viking Age and earlier. They didn't build in stone very often, in the way that people in southern lands did. Not that they couldn't build stone structures, but they lived amongst vast trackless forests and were absolute poets at shaping timber.
Trees were a big deal to the ancients of Scandinavia!

Which brings me back to the greatest tree of all – **Yggdrasil**!
As we have learnt in previous chapters, the stories tell us that this unthinkably huge tree stood at the centre of the world, connecting the great city of Old Asgard on the ground to Old Asgard in outer space, the original vast power centre and homebase of the Aesir people in 'Ásaland' aka 'Ásaheim' in 'Turkland', modern Türkiye. Yggdrasil, Snorri tells us, was a strongly rooted bearer and connector of many worlds, some roots seeming to be dug down

deep under the Earth, and some seeming to have been spread out wide and high in the sky.
The tree was said to spread its branches over and above the whole world, way above the clouds, in that place that we now call 'outer space'. I have shared visions of the great tree earlier and would now like to add this particularly relevant passage, Chapter 6 of 'Hálfdanar Saga Svarta' (Halfdan the Black's Saga), from Heimskringla. (Halfdan the Black's Saga tells of 'historical' events in the Viking Age, much later than the very ancient 'mythical' stories in the Edda. My translation.).

'Queen Agnhildi dreamed great dreams, and she was reputed to possess profound wisdom. There was one dream which she dreamed, in which it appeared to her that she was standing in her grassy garden and plucking a thorn from her garment. But when she held it, the thorn grew so that it became a mighty shoot, one end took root in the earth and soon became strongly rooted, while the other end reached high up into the sky.
And next, a tree appeared to her so immense that she could barely see over its top.
It was indeed miraculously/wondrously magnificent. The innermost part of the tree was red as blood, while the trunk was beautifully green, and the branches white as snow. Then there were many large branches on the tree, some high above and some low below. The limbs of the tree were so vast that they seemed to spread over all of Norway and even much farther.'

This wonderful passage appears to me to be both a prophetic dream vision of a Royal mother, gifted with the second sight, a Seer, seeing the future reign of her famous son, Harold Fairhair, as well as being a profound vision seeing far, far back, into a much

more ancient time, where the Queen sees and clearly describes what was once the original Yggdrasil.
With my Paleocontact hat on I am immediately put in mind of the theoretical concept known as a Starbridge. This is a concept that is considered technically possible, though our current technology does not allow us to create the incredibly strong and long structures needed to build one.
It is basically the concept of connecting an extremely long, cablelike structure, up to 100,000 km in length, firmly attached to the ground, with the other end of its immense length way out in space, allowing it to turn in geostationary orbit with the turning of the Earth. Once this cable is in place, much stronger structures can be built along its considerable length, (reaching halfway to the Moon). One of the main advantages of such a Starbridge is that large masses could be lifted from the Earth into space, allowing construction of a myriad of further structures etc., at a small fraction of the cost incurred by our current rocket technology.

It seems to me highly possible that such a structure once connected the land base of Old Asgard in Anatolia, Türkiye, to the great complex of space stations, satellites and massive energy collecting panels that was 'Old Asgard in the Sky', just as Snorri describes in the Prose Edda. A structure that looked like the biggest tree ever seen, the tree that the Norse people called 'The World Ash', Yggdrasil, 'Odin's Horse'.

I was particularly taken with the Queen's dream revelation that the great tree had three colours, red, green and white.
Firstly, she tells us that, 'The innermost part of the tree was red as blood' (Inn nezti hlutr tréssins var rauðr sem blóð).
This is an unusual thing to say, because we don't generally describe the insides of a tree when we look at it. It sounds as if the tree was

somehow open at the bottom, perhaps with enormous leg-like structures spreading out and digging deep into the ground to help it stay stable. Perhaps an observer could look up from below, and see bright red energy moving through the inside of the tree, perhaps some kind of red-hot plasma, or an unknown energy being drawn down from the great solar collecting panels, spread out over the world in space?

The green trunk that is described could represent a greenish protective covering, perhaps advanced metal-like materials, weathered to a dull green, maybe with a sort of gunmetal green patina?

The white colour of the higher branches could be a painted white colour, or they could be brightly lit, or even a silver metal that gleams white in the intense light of the sun above the atmosphere?

Something that really struck me, when I first read this passage, is the possible connection to the somewhat sassy description given to Gylfi, when he was speaking to the three High Ones. 'High' tells him that Bifrost is, 'like the rainbow', but that it has three colours. I feel there has to be a connection with this dream and that statement, as it seems that the stories of the great bridge and the great tree are perhaps a little mixed up. Possibly they were two parts of one great structure? And as we shall learn in the chapter after next, there appears to have been a lot of flying going on in that amazing time, and therefore it would make sense that there must have been lots of lights on this great tree structure, to make it more visible to 'ancient aviators'.

In 1964, Soviet astronomer, Nikolai Kardeshev, proposed a method for measuring the technological advancement of a civilisation, by gauging the amount of energy that civilisation can harness and use.

This became known as the Kardeshev scale, and it divides civilisations up into three categories - Type One, Two and Three, (with Carl Sagan proposing that there should be a more nuanced categorization indicating intermediate rankings).
Some say that we are currently a Type Zero global civilization, moving inexorably towards Type One. Other scientists consider us to be around 0.7.
So, what is a Type One civilization?
Professor Michio Kaku, Theoretical Physicist and Futurist, writes in his influential book, 'Physics of the Future'-
'A planetary civilization or global civilization is a civilization of Type I on the Kardashev scale. This type of civilization is likely to be reliant on renewable energy sources such as stellar (solar) power, as well as powerful non-renewable sources such as nuclear fusion.'

My contention is that Old Asgard, Yggdrasil, and Old Asgard 'in the sky', were indeed the homes of the 'gods', (the Aesir and the Vanir), and a wonder and beacon for the whole world to see. As is written in Gylfaginning Ch 9 - 'Þar næst gerðu þeir sér **borg** í miðjum heimi, er kölluð er Ásgarð…Þar byggðu goðin ok ættir þeira, ok gerðusk þaðanaf mörg tíðendi ok greinir bæði á jörðu ok í lopti' - (Next they built for themselves a stronghold in the middle of the world, which is called Asgard. There lived the 'gods' and their families, and in Asgard many very unusual events happened, both in Asgard on Earth and in Asgard up above the sky in outer space').
An interesting point is that, in the Old Norse, the word 'borg' tells us that Asgard was a fortified city, and according to my argument we would have to conclude that Asgard in space was also fortified. Which points to enemies who are being defended against doesn't it, enemies capable of attacking such a formidable and highly technical people.

Enemies who were perhaps extraterrestrial, or like the Aesir and the Vanir, remnants of a previous very high-tech human civilisation, forced to go off world for a period because of the cataclysmic great flood.

The agrarian or hunter gatherer peoples of Earth, those not in on the secrets of Asgard, would of course have had a naturalistic understanding of this vast tall and complex structure, and would have logically described it as a gigantic tree.
We can imagine that it would have been clearly visible from a very long way off, and at night would have been able to be seen from even further away.
Its bright branches in the sky would be noticed by everybody in every country of the world, (which is an interesting topic for further study).
Anybody seeing such a colossal wonder would have naturally considered that this was the very centre of the world indeed!

The idea of a worldwide outer space energy collection system makes great sense, drawing in the full unattenuated power of the sun, producing unthinkable quantities of energy.
This is a step down from the theoretical construct called a Dyson sphere, a Type II civilization concept, wherein a vast spherical structure or swarm of structures surrounds a sun, gathering power from it.
The Type I concept that I am proposing would operate in a manner surprisingly similar to the way an actual tree operates.
The massive far spreading head of 'leaves' (energy gathering panels similar to, but more advanced than, our familiar solar panels), spread out world-wide above the sky, gather in light, heat and cold, which a very advanced civilization could then convert into energy,

channeling it down through the 'trunk' and into the 'roots', to be used for the needs of all.

If this interpretation is correct, somewhere in the ancient past between the end of the last ice age,(c.12,000 years ago), and the Bronze Age/Iron Age, there was indeed a Type One civilisation here on Earth, and the Old Norse 'Edda's' and other saga's, particularly the early sections of Heimskringla, are describing just such a civilization and people.
I would also contend, along with many other writers and open-minded thinkers, that there are records and memories of this Type One civilization to be found in cultures all over the world.

Old Asgard was located in Anatolia/Turkiyë, the original home of the Sumerians according to the Encyclopedia Britannica, and not a terribly long way from Ancient Babylon, where the famous 'Tower of Babel' was located.

In the first book of the Bible, Genesis, in Chapter 11, we are told - 'Now the whole world had one language and a common form of speech.
And as people journeyed eastward, they found a plain in the land of Shinar and settled there. And they said to one another, "Come, let us make bricks and bake them thoroughly." So, they used brick instead of stone, and tar instead of mortar.
Come," they said, "let us build for ourselves a city with a tower that reaches to the heavens, that we may make a name for ourselves and not be scattered over the face of all the earth."
Then Yahweh came down to see the city and the tower that the sons of men were building. And Yahweh said, "If they have begun to do this as one people speaking the same language, then nothing they devise will be beyond them.

Come, let 'Us'(plural) go down and confuse their language, so that they will not understand one another's speech."
So, Yahweh scattered them from there over the face of all the earth, and they stopped building the city.
That is why it is called Babel, for there Yahweh confused the language of the whole world, and from that place Yahweh scattered them over the face of all the earth.'

I have replaced the standard word used in English, Lord, for the word that is in the Hebrew – Yahweh, the word for the leader of the Elohim, the 'powerful ones' ruling over the people of Israel. According to Paul Wallis, this word Yahweh features in later redactions, (the ones we read now), of the earlier Hebrew scriptures, which used the plural word Elohim, rather than the singular name 'Yahweh' which replaced it.
This is why the retention of the simple passage, 'Let us go down and confuse their language!' is so amazing!
All the Bible translations I've ever read, (and I've read a lot), always include this 'Us', even though it is emphatically plural. On the one hand we have this single powerful being, Yahweh, and then we find him talking to others who appear to be on the same level as him. We have to ask ourselves 'why would the Lord of the universe have to go down to have a look?'. Surely that divine being can already see what's going on, being omnipresent and omnipotent? This sentence clearly states that someone, (and his compadres), very powerful yet not omniscient, went down, obviously from the sky, or from outer space, to have a closer look at what these annoying, overly smart humans were up to.
What they found was a unified, highly skilled, (and technically very advanced), human group, not only planning, but about to complete the seemingly impossible task of building a tower that reached right

up into the 'basamayim', meaning 'the skies/up above the sky/where the stars are'.
(Once again, that incredibly dishonest and disingenuous archaic English word, 'heaven', is used in most English translations of the Bible, in the same way that our Old Norse friend 'himinn' is also mistranslated into a word that consciously means a different spiritual dimension, rather than what it plainly means – 'high up in the sky where the stars are'!)

Yahweh, and the group of powerful party poopers that he brought down with him undoubtedly had a good chat together afterwards, perhaps hovering in their 'chariot of fire', and decided that this was not on.
"Egad and By Jove, who do these primitives think they are?
If they have begun to do this as one people, all speaking the same language, then nothing they devise will be beyond them!".
Including getting some of their people up into the sky/outer space and having a good look at who these Elohim really are.
The word Babel is usually regarded as meaning 'confusion', yet Paul Wallis considers that it could mean a 'Gateway to or for 'The Powerful Ones'!

That won't do! The humans needed to be kept in their place, and so, somehow, Yahweh and his Powerful Ones must have used a horrid, invasive, brain manipulating device, greatly disrupting the cognition of this multitude of hardworking and hopeful humans. Which is pretty uncool!
These very smart humans were building themselves a 'bridge to the stars', hoping to spend time with these marvelous Sky People, their creators.
The Bible doesn't say that they wanted to attack or act against the Elohim.

Yet as we heard above, the Elohim commander and his army wanted to keep the humans 'in their proper place'. They must be taught to 'know their station in life'.
Whatever the device they used, it must've been very exotic technology, and it caused a great mass of human beings to completely forget their single unified language, overwriting the verbal areas of their brains so that they suddenly began speaking many different distinct, (and presumably invented), languages.

I have always found this story extremely grating since I was a kid. It seems mighty unfair of 'Us', aka the Lord, aka God, to do this to people who were working so hard to improve themselves, to take the race up into space, and one assumes to emulate their 'betters'.
The usual explanation from a Bible teacher, or a Minister of Religion, was always something along the lines of "those people were all really nasty sinners Dave, and they didn't deserve to be allowed to become technically super sophisticated.
Obviously if 'the Lord' did this, then he had an 'almighty' good reason for it".

I never really bought into that explanation, which was a standard answer excusing many very nasty, dark and unholy deeds 'Us' got up to in the Old Testament.
Even to a child's mind there was a natural abhorrence to cruel and often murderous actions, indeed high-level oppression, often committed against innocent children and animals. Certainly not the type of actions that Star Fleet Command would approve of!

Looking at the story as a free-thinking adult, it is rather obvious that something profound was happening in the ancient past. Our human ancestors were thinking deeply in a self-directed manner, seemingly creating amazing science, engineering, mathematics and other knowledge. It is also very possible, as we considered in the last chapter, that they were being helped and taught by sympathetic and caring advanced peoples (Odin, Mimir and Kvasir amongst others).

One might not be cynical to think that we could still be in a similar situation.

My theory about the Old Norse 'World Tree', Yggdrasil, being a massive structure reaching to outer space, seems to have obvious similarities to this story of the Tower of Babel.

In Snorri's description of Asgard, which you will remember from the adventures of the Wizards, he states that the great city was divided into 12 sections, essentially like a giant clock. It was ruled over by twelve leaders **and people there spoke twelve languages!**

It makes me wonder whether this great city, with its sister city up in space, connected by the massive towering 'tree', could indeed be another 'Tower of Babel', a second tower, created after the first was presumably destroyed?

Maybe the descendants of the people who were scattered, with their many new artificially implanted languages, came together in another place, to the North of Babylon, for the purpose of restarting the great project?

Asgard!

Isn't that a strange yet tantalizing thought!

It makes sense don't you think? The Bible doesn't say that 'Us' killed all those geniuses who were building the Tower of Babel, it says that 'they' scrambled their language centres and sent them off in all directions. It doesn't actually even say that they destroyed the tower.

The Tower of Babel, (if we accept that it really existed), must have been something very similar to the high-tech version of Yggdrasil that I am describing.
What if these Aesir, and eventually their 'frenemies', the Vanir, were the descendants of those great grandsons of Noah (or the Sumerian Noah, Utnapishtim), who planned and executed the original great Tower?
People who were probably/possibly hybrids of a higher humanoid race, and those chosen humans (remember the story of the horny sons of God and the fair daughters of men?).
What if they restarted the great project in the area of modern Turkiyë, and this time achieved it.
Were they able to come to an agreement with the bullying Israelite Elohim, and their leader Yahweh?
Perhaps they developed weapons that were the match of their opponents?
We don't really know, but we can certainly continue to look at the evidence and come to our own conclusions.

As I have mentioned, part of this great structure reaching the stars is the Bifrost Bridge, and we are introduced to it, (as you will remember), in Gylfaginning in the Prose Edda, where Gylfi asks Odin 'what way is there to outer space from the earth?'.
He receives a mocking answer from Odin (High), saying that this is a pretty dumb question for someone 'in the know' to ask. The bridge's attributes are then laid out, and to finish off, Odin mentions that it will break eventually when the sons of Muspell ride over it (at Ragnarok).
Gylfi, being the cheeky young Wizard that he is, sasses Odin back saying -
'Eigi þótti mér goðin gera af trúnaði brúna, er hon skal brotna mega, er þau megu þó gera sem þau vilja.'

(It does not seem to me that the gods built the bridge with much trustworthiness, if it is fated to break, when they have the power to make things as they wish.)

He is surely overawed by his surroundings in the great 'hall' in the sky, perhaps looking down at the globe of the Earth below, standing before the three daunting rulers who appear to be identical triplets, and yet, he is a Wizard King, undoubtedly a man of great pride.
It sounds as if he is starting to wonder whether these beings sitting before him are really the omniscient and omnipotent gods they claim to be.
We can almost hear the gears in Gylfi's head grinding - "If these are gods who have built this bridge, why would it have any chance of failure?".
It seems that, in the end, they convinced him, because we are told that he went back home and told everybody all the stories and experiences he had been exposed to.

So let's travel together up the great 'World Tree' starbridge, via the Bifrost, (the built-in high-speed elevator).
Rapidly passing many slow-moving heavy loads being winched up Yggdrasil, we arrive at our stop, as we see the blue atmosphere of Earth giving way to the blackness of space. The scrolling elevator light panel gives a ding and displays 'Welcome to Himinbjorg'.

The Prose Edda tells us that 'There is another place, which is called Himinbjorg. It stands at the edge of space, where the bridge tails off, where Bífrost comes to outer space'.
Its very name, 'Himinbjorg', means either 'Outer Space Mountain' or 'Outer Space castle/fortress'. The idea of it being a castle rather appeals to me, and makes more sense in this context.

I picture Himinbjorg as a massive space station, in geostationary orbit, acting as a counterweight to the starbridge Yggdrasil. (The theory of star bridges tells us that it would need to extend considerably past where this massive space station, Himinbjorg, is situated just on the edge of space.
The theory indicates that there could be multiple further extensions, perhaps extending out 100,000 km!)
Once we are there, we need permission to enter from the guardian of this great space station, whose name is Heimdallr.
He is an extremely interesting character, who we are told is the father of mankind. This is very interesting, as there are a number of beings in the stories who are said to play the same role. Some important facts about him - his job is to guard the space end of Bifrost, and to protect it particularly from the aggressive enemy, the Giants (Jötun).
In Gylfaginning, when Gylfi/Gangleri was asking about the great bridge Bifrost, High/Odin says to him - " That which you see as red in the bridge, is fire burning. Up to outer space the Frost Giants and the Mountain Giants wish to go, and if all of them could freely travel up the Bifrost, they would certainly travel!".

That's all that Odin says of the matter. So this fire burning is obviously there to stop them. Is it just a wall of fire? If we continue with our realistic approach to these stories, this doesn't seem likely, as fire won't burn in the very high atmosphere and certainly not in space. So this description really sounds like a weapon or weapons firing, perhaps projectile weapons like we use or perhaps some kind of lightning energy weapon on a large scale, as the Aesir will demonstrate soon on that great Swedish lake, Vänern.
And it would seem to make sense that this would be part of Heimdallr's job, to protect Asgard against these dangerous enemies, if they were to try to access Asgard in the sky.

Perhaps Heimdalr gave Gylfi a demonstration whilst he was there, showing off his array of fire weapons, always ready to blast Giants to perdition.

Heimdalr also has the gift that sets aside Odin and many other Aesir, the gift of 'spádom', (second sight and precognition), as well as extremely developed senses of hearing and sight, (he can hear grass growing down on earth from his post in space, which must be pretty loud for him, because there's a lot of grass growing down there!).

Like Odin, he has the ability, from his post in orbit, to scan the whole Earth, and detect any uprisings or problems which may affect Asgard, and the plans of the Aesir.

Obviously, these gifts, especially the world spanning surveillance, could be purely technological, however the old stories really indicate a mixture of technology and innate organic paranormal superpowers.

Like the Vanir man Kvasir, the incredibly wise and seemingly benevolent being born to all of the Aesir and the Vanir from their saliva, Heimdallr is said to be the son of Odin, and of nine mothers. Obviously, this doesn't make sense in a natural way, but once again I believe that what we are seeing here is a synthesis of human and machine, and some kind of exotic DNA splicing that is beyond our understanding at present.

There are even suggestions that the nine mothers could be the nine daughters of our Jötun Wizard friend, Aegir, and his wife Ran.

Similarly there is an ancient story from Babylon, telling of a powerful being called Kingu, who was also said to be the one from whom human beings were created. After losing a ferocious battle between the gods, he was selectively killed, and his blood mixed

with the saliva of many other gods to create humans, and there are said to be multiple 'birth goddess's'.
Does this multiple birth goddess's story recall embryos being created and then implanted in multiple human women, or perhaps humanoid 'goddesses'?

Heimdallr is called 'the whitest of all the gods' (he was very pale?), the 'golden toothed one' and 'the head is called his sword'. Quite a strong strange image of him being perhaps completely naked of all hair, and as white as a ghost, similar to the boy in the movie 'Powder'.
Combining this with golden teeth would make him quite a striking character visually.
'His head being his sword' brings to mind the saying 'The pen is mightier than the sword'. His mind is his sword, which again puts us in 'mind' of those other two great super minds, Mímir and Kvasir.

Getting back to Yggdrasil now, the Prose Edda tells us that its 'roots' seem to extend **above** the tree.
It really sounds as if this great space station acts as a gateway connecting Asgard on the ground to a great complex in space that extends to three different places.
We are told that three great tree roots **support** the great tree and extend very very far indeed.
This idea of 'roots' supporting the tree above itself really only makes sense if we think about this Starbridge configuration, with the three supporting roots extending perhaps halfway to the Moon.
The first of these roots extends out to where the Aesir live, the second extends out to where the Frost Giants live, and the third extends over what is called Niflheim. Our friend Mímir has his famous Well underneath this second root, the one that reaches out

to where the Frost Giants, (the Hrímþursum/Rime or Hroar Frost Giants) live.
Snorri goes on to say that this 'Well' has wisdom and intelligence contained in it. Like a massive master data centre and an artificial intelligence hub.

There is a second well, which is considered to be very holy, called 'Weird's Well' (Urðarbrunnr), and Snorri writes that 'there have the god's their 'judgement place', and every day 'ride the Aesir there, **up** over Bifrost'.
So we might say that the Aesir head off to work on this same highspeed elevator every day, **up** at the end of the great trembling light Bridge Bifrost, to hold their court or special meeting place at 'Weird's Well'.
Next, we are told that there are many beautiful places in outer space, (himinn), and one of them is a hall standing beside this 'Weird's Well', where three maidens (meyjar) live. They are called Norn's. Their names are Weird (Urðr), Verdandi, and Skuld. (The word 'meyjar', (maiden's), literally means very young women, in particular virgins, and this is a significant fact).
Many world mythologies consider that young innocent virgins have a purity that allows them unusual psychic abilities. One story says that they are the only people capable of taming a wild unicorn, considered a very dangerous creature in legends.

The name 'Weird' in this context, (weirdly enough), doesn't mean what it does to us. In the old languages of Norse and Old English it is spelt Urðr and Wyrd, and it has the sense of 'a fate that is inescapable'.
Weird's Well appears to be very much the same sort of place/thing as Mímir's Well - an ancient, very high-tech data and information centre, run by AI beings like Mímir and Kvasir.

The job of the three maidens is to shape men's lives, to set or direct their fate you might say. Doing a job like that seems mighty capital 'G' godlike doesn't it?

We are told that there are some Norns who visit everyone on Earth when they were born, to shape their lives. There are also other Norn's, and a quotation in the text of Gylfaginning says that Norn's do not have a common ancestry, that they are daughters of Aesir, Elves and even Dwarves, fulfilling roles given to them, and we can presume that these girls are hand-picked to fulfil these roles. Perhaps the two wells are vastly powerful quantum supercomputers, and these young girls act as interpreters, or even perhaps as psychic partners to the AI machines?
For me the word 'well' conjures up very large crystalline viewing screens, that someone, (Gylfi or Aegir?), have interpreted as being akin to large, perfectly still, pools of water, a visual interface for these special maidens.

If we leave Himinbjorg and Weird's Well, following the second root, we eventually come to the homeworld of the Frost Giants, the Hrimthursa (Hrimþursa)), which is where 'Ginnungagap' once was. I suspect that this homeworld is a long, long way away. Perhaps this root is some kind of 'Stargate' wormhole connection. In fact, these roots are really sounding like they are all something like wormholes, taking travelers from above the Earth and out into the far reaches of space.
If you think about the way wormholes are depicted in science fiction films, they always have that twisting, turning, tunnelling feeling of tree roots don't they. They never seem to be straight.
Often in science-fiction books and films, alien people are asked if they themselves built the wormholes, and usually the answer is

something along the lines of 'no, it was a very ancient race who built these, nobody knows how long ago'.
Perhaps this is what we are looking at here?
Pure science-fiction conjecture at this stage of course, but this concept certainly seems to make more sense, in the real world, than actual gigantic tree roots growing out into space.

Try saying the word Ginnungagap slowly. Gin-nung-ga-gap. I love this word. Not only does it sound cool, but it's meaning is also cool.
It literally means 'the great yawning gap'.
One could hardly find a more fitting descriptor for the mindboggling 'gaps' of interplanetary and interstellar space.
To me it seems possible that somebody, (the originator of the tale?), was taken on a journey, and later described that awesome and terrifying gap which the craft traversed.
It is not hard to visualize the absolute cold of a world deep in space, deep in Ginningagap, a world of absolute frost where these 'Þursa', these beings lumped into the generic category 'giants' by translators, might originate.

The mind-boggling question is, how could the ancient human storytellers, who coined this descriptive word, have possibly conceived of the vastness of space, of the great yawning gap which is way beyond human comprehension?
Even at the speed of light, a craft would take 4.2 years to reach the closest star. It is extremely 'yawning' out their!

'Ein er með Ásum'.
(One (root) is with the Aesir).
A short but powerful sentence, that, when we think about it, seem to indicate that there could be a place of the Aesir, not just on the

earth, not just in the area of the great space station Himinbjorg, but also out, maybe very far out, in space. Could it be a moonbase? A Mars base (or one of its moons)? Or could it be the original home world that they (and we) came from? Perhaps a planet so far away that it orbits a far-off star in one of the constellations?
Later on this journey, I will tell you about some incredible connections pointing to the constellation called The Pleiades, and it's modern-day anecdotal connection to the tall, blue or green eyed, beautiful blonde people called the 'Nordics'.

The last 'root' mentioned, the third one, is called Niflheim. Its name means 'Homeworld of Mist or Darkness'.
It is first mentioned by Snorri in the early introduction to Gylfaginning, and it is said that this home world was created aeons before the Earth itself was formed.
This would seem to indicate that it is a very cold world, desolate, way out in the absolute cold of deep space. We have many ice worlds in our own solar system, such as Jupiter's moons Europa, Ganymede and Callisto, and my personal favorite planet, Pluto, (yes, I am one of those rebels who refuses to acknowledge it's unfair reclassification ha ha).
We also have the Kuiper Belt (beyond Neptune), and the Oort Cloud out beyond Pluto, many of whose objects are believed to be mainly composed of ice.
It is interesting to note that the Marvel comics and film universe, which I mentioned in the very opening of this book, paint Niflheim as one of the 10 realms, and characterize it as the base world of the Frost Giants, and of a place called the 'Cave of Ages', where (Marvel's) Odin imprisoned an entity known as Mangog.
They identify this realm as associated with death and the afterlife. Snorri's Odin, as 'Third', told Gylfi the Wizard King that, ' all things cold and harsh came from Niflheim'.

We learn that there is yet another well there, in some translations a spring, called Hvergelmir. This word breaks down into two words, 'hver', meaning a hot spring, a boiling cauldron or even a whirlpool (and this word is still used in Iceland to this day), and 'gelmir', meaning resounding or roaring, from the root word 'gjalda'.
Combined these words conjure up something roaring, swirling and bubbling, not unlike the hydrothermal power stations of Iceland. We are told that out of this place flow eleven great rivers, whose names we know, and some of the meanings of these names.
The first is called 'Svöl (cool), second is Gunnthrá (battle defiant), third is Fjörm, fourth is Fimbulthule (loud bubbling), fifth is Slíð (fearsome), sixth is Hríð (storming), seventh is Slyg, eighth is Ylg, ninth is Víð (wide), Tenth is Leipt (fast as lightning), eleventh is Gjöll (which, we are told, is next to Hel's gate.)

I think that it is very significant that the Marvel writer's considered the home of the Frost Giants to be Niflheim. Even though we are told that near the end of the second root is the home of the Frost Giants, we are also told a fairly long story in Gylfaginning about Niflheim, (on the third root), and what amounts to the origin story of these Frost Giants, the 'Hrímþursa'. In fact, it is also another origin story of we humans!

The story goes like this – those eleven rivers, which I named above, flowing out of Hvergelmir, are collectively called Elivagar. These rivers are poisonous, and as they flow very far from their source they begin to freeze. Icing up, the flow eventually comes to a halt, and the vapour rising from the poison freezes on the top and keeps building layer upon layer.
The story continues in this manner, talking about great cold and great heat and a nice pleasant zone in between. The Prose Edda

literally says 'but Ginnungagap was as mild as a windless sky'. 'And when the heat's breath met the rime so that it melted and dripped, life arose from those flowing drops – given force by the one who sent the heat.
It took the shape of a man, who was called Ymir. But the Frost Giant's called him Augelmir, and from him came the races of the Frost Giants, as it is told in the Shorter Völuspá (from the Poetic Edda).'

I don't know about you, but for me, all this talk of poison and dripping and flowing and layering of ice, and the input of force and heat, brings to mind the sort of science-fiction technologies you see in movies like 'Avatar', and 'Don't Look Up', and many others. I imagine great steel and plastic devices with a myriad of tubes containing yellowish poisonous fluids flowing, lightly frosted with ice on the outside of the perspex canopies, through which we can see beings in suspended animation.
The reason that this passage brings suspended animation to mind is that in the story we end up with a man, who was called Ymir.
He is the first of the 'Frost Giant's', the Hrimthursar (Hrimþursa).

Forgive me for my wild imagination, but I see perhaps a fleet of cryogenic vessels coming to earth, thawing out their frozen cargo, and onboard are these humanoid beings, Hrimþursa. Perhaps beings who have been sent here, across the infinite vastness of 'the yawning gap', on a pre-programmed mission of some kind.
To back up this theory, (and of course that's all it is), the next thing we learn is that there was a 'cow' named Audhumla onboard, conveniently ready to go, feeding this little guy Ymir (and maybe many others), with four 'rivers' of milk!
Constantly on tap. This all seems rather odd doesn't it.

Imagine that the beings are actually babies, protected in high tech cribs, carefully, robotically reanimated, even brought to term, until they are large enough to start taking other food, which also could be conveniently packaged and robotically presented.
(Think perhaps of a less dystopian version of the excellent film 'Mother').
These beings, these Frost Giants, these special versions of the race called the Jötun, could go on to become the ubiquitous enemies and sometimes friends and partners of that other humanoid race, the Aesir?

There is another extraordinary gem of information hidden within this narrative which once again, like the tower of Babel, harks back to those same very early biblical stories in Genesis, about the founding of the human race.
This is from Chapter 7 of Gylfaginning.
'Then High answered – 'The sons of Bor, (Odin, Vili and Vé), killed the Jötun (giant) Ymir. When he fell, so much blood gushed from his wounds that it drowned all the race of Hrímþursa/Frost Giants, all except one who escaped with his family and retainers. That one the Giants called Bergelmir.'
(Note : The name Bergelmir is derived from 'berg', which most probably in this case means mountain (as in English 'Iceberg') and 'elmir', an obscure word which could be related to gjalma
(roar or resound) or almi (protecting?).)

Now the most amazing passage -
'He travelled/voyaged **up** on his **Lúðr** with his wife, (and undoubtedly family and retainers), and remained there (where? in outer space?), and from them came the lineage of the Frost Giants, as is told here.'

Now, to back this story up, Snorri quotes this (probably) very old poem -

'Endless uncountable winters
Before the Earth was (re?)shaped
Then was Bergilmir born
He who was first mentioned
That one who is the wise Giant (Jötunn)
Upon whom the protective vessel (**Lúðr**) was laid.'
(Vafþrúðnismál/Vafthrutnismal 35, from the Poetic Edda)

There is a lot of 'wow factor' to unpack here!

I hardly need to say it, but you will have recognised the similarity to the biblical story of Noah, from the book of Genesis Chapters 5 - 9.

The 'flood of blood' idea is pretty gross and yet if, as it seems very likely, there was a massive life destroying tsunami 11,000 years ago, then there certainly would've been plenty of blood in the water, and the water would not be a nice crystal blue green, but extremely muddy red like all floodwater.

This Old Norse Noah's name, Bergelmir, seems to mean either 'Mountain roarer' or something like 'Mountain Survivor', which immediately puts me in mind of the story of Mount Ararat, where the biblical Ark is said to have come to rest.

It's also significant that this is exactly where the land of the Van is, where Paul Wallis and Matt Le Croix have made so many new discoveries related to this very ancient place.

The place where human civilization began anew, right next door to where the Aesir people also happened to live.

The key word here is the mysterious **Lúðr**, this 'protective vessel' that takes Bergilmir, his family and their retainers '**up**'.

If we continue to follow the chain of reasoning that I've been proposing in this chapter, the people who came to be called the Frost Giant's seem to have been brought here in cryostasis in the very ancient past and were quite possibly the first wave of advanced humans on earth. At some time a great catastrophe threatens, a 'great flood' perhaps (which is attested to and remembered in so many stories from cultures all over the world).

Perhaps a large asteroid was detected heading for Earth, warnings promulgated, yet the majority dismissed it.

If this occurred at the onset of the last great catastrophe, the sudden onset Younger Dryas Ice Age, then it could have been this civilisation ending event.

Whatever it was, something drastic happened, and one family group is either warned personally by powerful beings or just takes the warning seriously. They manage to engineer a high-tech emergency craft, or perhaps find one of the very ancient original craft that brought their people to earth. Maybe they are the only group able to make it to an emergency flying craft and get clear before the giant waves hit? They are lifted 'up', (possibly putting themselves into suspended animation), and then, after quite a long time, are automatically brought back down to earth.

They land on the top of a mountain (Ararat?).

Perhaps this is what Bergelmir's name commemorates, and maybe what some folks living near the mountain witnessed, to their terror and awe, a great old tech Jötun space-ship's landing rockets 'roaring' as it descended atop the mountain?

Plenty of this type of thing is later vividly described in the Bible's Exodus stories concerning Mt Sinai and Moses.

I have one last story about these icey folks I'd like to tell you –

Snorri relates that before the original Ymir was apparently killed by Odin and his two brothers, something rather odd happened. I expect you're used to that by now!

Ymir is said to have slept, and whilst asleep sweated, and then under his left arm a male and female grew, and then one of his legs had a son of the other, and all the frost giants are descended from these three. One female and two males.

Once again, this just sounds like a bit of a really old 'mythical' myth, a strange fanciful story, and maybe that's what this is.

However we are considering here that these people, called the Frost Giants, had quite possibly come to Earth in spaceships, and had been artificially raised.

If we can accept that scenario as a technological possibility, then there is another possibility that this further story suggests. The first cloned animal was famously called Dolly the sheep. She was cloned from a cell, taken from a mammary gland, proving that a whole organism could be cloned from a specific cell type in a body. The system of axillary lymph nodes in humans extends from the breasts to under the armpit, and thus puts me in mind of the possible use of cloning technology to create the subsequent generations of this species of Jötunn.

Maybe I'm stretching things a little far, yet this is all a thought experiment, and for me worth doing to break away from the standard explanations of these rather fantastic stories.

So now let's visit some of the other fascinating places up there in space, up above the clouds.

Some of them seem attached to Yggdrasil, and others appear to be set at a distance, some at a great distance.

First we learn of Álfheim, (Homeworld of the Elves), where Snorri tells us the people called the 'Light Elves' live. These beings are more beautiful than the sun to look at, and one of their dwellings is called Breidablik, as beautiful a place as one could find. Breidablik means 'Gleaming far and wide'.

Another dwelling is called Glitnir, which is also part of Álfheim, and its name means 'Radiant Place'.
Of Glitnir it is said that its walls and columns and pillars were of red gold, and its roof was of silver.
It up to us to choose to imagine this 'radiant place' in a sort of 'Lord of the Rings' wonderous fantasy story way, or as a great gleaming starship, saturated in artificial light, floating weightless in the void.

What strikes me about the descriptions of these places is that they are all said to display brilliant light, radiating far and wide, the type of lights that are commonplace in our 21st Century homes and cities, and in our science-fiction films.
Strong brilliant light unseen in ancient days except from the sun.
(It will be noted that a majority of UFO/UAP sightings seem to be associated with very unusual and extreme light, light that often has very unusual properties. Light that can seem to be in some manner 'alive').

All the people of Gylfi's day, (and right up to very recently in human history), knew only sunlight, moonlight and fire light. Anything different, or greater than these lights, would be a subject of extreme wonder, and would certainly be carefully noted.
If we can believe Snorri, these stories we are considering were literally first told to the Wizard King Gylfi.
It seems logical to think that, besides being told the stories, he could have been taken physically taken and shown these bright gleaming places.

Imagine what a mind-boggling experience that would have been for him!

Odin's HQ is called 'Valaskjálf', and one would assume that this name has something to do with both the famous Valhalla, 'Hall of the Valiant Slain', as well as being connected to that 'high seat' of Odin's, 'Hlidskjalf', from which he could sit, leaning out over the world, observing everything that was going on down below.
This word breaks down into two somewhat unusual meanings – Valr - meaning the slain, in some contexts also relating to choice or selection, and 'Skjálf'- to tremble or shake, as well as having the meaning of shelf or ledge.
Combining these words could indicate the meaning of a shelf, a seat where Odin could look out over the world, making it pretty much the same as Hlidskjalf, a place for observing the outcomes of battles, and choosing the slain. If we go with the alternate meaning of skálf, it could also possibly indicate a powerful platform in space, sometimes trembling or shaking with power, where the viewing platform was attached.

The word 'Heimskringla', (Snorri's great History of the Norse Kings), breaks down into 'heim' (home or world), and 'kringla'(round or globular).
By itself 'heim' is obviously related to our word 'home' (a lot of English words derive from Old Norse). When you combine heim's two meanings you get the meaning 'homeworld', which for modern science-fiction fans instantly conjures up the worlds of Star Wars or Star Trek, where different species usually reside on homeworlds. From the homeworlds they often preside over a number of other planets which have been settled by their people.

To return to Alfheim, the homeworld of the Light Elves, we realize that it is not a secret forest retreat or a hidden mountain cave on Earth.

These Light Elves seem to be a special race, maybe a higher, separate, more powerful race than the Elves on earth, who often seem quite human-like.

In the Icelandic literature the Earthly Elves are sometimes indistinguishable from the Aesir.

In his groundbreaking study of the paranormal in the medieval North, 'The Troll inside You' (pg 31), Professor Ármann Jakobsson writes - 'Old Norse álfr is a more unspecified term with a fairly broad significance, perhaps indicating 'any cultic paranormal being on a lower rung than the actual Æsir, the high gods of Old Norse myth and legend', (thus including the fertility gods termed Vanir but also apparently covering a variety of other beings). Thus the Old Norse álfr is used to indicate not only a specific race or species or even category of elves but rather any kind of paranormal figure clearly superior to humans'.

The Professor is indicating here that these old words are quite elastic in meaning, and I really like his definition of them being perceived by humans as 'paranormally superior'.

In his essay, 'The Extreme Emotional Life of Völund the Elf', he elaborates on this idea - 'It is also unclear whether he (Völund) has any supernatural powers. He does not need supernatural powers for anything he does, (even though we are told of him flying high up beneath the clouds). However, gods and supernatural beings often seem to have no special powers in mythic narratives. In the poems adjacent to Volundarkviða in the Codex Regius, for example, Þórr (Thor) seems lost without his hammer in Þrymskviða (Thrymskvida) and has to use ordinary cleverness to dispose of Alvíss the dwarf in Alvíssmál'.

I find it very encouraging that he has concluded that the sagas paint the so-called 'gods', and other related characters, as not supernatural, that is, not having a reality and powers outside this normal realm of our universe. They have paranormal powers that even mere humans sometimes exhibit, though at a much higher level than most of us.

Even the Mighty Thor is not exempt!

In one story he finds himself at a loss without his mighty hammer Miolnir! Like a soldier without his rifle, or a Viking without his axe or spear!

So these Light Elves, with their separate homeworld, appear to be a unique and separate category of 'elflike' beings.

This is where things get really interesting.

Gylfi, questioning the three Odin brothers, is told about the most beautiful 'hall' called Gimle (a hall being, in my paleocontact view, quite possibly a massive spaceship, a 'Mothership'), situated

'á sunnanverðum himins enda', that is, at the southernmost end of the sky/outer space.

Gimle is described quite mysteriously as being 'the most beautiful of all and brighter than the Sun'. So where exactly is this southernmost end of the sky?

Now we get some further clues.

Gylfi asks 'what will protect this place (Gimle) from Surt's Fire?', (a prophesied great catastrophe to come, wherein the Earth and maybe our galaxy is burnt up during the final battle, Ragnarok).

High (Odin) answers him by saying - ' there is another 'himinn' (sky/outer space region) south of and above this 'himinn' of ours, and that 'himinn' is called 'Andlang' (meaning - 'outstretched'), and there is a third heaven still further above that one, and that is called

Vidblain (meaning Wide Blue), and it is in that heaven that we believe this place (Gimle) is'.
Having happily got rid of the word heaven as a translation, what do we make of this use of the word 'himinn'?

Odin seems to be describing either solar systems around stars, or even whole galaxies. We are being told that there is this sky/outer space region south, and above us, and then another one, about which we are not given any further details.
Andlang means 'outstretched'!
Like Ginnungagap, ('yawning gap' or even 'yawning abyss'), 'outstretched' is a fitting though modest description of the unthinkable distances between planets, stars and galaxies!
Vidblain (Víðbláinn) literally means 'the wide blue or black', there being some ambiguity in the old texts as to the exact colour.
The oldest texts generally go with black.
Many past cultures, including the ancient Egyptians, Babylonians, Vedic Indians, and the Ancient Greeks, thought of deep space as an ocean, a black or blue ocean through which cosmic vessels sailed. To our modern minds this is not a difficult concept is it?

Our popular culture has given us vivid visions of this reality for many, many years.
So once again, these words, almost always mistranslated as relating to 'heavens', are literally describing, clear as day, a surprising understanding of what lies beyond the Earth. We have been led to believe, through our schooling, that ancient people didn't comprehend the sky, and the blackness of the night sky, as being anything other than some kind of massive dome set with little lights.
Yet properly re-translating the word himinn, and these place names (that are often left untranslated), reveals a shocking truth.

People have been out there!

We are told that only the Light Elves inhabit these two places, Andlang and Víðbláinn, for the time being.

Are these two star systems, or even two constellations, inhabited only by these special beautiful bright beings?

Very interesting isn't it!

We will delve even deeper into this question of star systems and constellations in the final chapter.

There are even more incredible wonders orbiting the Earth to be told of, as part of the great land base, vast starbridge and interstellar starport that was known to the Aesir as Old Asgard.

We will return to them in the upcoming chapter, 'Chariots of the Viking Gods'.

For now let's take the high-speed elevator down the shimmering Bifrost, back to Old Asgard on the ground, where, surprisingly, there is a lot of packing going on.

Asking around, we learn that the gods are leaving!

'THE GODS ARE LEAVING'

During my month-long research tour of Scandinavia and Iceland, one of the most remarkable things was the consistent finding of circular shapes in landforms, circular shaped carvings on rocks and standing stones, and on beautiful artefacts crafted by master smith's out of bronze, copper, amber and precious stones. They all seemed to have a unique theme tying them together.

The theme of bright sun-like flying craft, seen in the skies by witnesses with high artistic skills, who then chronicled these extraordinary experiences.

Great arrangements of rocks in circular, almost clock-like shapes, at important places where presumably very unusual events happened.

Places like the great table mountains, Halleberg and Huneberg, in Western Sweden, owned since before records began by the Swedish royal family, who still believe this is where the great migrating Aesir people rebuilt Old Asgard in the North.

Then, in the University of Lund Library Museum, Sweden, that Bronze Age 'sunwheel' rock showing two great flying sunwheels against a background of three-dimensional ' stars', with the faintly visible, yet clearly carved, soft conical shape emanating from its base.

A shape that looks, for all the world, like the kind of light reported by people abducted into round bright hovering spacecraft. A light that has the power to lift people not only up, but through solid walls!

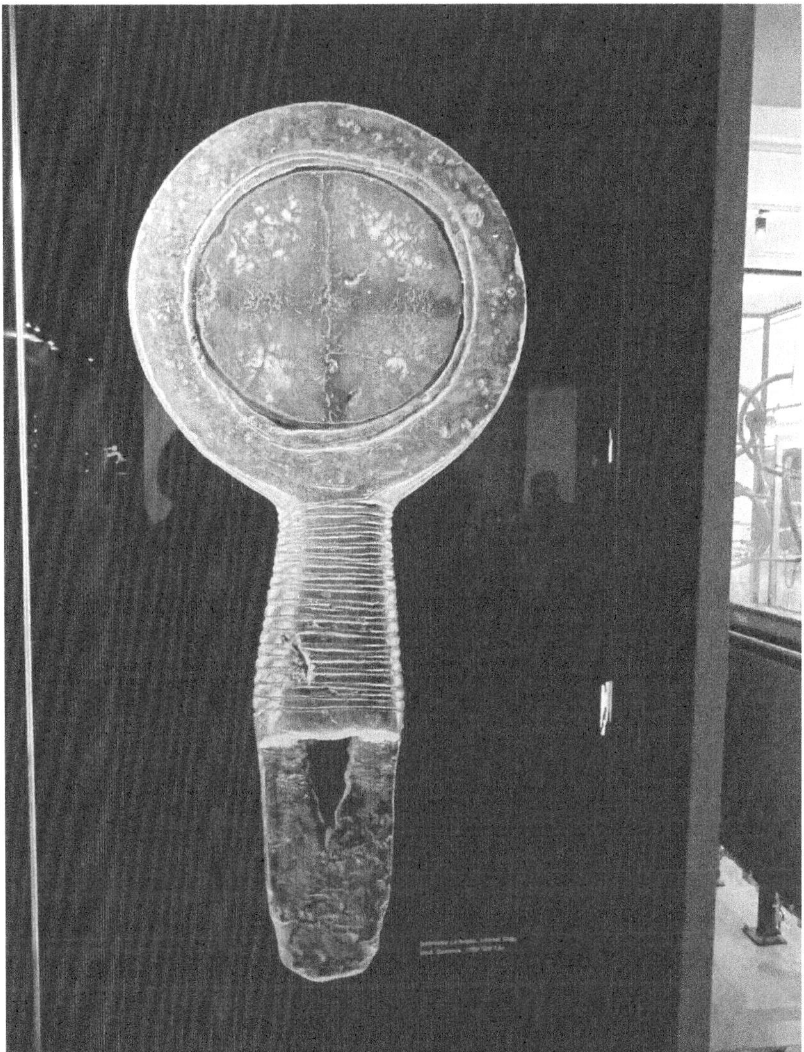

In the National Museum of Denmark, in Copenhagen, I photographed an intricate bronze, circular, sunwheel-like shape, hand crafted with great skill. In the centre of it there is a mysterious face, with bulging eyes that almost look as if they are surrounded by some type of goggles. Radiating out from around that face are triangular wedge shapes that run out to the circles edge. Below this sunwheel faced design there is what must surely be a representation of a great, flaring, ladder-like beam, reaching down to the ground. The object is from that same era as the sunwheel rock from Lund. Nearby was a similarly uncanny piece of three-dimensional art, a glass sunwheel, an extraordinary light-filled transparent red amber circle with a dark cross shape in it's centre, and descending below, a flaring ribbed ladder / stairway structure of glass.

The official position of archaeologists is that these flaring 'ladders' represent timber stands, practical affairs that would have held up large-scale sunwheel representations, for display and perhaps worship at religious festivals, or carried on a wagon pulled by horses for a similar reason.
As an artist I find this answer unconvincing. If these really represented a simple stand in the real world, why would you include it in these small size artistic, (and very creative), masterpieces?
Surely the point is to represent the real thing that you saw, even if you are actually simply representing the sun itself, or even the moon?
It puts me in mind of the Japanese traditional art of Kabuki drama, where the beautifully made props in scene changes are moved by people clad all in black.
These people are not supposed to be noticed, they are considered invisible, an artistic convention, as these stands are meant to be.

I believe that all of these sunwheel themed artefacts, for those with the eyes to see, commemorate the sighting, communication with, and perhaps voyaging in great circular physical craft.

Craft with crosses on their undersides, glowing brightly, and at times emanating a conical beam of light that behaves like a ladder. Craft witnessed by artists of the Bronze Age.

Then there are what I believe to be commemorative stone circles that I visited at Hlidarendi (Hliðarendi), in Southern Iceland, high up on a bare stoney hilltop, high above the funeral mound of the great Viking Age hero, Gunnar Hámundarson.

These two circles of stones, one larger than the other, seemed to be roughly laid out around two larger stones. My immediate feeling was that these were a cultural memorial to the two great landforms in Sweden that my friend Asgeir had taken me to – Halleberg (Valhalla) and Huneberg (Asgard), which in their turn appeared to be a cultural memorial to the great Aesir City of Old Asgard in Türkiye.

The rocks seem to be laid out as a tribute to Gunnar after his death, commemorating his journey to Valhalla. I had the distinct feeling that they were a forgotten feature of the landscape, or perhaps a local secret.

In chapter 78 of one of the great Icelandic stories of the Viking Age, Njal's Saga, a great bright light is witnessed by Gunnar's son Hogni, and by his close friend Skarphedinn, apparently hovering above Gunnar's haug (burial mound), brightly lighting up the surrounding area.

An event which was followed by what could only be described, in modern religious terms, as a transfiguration/resurrection event, and perhaps involving the 'alien abduction' of a great, recently deceased warrior.

VALHALLA

I will be telling this remarkable story in depth in my next book, 'Viking Superpowers - Way of Midgard.'

Later, on the day that I had climbed high up the steep slopes of Hlidarendi, my Icelandic friend took me to the nearby Saga Centre in Hvolsvöllur, which commemorates Njal's saga.
As we pulled up in her car I saw before the door a wide concrete ring, a large boulder in its centre, and a ring of small boulders around about it like numbers on a clock face.
Almost exactly mimicking what I had seen on the top of the hill at Hlidarendi farm!
My friend had no idea why this rock design was there, and told me that the man who had built and managed the centre for many years, and who set up this circle of heavy rocks, had recently passed away at just over 100 years of age.
How I wish I could have met that gentleman!
I suspect that a lot of pagan/heathen secrets passed with him.

The icing on the cake came when I visited, very late one night, the famous valley in Iceland called Thingvellir.
This is the ancient meeting place, the first parliament in the world, where the Icelandic freemen gathered to sort out their legal issues with each other. This valley is bounded on two sides by sheer lava stone walls, formed by nature in the most fantastic shapes.
Standing near the central place called the Law Rock is a little old church, the replacement of another little old church from the Middle Ages, and which undoubtedly replaced the original great heathen Temple, (the Church never missed an opportunity to replace an old sacred place with one of their own).
Walking behind this church in the surprisingly bright midnight, I was surprised to find a great sunwheel on the ground, probably

20 m in diameter, raised up just like the table mountain of Huneberg in Sweden, with a concrete cross shaped walking path stretched across its diameter.
I later discovered that this is a national burial site for very important figures in Icelandic history, yet my feeling was that, while what I was looking at was only perhaps 100 years old, it was representing an idea that was definitely pre-Christian.
To me it represents a memory of the great Asgards, the Old and the New, and the great sunwheels that brought the Aesir to the North.
A sacred pre-Christian memory reaching back thousands of years, not to be forgotten by the wise Icelanders.

Nearby, behind what is the Icelandic Prime Minister's summer residence, (Thingvallabaer), was another smaller circle, and in its centre what seems to be a tall, very conical, bushy tree. From the air it looks for all the world like a classic flying saucer shape. The summer residence, the great sunwheel and the smaller round shape were designed by the famous Icelandic architect, Guðjón Samúelsson, in 1930, to commemorate the thousandth anniversary of the founding of the Althing in 930 A.D.
The road running beside this complex is called Valhalla Way!

When I came back to Australia and collated my information and experiences, a clearer picture of what was going on in the mythic stories started to emerge.
I learnt that this sunwheel motif, found all over Scandinavia, also occurs as far south as the royal tombs of Bronze Age Anatolia/Türkiye, (home of Old Asgard, and the Aesir and the Vanir peoples), and as far afield as the yurts, (demountable round felt huts), of Mongolia!

Online I discovered a treasure trove of photographs of Bronze Age rock carvings in Scandinavia, (particularly Sweden), as well as in some of my older books, and what I found blew my mind.
Mainstream scholars consider that these carvings are very difficult to decipher, lacking as we do knowledge about the gods and spiritual beliefs from thousands of years ago in the North.
Yet with clues from the sagas and Eddas, my personal discoveries in Scandinavia, and applying my trained 'artist's mind', I quickly began to discern clear pictographic symbols and messages in these carvings.

These Bronze Age carvings seem to back up Snorri's accounts of the adventures of the Aesir and the Vanir peoples, from the Prose and Poetic Eddas, and Heimskringla.
In fact, the carvings lead me to believe that Snorri's stories could well be preserving actual events from two to three thousand years ago (and possibly older)!
When you think about it, that's not really so surprising.
The stories of the Judeo-Christian Bible, and the stories of many other very old religions, have also been preserved for similar lengths of time.
Text based civilizations like ours, can often be quite biased towards peoples who are 'illiterate', who don't keep written records.
Yet the great tradition of remembered and complex rhyming in which these original, (sung), poetic stories have been preserved seems to be almost as reliable as the written word.
In the same way, the language of drawing, painting and carving is sometimes held in lower regard than pure text, even though it is also within our cultural corpus that 'a picture is worth a thousand words'.

On a great broad, smooth stone slab in Tanum Municipality, Bohuslan, Southwest Sweden, what seems to be a world changing event is chronicled. The original, painstakingly carved into the stone, must've taken a very long time to complete with the tools available in the early Bronze Age.

Originally, in the same way that today's archaeologists have done, the carvings could've been augmented with coloured paint, making the story easier to 'read' for subsequent generations. The scene is depicted from an elevated position, and although the figures are laid out flat and full length, as are the ship shapes and other items, the whole picture has a feeling of perspective. The objects closer are bigger, and as they move away, they get smaller and smaller.

Surrounding the central picture are other scenes that seem to be speaking of separate events, perhaps happening at the same time, or at other times.

As a trained classical artist, having many years experience in comics and illustration creation, my assessment is that the artist or artists who created this great tableau were highly skilled. As simple as the ships and figures appear at first glance, they are graphically sophisticated, symbolic rather than realistic, and represent a developed pictographic language.

Having lost the direct keys to the language, the keywords as it were, we must try to use all our intuition, as well as the stories that have been left to us, to decipher them.

If these pictures, or at least some of them, are indeed depicting paleocontact, then the artists have done a magnificent job. Even across the great gulf of 3000 years we can be sure about some pictographic' words such as man, woman, ship, cow, dog, horse and others. This language relies on our shared visual experience of the world.

The first thing we notice on this great stone canvas is a group of large, sophisticated 'stick figures', humans or humanoids, standing in the centre foreground. They are much larger than the surrounding ships.

This may represent the relative size of the beings, or it could be purely an artistic device, letting us know that these are the most important beings in the picture, the central focus, and apparently the reason for the whole large gathering.

Five figures in all, each bears in the centre of their bodies a sunwheel symbol.

At first glance these look like the much later traditional round Viking Age shields, yet it is much more likely that they are symbols in this pictographic language, simply stating, 'this is a person from the sky, this is one of the sky people, the star people, the 'Powerful Ones' who came to visit us'. The accepted view is that these are symbols of the sun, and thereby of the sky.

These 'Powerful Ones' are holding unusual double headed axes in the air. The interesting thing is that there is a zigzag quality to the carved lines running down from the axeheads and connecting to the raised arm of each figure.

'Lightning bolt' is the first word that comes to mind!

The Sky People figures seem to be showing off their frightening powers, one would assume to confirm in the minds of the locals that they are indeed the old gods of legend, come to earth to visit their people.

And what more shocking demonstration of their awesome weapons than to emit blasts of lightning-like power.

It's not a great stretch of the imagination to think of the classic image of the Thunder God, the Mighty Thor, blasting away with his power hammer Mjolnir!

Another obvious aspect of these figures is that three of them have large, slightly curving and erect penis's, and two of them don't.

These penis symbols are found all over the ancient Scandinavian carvings, and appear to essentially indicate the word 'male', and possibly 'powerful ruling male'.
When we think of the well-known story of the 'spring wedding', between Sky Father and Earth Mother, the purposeful impregnating of Earth girls by these powerful males from the sky, then the symbol would seem to be also indicating that this is a part of their purpose in landing here.

As if to emphasise this obvious imagery, directly below the feet of the figure furthest right is a circular shape, having a curving line coming up from the bottom to a small circle in the centre. This shape seems to be indicating the end of a penis, seen from the

front, a design that, surprisingly, is mimicked almost exactly in at least one of the great burial mounds of the same period.
This is the Kivik 'King's Mound' from 1400 BC, located in South Eastern Scania, Sweden.
Of the two figures which I perceive to be female, one also carries the same powerful weapon as the males. The female figure with the power weapon has a variation on the sunwheel symbol, with what seems to be only half a cross within a circle. On other stones of the same period females are indicated by a dot carved between the legs, just below the groin area. This female figure doesn't appear to have one of these dots.
The fifth figure, somewhat smaller than the others, is also sans penis, yet has the full sun wheel symbol, but no axe/lightning weapon.
Surrounding these Sky People are ship symbols of all different sizes. Close to the viewer floats a large ship with little mark's representing either one or two warriors each, and there are 30 marks on the deck, so this is either a thirty or a sixty man vessel.

By the later Viking Age standards this is quite a big warship, and could represent the warship of the leader of the Earth people. On the left and right of the figures are a number of small ships, with maybe 20 people on each, and then lined up in the distance are at least 25 small ships. It seems that the whole community has turned up, and a show of human force no doubt is represented by all these warships.
No-one would wish to miss seeing these powerful people.

Above the tall figure, second from the left, there appears to float a strange object, up in the sky, above the heads of the Sky People. Higher up on the great rock mural, at the far top right, there is the exact same strange object, this time a little bigger, as if the viewer has zoomed in.

It's circular, coloured in vivid red, and emanating from around the circumference of the circle, (perhaps a globe), are unusual, three pronged shapes, which seem to represent flames, bright light or flashing/strobing light.

Beside this floating object are two female figures, (who also seem to be floating), presumably Earth women, who we can recognise by their long, tied back hair, hanging down their backs, down from their elongated heads.

These two women are reaching out to the circular shape. There is something about their slender elegant shapes, as compared to other more matronly female figures carved on other rocks, that suggest that these are young fertile women.

These pictographs seem to be telling us that there were bright floating circular craft present with the Sky People, and it could be that we are witnessing them taking these females on board. In the foreground, in a nice naturalist touch, we see what appears to be a dog, with his long tail and up pointed ears, and the dog's attention is taken by three very intriguing little animals. These creatures have two legs and very long necks, they don't have ears as the dog does, but they don't appear to represent birds. I hesitate to say this, but the first animal that comes to mind when you look at these carvings would be some kind of small dinosaur-like creatures, something like velociraptors perhaps. This of course is a strange thing, but perhaps if we can accept that this ancient carving is telling us about people who came from the skies with lightning weapons, who had flying floating bright craft, maybe we could accept that they had with them unusual creatures, perhaps companion animals, but from a different world, from a different planet? I rather like that idea!

Up near the top of the rock mural we see a number of very large beasts that appear to be either cattle, or perhaps the extinct giant cows called aurochs. There are three bulls, and two cows, two reindeers (or elks), and a number of what might be horses, and their colts or fillies.

The cattle are being herded or hunted by a person with a long stick/ spear.

A figure stands near him with a bow and arrows (protecting the herd from predators?).

Perhaps these animals are part of a tribute of breeding animals, of food, or to be sacrificed to these 'gods', who have so marvelously descended from the sky.

There are two four-wheeled wagons represented, and on the far left of this great canvas of stone we see two large sunwheels, maybe the very large landed craft out of which these people came. Near these craft stands a tall Sky Person, possibly on guard, and he holds a bow and arrow. Maybe he has asked one of the human Warriors if he can try out this interesting, primitive, yet effective weapon. There are a number of the smaller ships close to these two sunwheel craft.

Another fascinating little detail in this picture is three shapes, for all the world looking like large modern boot prints, showing a distinct heel shape, separated from the front of the boot by a straight line. Just like in a modern boot. One might say they look like moon boot prints, and nearby each one of these boot prints is a little figure, with the circle shape on the body, which could indicate that this is also one of the Sky People. The interesting thing about these prints, and the little Sky Person, is that they appear near human ships that are off a little bit in the distance.

It looks as if beings are inspecting the Earth people's ships. In the final chapter, 'The Smoking Gun', I will have more to say about these boot prints, helping to put all this evidence together in what I hope you will find quite an astounding way.

All things considered, this ancient tableau seems to be clearly telling the tale of something very extraordinary indeed, something that actually happened to the people of that area of Sweden, way back in the Bronze Age.
Could it be that this is a true record of a primal paleocontact event, made at the time, of first contact between two peoples, an introduction which clearly sets the stage for their future relationship?
Is there the possibility that our friend Gylfi, (aka Gangleri), the Wizard King of Sweden, could have been there personally, leading his people through this inevitable event?
Considering the stories I'm about to tell you, from both the Prose Edda and Heimskringla, (the History of the Norse Kings), I think you might have to agree with me that this is all a very real possibility!

So let's fly in our personal Sunwheel back to the centre of the world, Old Asgard, the great city on Earth and in the stars, which we have come to know so well, and catch up on the latest exploits of these Sky People, the Aesir and Vanir.
Snorri has told us so much about this great and beautiful and mindboggling place, Old Asgard, yet we don't really know how long ago it was first built. The obvious biblical parallels in the stories indicate that it could well have been there, in the area of Troy/Anatolia/Türkiye, way back into very ancient times. So let's imagine that we are back there in the early Bronze Age, in the time just prior to when that extraordinary, commemorative stone carved artwork was created in Sweden.

We hover above Old Asgard's spaceport Earth base station, and as we glide down to land, we notice that it is a hive of activity.
A great fleet of sunwheel craft, and smaller flying vehicles, are being loaded with machinery of all kinds, including land vehicles equipped for rough cross-country trekking.
Families and larger groups of people, wearing their special flying suits, are loading household goods, (and even household pets in carry-cages), into sun wheel craft.
Some people, perhaps aristocracy, are wearing very spectacular formal outfits, and are taking up their assigned seating in personal craft.
It appears that a large-scale migration is underway.

This is what the Prologue to the Prose Edda tells us -
'Óðinn (Odin) had 'spádom' (the paranormal gift of seeing the future (clairvoyance)), and so did his wife, and from those visions found he this, that his name would be remembered in the northern half of the world, and exalted above all kings. For that reason, he was determined to start his journey from Türkiye, and had with him a great number of troops - young and old, men and women— and many valuable, precious and treasured things. But wherever they travelled **over** lands, their marvels and glory was widely celebrated, **so that they were thought more like gods than men**. They did not stop their journey until they came north to that land now called Saxony. There Odin dwelled for a long time, and he took possession of that land far and wide. There set Odin to rule over these lands three sons of his.'

It is telling to read that 'wherever they travelled **over** lands, their marvels and glory was widely celebrated'. The old Norse makes it clear that they travelled **over** the lands, in the same way we would say that we would fly over the lands. Travelling on the ground we would tend to say 'travel **across'** lands.

Wouldn't it be fantastic if we had some stories about those marvels that the ordinary humans saw!

Simply the act of flying over the lands in great, bright, sun wheel craft would be enough to cause endless 'marveling'. Even though the text says that they didn't stop until they came to the north, perhaps they did land in certain places, maybe just to impress people. It's not too hard to imagine the 'marvelling' that would be caused, even by you and I, if we were to suddenly arrive at a populated settlement, in say 1000 BC, and start openly displaying ordinary items from our everyday life.

Our cars, (their motors, glass, tyres, noise and headlights), our sound systems, our smartphones. Imagine setting up a wide screen in a forest clearing, and projecting videos of our most amazing movies! All things we take for granted, as if we have always had such marvels.

Even our ancestors 100 years ago would absolutely marvel at these things!

Consider also that this great flying migration would often be witnessed by many people at one time, the gold standard for sighting events, and you can imagine how fast the news travelled ahead of them.

Every artist worth his or her salt would be getting out their stone carving tools, striving to visually describe what would be very difficult even for us to describe, especially if all we had was wood and stone as art materials.

(Ironically, the sort of materials we would use now, paper and pens or even computer printouts or digital files, would not last the thousands of years that these stone pictographs have.)

The poets and storytellers would be working overtime crafting elaborate odes to these unexpected and utterly marvellous visitors!

On a less pleasing note, it's interesting to read that, right from the very start, the Aesir showed an extremely cavalier and uncaring attitude towards the rights and feelings of the Earth people, as they took their lands.
They take land as by 'divine right', by the old principle of 'might is right', by dint of their far superior technology, and undoubtedly due to the overwhelming psychological effect of their 'God-like' appearance.
Sadly, this bullying authoritarian style has been a mark of cultures since the very ancient days, and not just of the 'civilized' and technically advanced cultures.
It is clear from the records, both written and carved, that the Sky People, the 'Elohim of the North', were just as 'human', and mixed in their attitudes towards others as we still are in our 21st century world.

Snorri carries on his narrative of this great event by getting down to very specific details, (adding credibility to the narrative) -
'One (son) was named Vegdeg, he was a great king who ruled over East Saxland (part of modern Germany). His son was Vitrgils. His sons were Vitta, father of Heingest, and Sigarr, father of Svebdeg, whom we call Svipdag.
Another son of Odin was called Beldeg, whom we call Balder. He ruled that land, that is now known as Westphalia (Western Saxony). His son was Brandr, his son Frjódigar, who we call Fróði, his son Freóvin, his son Uvigg, and his son Gevis, who we call Gave.
The third son of Odin was named Sigi. These, the great forefathers, long ruled over the land that is now called Frakkland

(France), and from them came that (royal) family c Völsungs. Numerous mighty (genetically related to the Aesir) lineages sprang from them. Then Odin began his journey northward, and came to that land that they called Reiðgotaland, (the Land of the Goths), and claimed all the land that he willed. He set his son over the land who was called Skjöldr. His son was Friðleifr. That is where that family came from, that are called Skjöldungs, they are the Danish Kings. And that is called now Jutland, which then was called Reiðgotaland.'

As we peruse this long list, it becomes apparent that, if these stories are actually true, the Aesir under Odin had a major founding influence on the ruling family dynasties of Western Europe. We are even told, (in Heimskringla), that Odin and the great Aesir migration went initially to Russia (ON Garðaríki) before heading to Saxland.
There is no information about the names of the dynasties set up there, but undoubtedly there must've been knowledge of this at one time. Maybe the Russians have got it hidden away in the vaults?

We are given the specific names of many sons of Odin, who we can presume were often married to the daughters of the most powerful of the conquered people in these wide territories that the Aesir 'landed' in.
The founding dynasties of the ancient rulers of Russia, of France, of the Eastern and Western Saxons, and of the peoples of Denmark and Jutland!
No wonder royal families often considered that they ruled by divine right!
There is undoubtedly a whole field of fascinating research worth delving into concerning each one of these dynasties!

This exciting and eye opening account of the Aesir leaving Asgard, and migrating north, is also told in Chapter 5 of 'Ynglinga Saga', the first book of Heimskringla.
It is essentially the same story, but with certain added details which make the account even more compelling!
Firstly, we are told that Odin had large possessions in Tyrkland, 'Ásaheim', the home of the Aesir people.
Next we learn that Odin not only had 'Spádom', the gift of seeing/clairvoyance, but that he was 'fjölkunnigr','one who had great knowledge' of the powerful secrets of life, both paranormal and what was really happening in the world (and in space)!
A Wizard!

He knew ahead of time that he would be famous in the North, and that his descendants would have great possessions there.
We learn, significantly, that he hands over rulership of Old Asgard (presumably the whole box and dice - Asgard on the ground and Asgard in the sky/outer space), to his two brothers, Vé and Vili, aka Just-As-High and Third.
One assumes that he takes his beautiful wife Frigg north with him this time!
(I can promise you a lot more fascinating stories and information about the three brothers and their further adventures in my next book, currently in production.)

The Prologue of Snorri's Prose Edda continues -
'After that he (Odin) travelled north, to the place that is now called Sweden. There was a king there who was named Gylfi. But when he (Gylfi) heard of the travels of 'the men of Asia', who were called the Aesir, he went to meet them and offered Odin as much power in the kingdom as he himself had'.

Now of course we know that this young King is the very same Wizard King who was duped out of a great mass of his land by the beautiful Aesir woman, Gefjun.
The same heroic human who, against all odds, travelled all the way south to the vast 'Earth to Orbit' megapolis that was Old Asgard, and gained himself an audience with the frighteningly high-tech Odin and his two identical brothers.
Gylfi knew exactly who he was dealing with!

So let us thus imagine that it was this hero, Gylfi, who was the King on that large Bronze Age sailing ship, at anchor in the foreground of the great rock carving at Tanum Municipality, Bohuslan, greeting with all reverence and fanfare those Sky People with their lightning weapons.
He knew better than anybody else that these people were way too powerful to resist.
He and his hundreds of hardened elite warriors could do nothing more than stand back and watch.
The only smart thing to do at that point was to offer Odin 'as much power in the kingdom as he himself had'.
I can guarantee however that Gylfi wouldn't have been happy about any of this, but he also knew which side his bread was buttered on.
He had undoubtedly spread the stories that they had given him to spread, and prepared the hearts and minds of the people of Sweden for this inevitable invasion.
The marvels that attended the Aesir were therefore expected, and surely celebrated, and Gylfi, we could assume, was well looked after for his service.
Yet he was not a pushover, and as a great Wizard and leader of his people he would have looked for ways to quietly resist.

Heimskringla's 'Ynglinga Saga', Chapter 5, tells us that 'Odin and Gylfi contended with each other in contests of (paranormal) skills and powers, through cunning stratagems and psychic illusions, but the Aesir consistently emerged victorious and stronger'. This is a classic bit of information, because it shows that the humans, the Earth people, didn't just give up easily, but that Gylfi, and presumably other wizards, instead of resisting directly, kept testing the Aesir using their paranormal abilities, looking for weaknesses. No doubt Odin and the other Powerful Ones gained a measure of healthy respect for these people, realizing that they might not have had the advanced scientific technology, but that they had very strong powers of consciousness. Maybe Odin even realized that these particular humans had some subtle advantages over the Aesir, making them even more attractive as mates and breeding partners.

Returning once again to the Prologue of the Prose Edda, we read this fascinating passage - 'And such good times accompanied their journey, that wherever they dwelt, in any land, there came prosperity and peace. And all believed that it was they who caused it, for the noble (native) folk of the lands saw that they were unlike other men they had known, both in beauty and in wisdom.
In one place, Odin found beautiful meadows and good conditions, and there he chose a site for a stronghold, which is now called Sigtúnir. He appointed chieftains there, in the same way things had been set up in Troy, and placed twelve headmen in the stronghold to uphold the laws of the land. In the same way he re-established all the laws that had previously existed in Troy and to which the Turks (the Aesir) were accustomed.
After that, he went north, until the sea met him—the sea which they thought surrounded all the lands—and there he placed his son over the kingdom that is now called Norway. He is called Sæmingr,

and the kings of Norway trace their lineage to him, as do the jarls and other noblemen, as is said in Háleygjatal.

But Odin had with him another son named Yngvi, who became king in Sweden after him. From him are descended the lineages known as the Ynglings.

These Æsir took wives from the natives of the land, and some married off their sons to native daughters. And these lineages became so numerous that throughout Saxland and the entire northern half of the world, their tongue—the tongue of the men of Asia—was the native language in all those lands.

And it is thought that one may perceive from this, in that the names of their forefathers are written down, that those names have followed this tongue, and that the Æsir brought the language with them north into this part of the world: into Norway and Sweden, into Denmark and Saxland.

And in England there are ancient names of lands and places, from which one may understand that they were given in a tongue other than the one spoken there now'.

Paul Wallis wrote about this surprising statement, regarding the language of the Aesir from Old Asgard becoming the language of the people of the North.

In his bestselling book 'The Invasion of Eden', Pg 44, Paul notes - 'In the ages since, the case for Sturluson's geo-linguistic connection has been strongly argued by eminent academic figures, Swedish geographer Philip Johan von Strahlenberg, Norwegian Professor of Linguistics, Georg Valentin Morgenstierne, and Swedish historian Sven Lagerbring.

In the 21st century, Professor Gregori Vahanyan has demonstrated in detail the deep linguistic affinities of Swedish with the language of ancient Armenia. In short, we have data from a whole cluster of academic fields pointing to ancient Armenia as a significant source of language, cultural thought, technological advancement, and human migration. Certainly, an uncanny concentration of archaeological firsts point to ancient Armenia as a powerhouse, stretching from the common era to many thousands of years before present.'

Another subject absolutely worthy of further investigation!

It is significant that the 'Æsir took wives from the natives of the land, and some married off their sons to native daughters'.
This not only shows the genetic compatibility of the two races, but also must surely be a mark of respect for the Earth people?
It is also worth noting that the default in Scandinavian cultures, even in the later Viking Age, was a dislike for being ruled by overlords.
People preferred loose groupings of free equals (despite the age-old inequality between wealthy and poor).
The setting up of these kingdoms will eventually be the downfall of the old ways, because it was those very Kings in the late Viking Age who sold out their people, and their spiritual and historic beliefs, to the authoritarian church, forcing them to give up their old ways and attachment to their old 'Gods'.

We now come full circle back to that fateful original encounter, between Gylfi and the beautiful 'travelling woman', Gefjun, the secret Aesir leader.
I would bet that you have thought, at some point, where did this woman come from? Why did she just happen to turn up in Sweden, so far from Old Asgard, and put herself in the way of the young Wizard King of Sweden?
Was she just acting off her own bat?

The surprising answer is once again found in Heimskringla, in Chapter 5 of Ynglinga saga.
We have learnt that Odin and all his people had travelled up through the European world, founding ruling families, and that they arrived in Saxony and took over/set up at least two kingdoms there.

The saga tells us - 'then he (Odin) travelled north to the sea, and took himself a living place on an island. That is called now 'Odin's Sanctuary', on the island of Fjóni (Fyn), (the island between the Danish mainland and the island Gefjun creates, 'Sealand' (Zealand).)
Þá sendi hann Gefjun norðr yfir sundit í landleitan –
' then sends he Gefjun north over the sound on a land grab'.
So it was Odin who sent the beautiful lady!
I love this, because it is very pragmatic - a secret mission to seduce the most powerful man in Sweden, take a huge chunk of his land, (by semi-legal means), and convince him to head south to Asgard. Gefjun was a sort of Bronze Age 'red sparrow'!

Next we discover that, to add insult to injury, poor old brokenhearted Gylfi, (he surely fell in love with the very 'Love goddess' herself), has his nose rubbed in it.
The beautiful Gefjun goes to live on the island that she created from his land, and there she marries an Aesir named Skjöldr, who is, you guessed it, the son of Odin. (Odin was a virtual 'son machine'.)
Finally we learn that 'Odin took himself a dwelling place by Löginn (literally 'The Lake'), there that is now called Old Sigtúnir, and he made there a great temple and practiced spiritual gatherings according to the customs of the Æsir. He acquired extensive lands there as far as the place he named Sigtúnir'.

'Sig' means 'Victory' and 'túnir' means fortress or enclosure. Victory over whom we might ask?

Perhaps this is an indication of the power of the Earth people's Wizards, and the fact that there might have been a great secret resistance to the Aesir invasion, and even battle fought on a paranormal rather than on a physical level? There has to be a reason why Odin would be praising his own victory. It certainly wasn't a victory fought physically according to the story.

Snorri informs us, on the first page of Gylfaginning (The Prose Edda), that 'the Lake' was called Lake Mälar, which is in eastern Sweden near Uppsala, and that ' the inlets in the lake correspond to the headlands in Zealand'.

This is obviously where he considered that Odin built Sigtúnir, and indeed the modern Signhildsberg, a manor near the town of Sigtunir, was formerly known as Old Sigtunir.

Many modern scholars, notably Heimir Pálsson, from Uppsala University, consider that it makes more sense that Löginn, (The Lake), would be referring to Lake Vänern, which from a modern mapping perspective looks far more like the actual outline and inlets of Zealand (ON Sealand).

Vänern is on the opposite side of Sweden, in the West, and after spending some time beside the lake exploring a 'lost city', on the mountainside of Valhalla (Halleberg), and looking closely at the old and modern maps, I personally think that this is correct.

There is also another incredible possible connection to Old Asgard here!

The name of this great lake, 'Vänern', the biggest in Sweden, is conjectured to derive from the Old Norse word 'Vænn', meaning 'very beautiful or desirable'.

It's where our English word 'vain' comes from.
Today it means 'overly obsessed with one's own beauty', but in the old days it just meant 'very handsome' or 'very pretty'.
The name of the Aesir's old friends, the Vanir, (from Lake Van in Türkiye, near Old Asgard), is related to this word, and etymologically it comes from Proto-Indo-European word 'wenh'- ("to love").
It is also related to Proto-Italic: wenos, which became Latin: venus ("loveliness, charm"), which of course is also the name of the Roman Goddess of sexual love - Venus. The great lady of the Vanir, Freyja, is the Norse version of Venus!

The Aesir woman Gefjun, Odin's secret agent, was also known by another name, (her Vanir name).
Freyja!
I think that Lake Vanërn, 'The Lake', is named after Gefjun to this day!

I would now like to revisit that great story once again - the seducing of Gylfi, the taking of his land, and the creation of Lake Vänern.
This time, however, we will take a look at a very rarely seen document, a veritable secret resource I believe, that reveals vital information that Snorri seems to have missed, when on his two year research tour of Scandinavia between 1218 and 1219 AD.
I was sent a photo of a small sign, discovered by my good friend, and fellow researcher, Asgeir. He found this sign in the Royal Hunting Museum, a quaint red painted timber building nestled in the forest on top of the plateau mountain called Hunneberg (Asgard), in Vänersborg Municipality, Västra Götaland County, Sweden.
It is printed in Swedish, and translated, this is what is says -

'Of her (Gefjun's) journey it is told in the legend that she came to Gylfi in 'Godsheim', (he was) the King of the land which is now called Svithiod (Sweden).
She received from him a piece of land, as big as four oxen could plow out of his land in a day. Thus Gefjun went to Jotunheim, the home of the giants west of Svithiod, and begot four sons there with a Giant. These she transformed into ox forms, and then yoked them to a plough. The plough dug in hard, so hard and deep, that the land loosened, and the oxen dragged it out to sea, but stopped when they came to a strait in the west, where, opposite 'Odense', they lowered the land.
(Note - The name 'Odense' is derived from 'Odin's vé', meaning 'Odin's sanctuary', and this is the very island where Odin first settled in Denmark, and the base from which he sent Gefjun on this mission!)

Thus arose Seland (Zealand), which island an ancient poet, Bragi the Old, with reference to the myth of its creation, calls 'the addition to Denmark'.
Skjöld (Odin's son), was made King there. He built a fortress, took Gefjun as his wife, and became the progenitor of Denmark's Kings, that is, Skjöldungar, (Skjöld's descendants).
Where from Svithiod (Sweden) the aforementioned land was removed, a very large lake arose instead, which was called Vani by the ancients, but in our days bears the name of Vänern. As a confirmation that Zealand and Vänern were thus acquired, when compared, the shape of the island of Zealand is strikingly similar to Lake Vänern.'

There is some fantastic and virtually unknown information to unpack here!

Firstly, I love this sentence - **'where, opposite 'Odense', they lowered the land.'**
Think about that wording for a second. If these are oxen (even giants ones), how would they 'lower' the land? Surely lowering indicates something that's taken up high and lowered down, doesn't it? This, for me, clearly hints that this massive amount of earth and rock was not dragged by oxen, but by great earthmoving machines which literally gouged the land out of Sweden, flew across the 'Sound', and **lowered** it right next to Odin's new base. This was to be the beautiful lady Gefjun's home, with her new husband Skjöld.
(Once again, let's take a moment to shed a tear for poor Gylfi, the jilted lover!).

Secondly, here we finally learn where King Gylfi lived and presumably had his homebase! Snorri doesn't tell us anything about this!
The Swedish royal family calls it 'Godsheim', and connects it with the table mountain they call Valhalla (Halleberg), which stands right beside Lake Vänern and Asgard (Huneberg).
This is double humiliation for Gylfi, because Odin not only took the beautiful woman he had fallen in love with from him, but now we learn that they took his very fortress, his royal estate!
No wonder he later gave them a fair bit of Wizardly paranormal resistance!
We don't hear anything further about Gylfi in the stories, so let's just hope that he wasn't disposed of, but was rather given a fine piece of land somewhere, and one of the beautiful ladies of the Aesir, or the Vanir, in marriage, to make up for the loss of Gefjun.
Maybe he disappeared, perhaps setting up a secret resistance movement, perhaps on a mountain, where he trained young wizards in the arts?

The third remarkable discovery is that the ancient Swedish Royal family is confirming to us that Professor Heimir Pálsson et al are right, that it is indeed Lake Vänern that was 'the Lake'.
It makes perfect sense that the Aesir would set up a great fortress city in those perfect defensive tabletop mountains right beside it. The Royal Hunting Museum poster finishes off with this information -
'After a long journey, he (Odin) finally found excellent land and plains at Hall, the mythical mountain we call Halleberg today. There he had Asgard and Midgard built, as well as one of the largest ancient fortress cities in the whole of 'Svíþjóð' (Sweden)'.

Not in the East of Sweden at all, (as has generally been believed, including by Snorri), but over in the West, right beside and below 'The Lake', Vänern, on two absolutely perfect natural places to build fortresses (above and below the ground)!

New Asgard!

So, let's wind up this chapter with a creative re-imagining of that incredible day when the 'god's' came to Sweden, vividly captured for us by Snorri Sturluson, by the curators of the Sweden Royal Hunting Lodge Museum, and by the unknown Master stone carvers of Bronze Age Sweden.

The great lake Vänern stretches out like an ocean, its far side hidden from view.
It is a glorious spring day in Western Sweden.
Warships, packed with warriors, lie at anchor, stretched out in lines side-by-side for hundreds of metres, on both sides of an area of water left empty. The King's flagship floats close to the land,

where stone towers stand guard over the entrances to the great Bronze Age fortress behind.
The sounds of drums, and the deep throated music of the long curling bronze Lurs, the horns of war and peace, reverberate across the water.
Audible gasps and shouts rise to a crescendo as people point to the sky, where several great, brightly shining discs float through the air. Some bear cross-like shapes in their centres.
Tremors of fear course through the stoutest of hearts, and there is much involuntary high-pitched screaming and crying.

Two of the great craft soundlessly settle on a cleared area of land to one side of the stone towers. The largest craft lowers and seems to float just above the water, in the central area surrounded by ships.
Its great brightness diminishes, until people can see that it appears crafted from a strange grey metal, one they have never seen before. There is a hush of expectation.
Openings silently appear on four sides of the craft, and beings that look almost human emerge. They walk up the slightly curving top of the craft, and stand at the pinnacle. Somehow the beings shed what look to be shining multicoloured skins. The people see what now appear to be three men and two women.
They have bare skin like the people, and even from a distance they are all obviously strongly built and beautiful.
The King's warship begins to row, and turns towards the craft.
At the prow, the King, who is a great Wizard, stands and gazes towards the craft and the strange people standing on it's top.
His rowers now back paddle, slowing the ship, and as the prow nears the floating craft, something slides and projects down from the flying craft towards where the King stands.

Gasps are heard as he steps from the ship onto the projection, and fearlessly walks up to the five beings. The people are amazed to see their proud King kneel and bow before the beings, and then they see the beings taking him by the hand and standing him up.
The King is handed a type of wand, and suddenly his unmistakable voice booms out like the voice of a giant, able to be heard by all the fleet, and those on the land.
He tells the people that these are the very gods that he had met, years before, in his celebrated journey to the centre of the world. Everyone has heard these stories, and everyone has been excitedly preparing for this extremely unusual event, ever since the king, by his great wizardry, received word of the coming of these beings.

The people see that the beautiful men and women carry what look like short handled double headed axes, slung at their waists.
As one, they lift these axes above their heads towards the sky, and each emits a blinding streak of energy, like straight lightning, accompanied by an ear shattering thunder. The great sound reverberates across the water and bounces back from the cliffs. Once again voices raise in terror, and some ships begin to paddle away from the scene.
The King calls them back using the wand, and calms the people. He explains that great as his magic is, he is not a match for the wizardry of these gods.
One of the 'Gods', a superbly beautiful green eyed woman, is recognised by the King, and some of his close retainers.
She steps forward, and asks him to select a large rock on the shore. He points to one that is not particularly sacred, and the beautiful woman stretches out her arm and her short axe-like weapon.
Another great shaft of light, and an ear shattering crack of thunder. The rock is pulverized into a million pieces.

The King's strong voice booms out again.
He explains that the people must accept that these great and powerful beings, these gods of their ancient stories, have come to live amongst them, and that this is truly an historic and unforgettable day. He assures them that nothing but good will come from this, as long as all are suitably obedient.
The King is pleased to see that the majority of his warriors and women are standing strong, though there are many people who have understandably fainted in fear and shock.

More flying craft appear in the sky, these also looking like suns, but of a fluctuating orange hue, seeming to be edged with flickering flames.
The King speaks a command and two ships row forward. It is seen that on board the ships are some of the most beautiful, talented and intelligent girls, daughters of the people.
Their bodies are specially painted, and wear fine ornaments, and the girls' hair is braided into long ponytails, hanging way down their backs, the tradition of their people. These young ones are visibly frightened, but stand courageously together.
One of the new glowing ships floats in close, and a strange shaft of light emits from below it, enveloping the young people. They are lifted up and taken into the craft, which has opened up below.
The King, once again using the wand, tells the gathering that these young ones will not be harmed, and that they have been specially selected to marry with the Aesir's sons and daughters, to be founders of new royal families.

That night the greatest feast ever seen is prepared, set out in the broad clearing where the other sunwheel craft have landed. The people have somewhat recovered from the extreme culture shock of meeting these beings, and having their world turned upside down. Now their senses are seduced by the impossibly exotic

music coming from who knows where, by great lights shaped like standing swords, blazing with a cold fire, by unimaginable varieties of food, set on tables that seem like polished white stone. There are exotic tame animals that the Aesir gods keep as pets, and small bald people, with strange large eyes and three toed feet and hands, who are serving food and drink wordlessly.
There is even a Wizard belonging to the feared Jötun people from the West!
He seems to be a good friend of these gods, and it is said that the superb and powerful mead is his personal brew.

The young, newly wedded couples are presented wearing marvellous clothes, cut in the traditional designs of the people, but with cloth that defies understanding in its fineness and beauty. Great relief is felt all around that they haven't been killed as sacrifices within the terrifying flying objects.
A great time is had by all, and only the young Wizard King is secretly despondent.
He knows that his time is over, yet he is already making plans.
Smiling, he encourages his people, as they watch the incredible flying show being put on in the sky by the Aesir, for their entertainment, at this first great Spring Wedding feast.

Let's leave them there for now, and proceed to the next chapter, in which we will have a close look at what these truly remarkable Northern stories tell us about ancient flying machines. Literally the Chariots of the Viking Gods!

CHARIOTS OF THE VIKING GODS!

I had been having quite a wonderful email exchange with Professor Jakobsson, and one day we started talking about elves (álfar in Icelandic and Old Norse). Ármann mentioned an essay he had written titled 'The Extreme Emotional Life of Völund the Elf'. Quite the intriguing title, and of course I had to find it and read it.

I had heard of Völund, and his Anglo-Saxon iteration, 'Wayland the Smith', names that carried with them a fine sense of mystery, but about which I realised that I knew relatively little.
After consuming Professor Jakobsson's very interesting essay, I proceeded to read the original story - 'Völundarkviða' (Volundarkvitha), from the Poetic Edda.
I then read 'Velents þáttr smiðs' (Velent (or Völund) the Smith's short story), contained in 'Þiðrekssaga af Bern' (Thithrek of Bern's Saga), which contains some very interesting extra information and plot twists.
What shocked me was that these stories, especially Volundakvitha, unequivocally talk about someone who created a working flying machine, and who uses it to escape from his enemies.
Scholars are unanimous about this fact, that Völund is not a supernatural being who could fly by himself.

It didn't take me long to start to find some pretty incredible supporting evidence, in the form of a rune stone from Sweden, known as Ardre VIII.
The Ardre image stones are a collection of ten rune and image stones, dated to the 8th to 11th centuries, that were discovered at Ardre Church, in Ardre, on the large island of Gotland, Sweden.

These stone masterpieces, beautifully carved spiritual depictions of stories from the old Viking Age faith, survived, ironically, because the fanatics of the church pulled them down, reusing them as paving under the wooden floors of the local church!
The priceless stones were only refound in 1900 AD, when the church at Ardre was being restored.
(For those who would like to see them, they are now in the Swedish Museum of National Antiquities in Stockholm).
Ardre VIII, amongst other important stories, (that back up the stories in the two Eddas and Heimskringla), depicts the figure of a man wearing a type of bird shape, with wings and a tail. Behind him sits a forge, complete with two sets of tongs and two headless bodies (which are a grisly part of the Völund stories).

Searching for 'Völund' in Google I found necklaces and broaches for sale in many different 'Viking' inspired shops, generally calling them 'Flying Völund broaches',(or even 'Flying Loki broaches' - that is another story!).
They all had that 'ancient' look, but at the same time somehow looked too good to be true!
Could there really be something from the Viking Age that looked like this?
They appeared for all the world like artistically stylized depictions of one of those incredibly brave maniacs, the ones who fly down mountain sides wearing flying suits!

Upon further searching I found that these jewelry pieces were based on a single real find, a beautiful Viking Age artefact, excavated from an archaeological dig in the small village of Uppåkra, Scania, Southwest Sweden.
Researchers there, in September 2011, had found the remains of a pre-Christian temple, a very rare find indeed, and within its bounds this extraordinary piece.
I felt like I had found the Holy Grail! (You can see my photo of this artefact on the front cover if this book.)

Here was an ancient artefact that appeared totally anachronistic. No human has ever been known to fly before the first hot air balloon flights by the Montgolfier Brothers in 1783.
This was no angel-like man with large bird's wings growing from his back, or even a muscular Icarus, naked and flapping eagle's wings created with feathers, wax and leather straps.
This was a man in a machine, wearing an aerodynamic helmet, a pressured ring suit, sturdy flying boots, gloves, solid knee and elbow protectors, a man literally strapped into a wingsuit.
Not only that, but at the figures base, behind his back and just above the large 'bird's tail' style 'elevator', (the flying surface at the tail of aircraft that causes the tail to lift or drop in flight), were bulbous tapering flame shapes, curving to left and right.
On close inspection I saw that these flame shapes come to two flat points at their ends.

Some commenters on my Viking Superpowers channel have suggested that these two shapes were merely straps, reaching down under the figures legs, or that they were some kind of claws.
I can certainly appreciate their thinking. It's a huge challenge to accept this idea, that a Viking Age (1000 A.D) representation of a man in a flying suit could have two flames emerging from the base

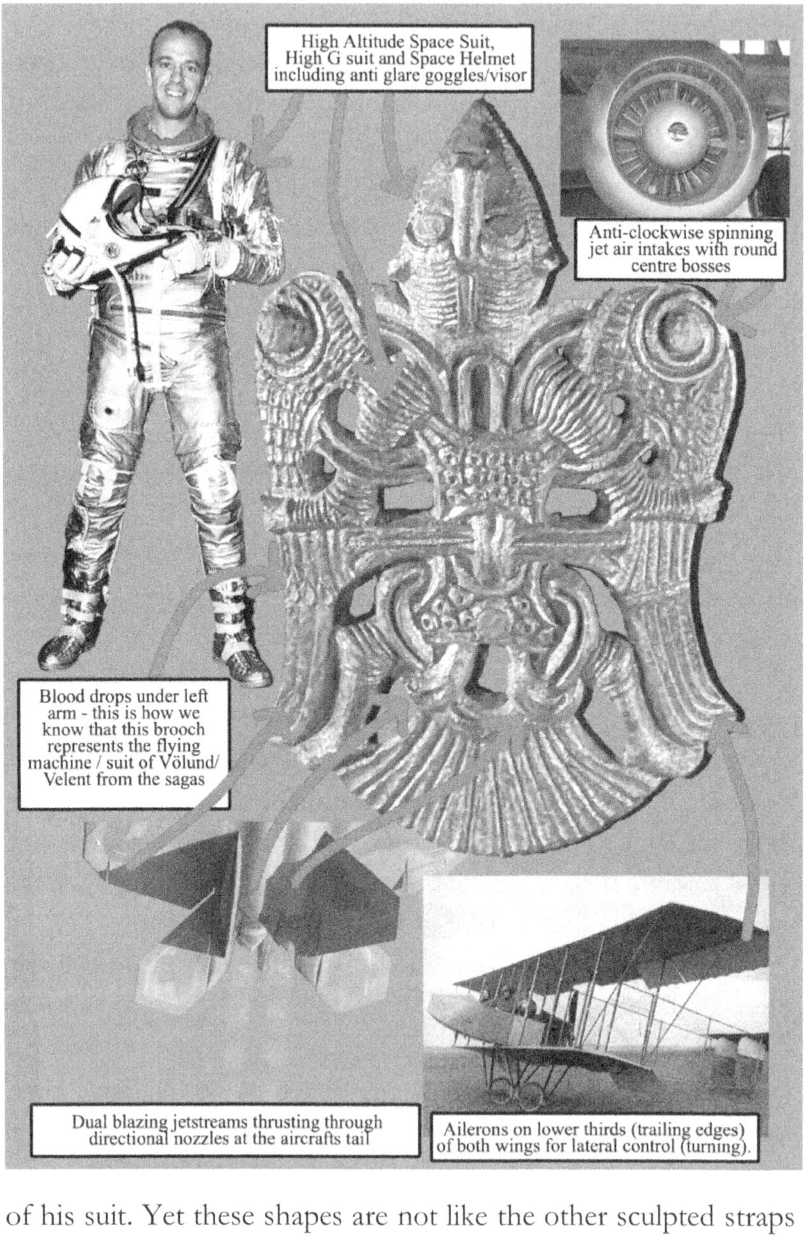

of his suit. Yet these shapes are not like the other sculpted straps on the body. They bulge and taper in just the way I myself would sculpt them to represent tongues of flame, whether in wood, stone, clay, or in this case, metal.

Instead of having symmetrical grooves running the length of them, the way that the obvious straps on the contrivance do, these bulbous tapering shapes only have a short curving gouge on top of, and near to, the tapered pointed ends.

These ends do not dive down under the figure's legs, they instead slightly overlap the back of the legs.

As for these shapes being claws, I can see some resemblance to claws, but I immediately have to ask, why would there be claws back there? Why only two of them, appearing from the backside of the figure and overlapping **above** the tail?

I really can see no reason to interpret these shapes as claws or even birds feet.

As I observed them closely, I noticed that the tips of these shapes seem to split into two sharp ended tongues.

Tongues of flame!

A lot rides on the interpretation of these little shapes. I have painstakingly gone over every single photo and video I took of the object whilst in Sweden, as well as looking at every image I can find online. Interestingly, the first image that I ever saw is the clearest, and I assume that the photographer was given permission to photograph it outside of the perspex case. You can see my photo of the broach on the cover of this book, and I would encourage you to search for photos yourself, and see what you think.

I've also made a video on my youtube channel about this object titled 'The Sky People'.

As far as I'm concerned there is no doubt.

The question is, why would even the most creative ancient artist think about carving two flames coming from the base of the backpack of this wingsuit?
There is no mention of flames in the stories. Nobody who has ever read this story in the past would have thought about flames at all. It has always been treated as just a typical fantasy flying story, a marvelous tale for the 'simple minds' of 'primitive peoples'. Finally coming to light after 1000 years, seemingly just at the right time, this masterpiece challenges everything we think we know about the ancient history of the North. What on earth was really going on?
I see these flames (as well as the other practical aeronautic features), and I'm led to believe that there was once a highly detailed story, passed on for well over 1000 years, about a flying contraption, lifted by two streams of roaring superfast flames, emerging from the bottom of the wingsuit.
Undoubtedly this was considered a holy story, a story of a strange inexplicable power, and only modern people like us, who have been fortunate enough to grow up with jet aircraft and rockets, can recognise what these sculpted flame symbols mean.
(Consider that jet engines weren't even invented until the 1940s!)

I know I am really emphasizing this, but think about it.
This detail on the flying broach is as surprising as it would be if these two flames were actually mentioned in the old stories. If we can accept, (even just for the sake of it), that this remarkable artefact is representing an ancient high-tech jet engine system, with two jet nozzles, (perhaps even capable of swiveling to maintain controlled flight), then we can look for more jet related information in it's design. Sure enough, when we look at the top of the two wings, we see two spiralling round shapes, shapes that have in their centres rounded, tapering bosses, or knobs.

They look for all the world like jet aircraft intakes, and the spiralling, (to me), is an artistic device indicating that these spin and suck air into the motors.
Once again, a strangely modern design to place at the top of great bird wings. I've never seen real birds with air intakes, and when you look at the broach, there are really no other random artistic designs sculpted just for the aesthetic or artistic effect.
These spiralling knobbed shapes really seem to be indicating something technical and engineered.
Jets need masses of high-speed air!

When we look at the design that is on the figures backpack, we see short round pipes protruding from the squarish shaped pieces.
These, from an engineering point of view, would seem to be illustrating perhaps a fuel tank at top, and then the lower section being where the two jet engines would be encased.
The small pipe-like protrusions in the design could be something like attitude correcting thrusters, a necessary part of controllable spacecraft, and very high altitude aircraft.
This assemblage connects at six points to the top two thirds of the wings, and at the base, a roughly heart-shaped assemblage connects to and seems to stabilize and control the elevator surface, the flat spreading bird's tail shape.

It is obvious that these wings are intended to be rigid and not flapped by manpower.
(The ancient dream of humans having the strength and speed to flap bird-like wings, to lift their heavy body weight, was disproven tragically by some early aviation pioneers).
The pilot grips the outside leading edges of the wings with his sturdy gloves, his arms on top of the wings rather than underneath,

as they would be if he was intended to flap the wings with arm strength.

Next we come across another completely anachronistic piece of engineering design.

Two thirds of the way down each wing we see a line creasing straight across the wings. This in itself is quite strange. Why would bird wings have a very straight double line cutting across them like this?

If we keep to our manufactured aircraft concept, then this makes perfect sense, because modern aircraft since the First World War have had what are called ailerons.

These are small, wing like surfaces, usually near the ends and rear, (trailing surfaces), of wings. Ailerons lift and drop on alternate wings, interrupting the airflow, and causing the aircraft to bank (turn), left or right.

Even though the Wright brothers first powered aircraft flew in 1903, it took until the early years of the First World War for the concept of ailerons to become standard. So what are ailerons doing on this thousand year-old sculpted flying artefact!

As I mentioned earlier, the pilot appears to be wearing a ringed suit, which is a very unusual thing. I am not aware of any suit of armour from any period of history that looks like this. The only suit that comes to mind would be an astronaut's pressurized spacesuit, made to keep a pilot alive when exposed to outer space or to very high altitude. Rings are a very strong structure, and would provide the support needed to withstand a strong pressure difference between the internal environment of a suit, and the external environment. Besides the very sturdy 'space' gloves, there are also elbow and knee protectors that are part of the suit.

The high sturdy heeled boots on the figure would appear to be protecting the pilots lower legs from being accidentally burnt by the jet blast.

Now we come to the helmet. We don't see a man's head with a typical war helmet on. Instead, we see a streamlined, hard edged wedge shape, with an indication of a nose and a mouth, and either stylised round eyes or… goggles?

Once again, we ask ourselves, why is it so? Why would people in the Viking Age or earlier think that somebody who flew would need to have a big solid aerodynamic helmet?

People understood that you needed a helmet in battle, because enemies were trying to crack your head open with all sorts of heavy metal objects.

But this is a picture of somebody flying up in the air to escape from his captors.

We need to remember that before the motorcar and the aircraft, many scientists considered that travelling faster than about 45 miles (60 kilometres) an hour would make it impossible to breathe. Very few people had ever travelled faster than a galloping horse. So how would somebody conceive of the needs of somebody flying as fast as a bird or faster?

If we do once again consider this could be a depiction of a real ancient high-tech flying device, then this helmet makes perfect sense. It could be both a streamlined protection for the pilots head and neck, and also part of a breathing device, providing oxygen as he flew up high into the clouds, which both these ancient stories clearly say that he did!

So… let's ask ourselves, when we think of an elf flying, does a suit like this come to mind? No, no it doesn't. I would bet that a slender, pointy eared Orlando Bloom character would appear in our minds eye, wearing a figure hugging silk suit of a greenish colour. All in all, the figure and wingsuit modelled in this broach is completely out of place. Anachronistic to the max.

I am using (even more) imagination here, and going out on a limb, but I really do wonder whether, within that once great heathen temple, the original flying suit might have been on display, an exceedingly holy relic?

Did the craftsman who made this broach base it on that carefully preserved 'holy' relic? Imagine the wonder for many many generations of worshippers, to see such a mysterious and inexplicable machine preserved there.

Maybe the Goði, the high priest, even started the jet motors every couple of years, to show the people the terrifying and awesome power of the Aesir, the Álfar, the Vanir?

Maybe the precious jet fuel was guardedly hoarded, maybe the starting sequence from warm up to 'flame on' was a holy secret passed on from high priest to high priest over many generations?

Of course this is exactly the sort of 'heathen wonder' that the fanatics of the new Roman State religion would have destroyed, as the work of the devil, (or had carted off to Rome, to be buried in the catacombs of the Vatican with other mysterious heathen treasures!).

As you can imagine, I absolutely had to see this flying man brooch for myself!

In mid 2024 I had the opportunity to travel to Scandinavia, and I made a beeline to Uppåkra, and thence to the Library Museum of The University of Lund, where the broach is on display. In Uppåkra I checked out what could be seen of the excavation, and the scaled down reconstruction of the 'Hof' (not 'The Hoff'), the

once great Viking Age temple, that had been a hub for spiritual pilgrimages from all over Sweden.
I checked out the display and shop next to the reconstructed temple, and the friendly lady behind the counter was interested in where I had come from.
I told her that I was an Australian, and why I had visited, and then I went out on a limb, and told her my theory about the broach being an actual powered flying suit.
She grimaced and shook her head, and assured me that it was 'definitely not some kind of ancient alien device'. It seemed that many other people had made this paradigm challenging suggestion, and I assume the poor lady was feeling a bit over it!

A little later I met a local archaeology student, outside near the reconstructed Hof (temple), and we ended up talking paleocontact together. We decided to share a taxi to the nearby city of Lund, as we were both keen to see the original Völund artefact.
It was so cool to discover how open minded she was, and it turned out that her archeology classmates sometimes discussed the possibilities of paleocontact together.
In fact I met plenty of similarly open-minded people in Scandinavia and Iceland, and that's exactly what I've experienced in the comments section of my YouTube channel, with many subscribers and viewers being from these Northern countries.
There has indeed been a lot of very strange stuff happening in Scandinavia, for a really long time, regarding UFOs etc.
They, like we in other parts of the world, are pretty keen to find out the actual truth.

As with a lot of masterpieces, I found the broach surprisingly small, maybe 2 inches in length, but I wasn't disappointed at all seeing it in all its three dimensional glory. The very old story of Völund is

thrilling, (and somewhat horrifying), a story that is not much like a modern fairytale, (though not unlike some of the very old and aptly named Grimm's fairy tales).
Especially in the Old Norse, it reads like a hard-core realistic sci fi script, with humans and extraordinary humanoid beings and, (in my view),'high-tech' technologies.

The stories start by introducing us to Völund, and his two brothers, Slagfiðr (Slagfithur) and Egill. They belong to the mysterious race called Álf´s (Elves), and they are the sons of a Finnish King (the Finns were renowned Wizards!).
The original meaning of the word Álf is a bit of a mystery, and we don't really know if they are a separate race of pointy eared beings, as they are portrayed in our popular culture, or something else.
In the Icelandic sagas they often seem to be practically the same as the Aesir in the storytellers minds.
Professor Ármann Jakobsson writes in 'The Troll Inside you', (page 31), that 'the Old Norse álfr is used to indicate not only a specific race or species or even category of elves but rather any kind of paranormal figure clearly superior to humans - somewhat similar to the way a modern anthropologist might use the term 'god' (or 'deity') to mean 'a god' rather than 'God'.

Thinking about that recently, an interesting concept occurred to me, and I wrote to Professor Jakobsson to get his take on it.
'Hæ Ármann!
Hoping this finds you and yours very well.
I'm just filming my next video about flying in the Eddas etc, focusing on Völund and the broach from Uppäkra, and have been thinking about your 'Emotional Life' essay and 'Troll Inside' re Álf's, and it occurred to me that perhaps the word Álf might mean (in some contexts) 'hálf' an Aesir?

This occurred to me because I was thinking about his, (Völund's), eyes 'glittering like a snake', and that quality he has of being somewhat superhuman and super smart, and with a very ruthless edge, half human…Could it be that Álf was once a halfling/ half human sort of word?
I went searching in Zoëga (the Old Norse - English dictionary), and it has hálf-risi for half giant, and I learnt from your writings that the words Álf and Áss (singular of Aesir), are sometimes used interchangeably.'

I also wrote to him that in that old English 'Cockney' London accent, which is still somewhat part of the Australian accent, people say 'alf a mo' meaning 'half a moment'.
The Professor replied - ´Sadly, I think 'alfr' has Germanic relatives which do not support an alfr/halfr hypothesis. However, it is clear that the continents were called both 'halfa' and 'alfa' in the Middle Ages, so the theory is perfectly sensible. It is also not impossible that in spite of the etymology, some medieval Icelanders would have understood 'alfr' as linked to 'halfr'.
In his next reply he added - 'Today the seven continents are called 'heimsálfur' (parts of the world), and this word, 'álfa' or 'hálfa' (perhaps meaning 'part') also existed in medieval Icelandic.'

All of this led me to suspect that the Elves, (Álfar), could well be half human and half the humanoid race called the Aesir (or Vanir). People who were the offspring of the sons of Odin, (and other Aesir), and of Earth mothers and fathers?
These three Elf brothers are great hunters and skiers, and have just returned from a hunting expedition.
(If it helps to visualize them, it is probably not too far off the mark to think of them as somewhat like the elves in JRR Tolkein's books, (and the film versions)).

They live in 'Úlfdali', (Wolf Valley), where the three have a house. One morning they go down to the lake, 'Úlfsjár'(Wolf Lake), near their house, and find three very beautiful women there, (spinning linen for some reason).
We are told that these three are Valkyries, and that beside them, on the beach, rest their three 'álptarhamir'.
Most translators render this word as 'swan skins', and the impression given is that these girls are found sitting stark naked, spinning linen, having unzipped and slipped out of their feathery swan skins.
This interpretation obviously suits the fairytale version of the story, however I would like to offer a different version, one which will be backed up later when we look at some other amazing flying stories.

Old Norse 'Álptar' definitely means swan, but the word 'hamir' (plural of 'hamr') has a number of meanings. It can certainly mean 'skins', but it can just as correctly be translated 'shapes'. As with Völund, I think that these girls are not considered to be able to fly by themselves but are piloting some kind of flying machines. Calling the girls' flying machines 'Swan Shapes' is in line with modern usage.
Our aircraft are sometimes named after flying creatures, such as the powerful fighter planes the MacDonnell Douglas F/A 18 Hornet, the Swedish designed SAAB Draken (Dragon) fighter, and the Douglas A4 Skyhawk fighter..
(We won't mention the Grumann F-14 Tomcat…but then again the Goddess Freya did have a chariot pulled by cats!)
These 'Álptahamr' must have had some kind of resemblance to swans (graceful long necked flyers?).
The three virile young Álf men invite the three beautiful young Valkyrie girls home, presumably carrying or flying their Swan

shaped crafts up, and into the shed beside the house, (or maybe they built a special hangar later).

Next we are treated to an ancient poem about these events, and this is where, at least for me, the story gets really groovy.
The poem begins –

'Meyjar flugu sunnan Myrkvið í

gøgnum, alvitr ungar, ørlǫg drýgja; þær

á sævar strǫnd settusk at hvílask, drósir

suðrœnar dýrt lín spunnu.'

'Maids flew from the south, through
Mirkwood, young, wise in magic, to shape
fates; they sat to rest on the shore of the sea,
southern maidens, spinning precious linen'.

In his wonderful bilingual and very scholarly translation The Poetic Edda, a Dual-Language Edition, by Edward Pettit, published by Open Book Publishers, 2023, Edward Pettit translates **'alvitr ungar'** (line two) as 'young alien beings'.
This translation really gave me a start.
Obviously 'alien' doesn't have to mean little grey beings, with big heads and great big black eyes, or denizens of the cantina at Mos Eisley, but I'm fascinated by this translation. This scholarly translator must have had good reasons for this choice of words (which also appears in verse three).
The word 'Álvitr', on first reading, seems to mean something like 'wise in magic', and other translators have glossed it as just 'Valkyrie'.

However I also really like the 'young alien creatures' translation as well, as it conjures up the idea that these three girls were very extraordinary, not just for their beauty, but for their origins, accomplishments, and technology. They came from the mysterious south, and being considered Valkyries, it seems likely that they were full blown members of the extended family of the Aesir. They were certainly not wild Álf hunters like the three lads.

They have flown to this place 'to fulfill their fates'. They were on a mission, and though the introduction gives us the feeling that it is the young men who approach the girls, the poem seems to indicate that it was the girls that went and chose which man they wanted, which man they were assigned to you might say.

Verse two tells us –

'One of them Egil took in his arms— a
fair maid, shining-limbed.
Another was Svanhvit, who wore swan
feathers. And the third, their sister, clasped the
white neck of Völund'.

The girls made the moves here.

These beautiful young alien creatures appear to have been sent, perhaps by Odin, for a distinct purpose.

My theory is that they were not only to marry these elven sons of the Finnish King, and quite possibly to have children with them, (though not mentioned in the story), but were also to introduce them to Aesir high technologies.

A specialty in engineering flying machines and related equipment perhaps?

The young alien creatures stayed with the young men, apparently in love, for nine years. Then, one day, whilst Völund and his two

brothers were away hunting, the beautiful alien creatures received urgent new orders.
I can imagine them rolling out their Swan shaped craft from the hangar, filling their 'Mr Fusion' fuel cells with household rubbish, (a Back to the Future joke), and taking off on a new mission south to Mirkwood.
(Yes, the same Mirkwood featured significantly in 'The Hobbit' and 'The Lord of the Rings').

The three Álfar returned home, and we can only imagine how devastated they would have been to find their beloved wives gone. Obviously, the girls left no parting messages, and foul play would have been assumed initially.
Being the superb hunters that they were, the three Elf brothers would have noticed that there were no tracks leading away from the house, no signs of raiders, and that the three high-tech Álptahamr, (Swan-shaped craft) had 'flown the coop'.
Two brothers set out to find their respective wives, but Völund stays home, working on his smithing, certain that his girl will return.

'But Völund sat alone in Wolf-Dales; he
hammered red gold and set it with gems,
fastened and forged all his shining rings—
so he awaited his radiant bride, if she might
ever come to him again'.

A greedy local King, Níðuðr (Nidudur), of the Njárar, (a Swedish people), hears that Völund is there alone, and surmising that the brothers have great treasure, comes with his war band and captures Völund. The story indicates that they somehow drugged the mighty Álf and then tied him up.

The king has him hamstrung, which is a terrible torturous maiming that was done in the old times, cutting the large hamstring tendons behind someone's knees. Völund can never walk again, and is dragged off to Nidudur´s land.

There he is set up with a forge and his tools on an offshore island, and forced to create masterpieces of golden art. No one visits him except the king, who taunts him by wearing Völund's handmade elven sword at his belt.

Völund works hard and fast for a long time, producing an unending stream of beautiful golden and jewelled objects.

Enough time passes that the King, and his equally nasty Queen, seem to drop their guard, and it is then that Völund takes his revenge and escapes.

He kills their two young, but equally greedy, sons, and seduces his beautiful daughter, BǫðvildR (Bodvildur).

We later learn that she is now pregnant by Völund.

'"Well it would be for me," said Völund,
"to be standing on the meadows,
Free from Niðuðr's men who captured me!"

Laughing, Völund lifted himself aloft to the upper sky;
weeping, Bǫðvildr walked from the island, grieving her
lover's flight and dreading her father's wrath'.

Völund realises that the time has come to make his get away, because his revenge will be soon discovered.

How he escapes has always taken readers by surprise, as he laughs with the combined joy both of revenge, regaining his freedom, and taking to the air.

He knows that what he is about to do is going to boggle the small vicious minds of his enemies, King Nidudur and his unnamed Queen.
You might ask 'How does he 'raise himself aloft'?
Dr Edward Pettit, the Poetic Edda translator, asks this question in a related note.

'How VǪlundr takes to the air is uncertain. Possibly he made a magical feather-coat akin to those of the swan-maidens, **or some sort of flying machine.'**

Here we have the two views of mythology in a nutshell. As with all the other wonders I have described, one can either see these stories as magical fairytales, or as tales of actual people, and actual ancient technologies, their true nature obscured by the understandable incomprehension of the people who witnessed them.
You can see why the wonderful broach from Uppäkra so excited me! This is the very flying machine of the ancient story, clearly illustrated in 3D form!

Völund flies to the King´s fortress and lands, (no doubt noisily, if I am right about the jets), in the courtyard.
The Queen is awake, and hears the flight of the flying machine, and quickly walks to the end of the hall where the king is in bed. She shakes him to wake him, (it seems to me), and a great unnaturally loud voice booms from the hall yard outside.

'Are you awake, Níðuðr, lord of the Njárar?

We can imagine the king, shaken by this uncanny voice, running through the hall and out into the yard. He is confronted by this very peculiar contraption, perched on top of the hall yard wall,

seemingly part man and part bird, with a frightening, large, metal head, and glazed black, featureless eyes.
King Nidudur answers (from Pettit's translation) -
"I wake constantly, without will,
I sleep the least because of my son's deaths;
My head throbs—your counsels are cold to me,
I wish now to face Völund in judgment."

The king is making a connection between this bizarre being and Völund, and yet fails to recognize that this is actually Völund within.
Maybe he thinks that this is an apparition, or a dream?
He states, in his desperate turmoil, that he wishes to have it out with Völund.
In the next line the king begins questioning Völund, so it is obvious that he can now see his face, and that he recognizes him. So what has changed?
If Völund was wearing a flying helmet he would be unrecognisable to the king.
So then he lifts up his helmet, perhaps a visor, and the king sees his familiar face, once again validating what we see in the Uppäkra broach. It seems that the goggle-eyed helmet on the artifact is not an artistically stylized head, but a representation of a sturdy aerodynamic helmet!

The King and his nasty wife must have drawn back in amazement and dread, knowing full well what they were guilty of, and seeing Völund's unearthly powers on display.
"Tell me this, Völundr, wise one of the elves:
what happened to my healthy cubs?"
Here it seems that the king is actually showing respect, out of fear of Völund it would seem. Maybe Völund blipped his jet motors? It

would make sense that they would be running on idle the whole time, staying hot and making an unearthly sound, a 'dragon' sound that put terror into the people in the stronghold.
I expect that everyone had run out with the King and Queen to see what on earth was going on. Völund tells the king and queen the straight truth, though first getting their pledge that they will not hurt their daughter or Völund´s unborn child within her womb. He then admits to killing the two sons, and seducing and impregnating their beautiful daughter.

The King roars with fury!

' "You could say no words, Völund, that would cause me deeper grief, nor would I wish to repay you with any less.
However, no man is so tall that he could drag you down from horseback, nor so mighty he might strike you from below— there where you soar and dart amongst the upper clouds!"
Laughing, Völund lifted himself high up into the sky,
But grim faced Níðuðr was left behind.'

What happens here is obvious - the King explodes with fury, undoubtedly screaming at his warriors to shoot this wretched elf from the parapet. Once again Völund laughs, and 'lifted himself high up into the sky', which I would imagine meant opening his throttles full blast and 'zoom climbing' straight up into the sky, out of arrow shot, and then there he is, hovering **up near the clouds!**
This of course indicates that he is a few thousand feet in the air! There is no way that he did that by flapping his arms, is there! You would almost think that he must have had something like two super powerful alien tech jet engines to propel him that high,

(and fast), before the swift arrows of the King's Warriors could reach him!
Imagine the effect on the King, the Queen and their retainers!

I mentioned earlier that there is another version of this story told in the saga named Thidrek´s Saga of Bern (Þiðreks saga af Bern), where Völund is called Velent.
So, let's have a look there at what was written about Velent's (Völund's) creation of a flying machine. As you would have noticed in 'Völundarkviða', it wasn't really explicitly stated that Völund actually made himself a flying machine, leading the translator Edward Pettit to wonder whether this is a story of a supernatural flying suit, or an apparatus made by the master smith. In this second version, the story is unequivocal.
It's a flying apparatus, and we learn of ancient real world 'how to fly' instructions here that I think will blow your mind!

´There was one time when Velent asked Egil, his brother, to fetch him all kinds of feathers, both large and small, saying that he wished to make himself a flying device (O.N flygil, possibly from Flug-vél). Egil went into the forest and hunted all kinds of birds and brought them to Velent. Now Velent made a pair of wings, and when they were finished, they resembled most closely the feathered skin of a creature—perhaps a griffin or a vulture or that bird which is called the ostrich. (All very large birds, except for a 'griffin', a large flying lion-like creature).
Then Velent bids Egil **go into** the contraption he had made, to fly and test whether it would work.
(**Biðr Egil fara í** - Bids Egil go in. Not strap on, not slip into.
GO INTO! It's a flying machine with a cockpit,. and one assumes a fuselage, wings, controls surfaces, as we see in the wonderful Uppäkra broach).

Egil said, "How am I to take off, to fly, or to land?"
Velent replied, "You should launch yourself into the wind, and you shall fly both high and far. But you must land with the wind at your back."
So Egil went into the feathered frame and flew up into the air as lightly as the nimblest of birds, but when he went to land, he pitched forward, head-first toward the earth, and **came down very fast, nearly losing consciousness**—for the rushing of the wind **roared in his ears and temples.**
The text is clearly telling us that Egill, the novice test pilot, flies up high into the wind, (and I believe using the power of two flaming jets as per the Uppäkra broach), then descending, he loses control of the aircraft, and came roaring down so fast, possibly spinning, that he experienced what fighter pilots experience - high G-forces! Fighter pilots have G-suits and training to handle this, but it's very common for inexperienced people to lose consciousness under high G (Gravity). We have to ask ourselves, how is it even remotely possible that this ancient writer knows about this physiological experience, that can only be felt in a speeding turning aircraft?

Then Velent said, "Tell me, Egil my brother, was this flying device of any use?"
Egil said, "If it were as easy to land with it as it is to fly, I'd be in another country by now, and you would never see it again!"
Velent replied, "I shall improve that which is lacking."
(Once again, an incredible piece of very modern engineering and design thinking – this is his prototype, and he is here stating that he is going to improve the design having observed what happened to his brother).

Then Velent entered the feathered frame himself, with the help of Egil his brother. He went up on top of a house and launched himself into the sky, saying:
"I misled you when I told you to land with the wind behind you, for I did not trust you to bring it back if you knew how good it truly was. You should know that all birds rise and land against the wind."
This could be happening on the same day or it could be sometime later, after Völund/Velent has refined his protype that almost killed his brother Egil.
It's pretty wild that he knew about taking off and landing into the wind! That's not really intuitive knowledge is it? Maybe the writer spend a lot of time looking at birds flying, but still it took the pioneers of flight a long time to work all this stuff out, so how could this have been known so long ago?.

"And now, brother, I will tell you my plan. I intend to go home and speak again with King Niðung. But if I say something that displeases the king, and he forces you to shoot at me—then aim beneath my left arm.
There I have tied a bladder, and inside it is the blood of King Niðung's sons. Now you may strike your shot such that I take no harm—if you value our kinship."

This is the same brother, Egil, (spelt Egill in Volundakvitha), who Velent/Völund shared a house with, and who met with (along with their other brother Slagfithr), the three beautiful young alien beings on the beach. We learn in this second saga that Egil is the best archer who ever lived.
There is something hilariously realistic in the way these two brothers act.

Imagine telling your brother to land before the wind, instead of into the wind, so that he would crash land and not fly off with your fabulous invention. He obviously knew his brother well, and really, who wouldn't want a personal flying machine?

What I also find very interesting is that the story tells us that when the brother turned his head, looking towards the ground with the intention to land, the aircraft dived and crash landed.
This fits perfectly with an idea that occurs to me, (suggested partly by my Swedish ex-military friend Asgeir). If that special flight helmet that we looked at earlier were similar to the very latest modern fighter pilots helmets, Völund could just look towards where he wanted to go and his aircraft would go there.
This technology is at the very cutting edge here in the 21st-century. What is it doing in this ancient story that is possibly thousands of years old?

The odd story about the bladder of blood, tied under the left arm, is the major factor that conclusively identifies the Viking Age (10th C.) Uppäkra broach as representing Völund.
The place on the left wing that I identify as the turning point of the ailerons is where we see drops of blood illustrated.
Thus confirming that this second version of the story was known at least in the Viking Age, a couple of hundred years before the story was written down.

The saga continues -
'Now Velent flew to the highest tower in the king's stronghold. And the king came into his hall, with many men in attendance. But when he saw Velent, he said:
"Are you a bird now, Velent? You never cease to amaze."

Velent replied: "My lord, now I am bird, now I am man—and now I take my leave. Never again shall you hold sway over me—not in all your life. You and I once made a bargain: that you would give me your daughter's hand, and half your kingdom, for you thought yourself beset by dire need and foes at your gates. But instead, you cast me out and stripped me of all protection, because I defended myself and slew the man who sought to slay me first. For that, you maimed me, and repaid all my craft and service with evil.

"Yet even so, though I was bereft of strength and allies, I found my way. Many things have passed between us. You severed the sinews of my legs. In return, I slew your two sons—and the proof of that stands now before your very eyes. Look to your drinking vessels: within are their skulls, and all your finest table ornaments are fashioned from their bones. I do not hide this from you.
"And as for your daughter—the wrongs you once did me were repaid through her. When we changed garments, I did more than take her robe. I believe she now carries a child, and I claim it as mine. So ends the reckoning between us."

And with that, Velent rose and flew high into the air.

Then King Niðung said: "You there, young Egill - shoot Velent!"
Egill replied, "I will not harm my own brother."
Then said the king, "Then you shall die—either for refusing my order, or for being party to your brother's crimes. But your life may yet be spared if—and only if—you shoot him down."

So Egill nocked an arrow and drew the bow. He shot beneath Velent's left arm, and blood fell to the ground. Then the king and all his men declared, "That wound will be his death."

But Velent flew away, returning to Sjælland, to the lands of his people that once belonged to his father, Vaði the giant. Not long after, King Niðung took ill and died. His son, Otvin, inherited the kingdom, and he was well-loved by all, and especially kind to his sister.
Velent made peace with Otvin and wed the king's sister.
Now the king's daughter went to her bed and gave birth to a son. He was named Viðga. When Velent learned of all this in Sjælland, he sent word to King Otvin in Jutland, seeking a truce and settlement.

The king welcomed peace and granted him safe conduct for a parley. Velent journeyed to Jutland, where he was warmly received. King Otvin offered him a place in his court, but Velent said it seemed more fitting to return home to his father's land. Still, he vowed to remain a loyal friend and ally to the king.
Otvin agreed and pledged him his friendship.
And so Velent returned to Sjælland with his wife and their three-year-old son Viðga. The king gave them rich treasures and fine gifts, and they parted as dear friends.
Velent dwelt long in Sjælland, renowned throughout the northern world for his craftsmanship and cunning in all contrivances.'

I think it's really cool that the story has a happy ending in this version.
I do wonder though what other cunning contrivances he came up with? If only we could look through a Time Machine and see. I did however discover one of Velent's 'contrivances' within the saga as I was researching this chapter, which I'm going to tell you about very soon.

The fact that the story has a classic happy ending, with Velent/Völund marrying the Princess, loving their little son, and retiring to his old haunt rich and prosperous is very cool.
I have no doubt that sometimes he dreamt of his beautiful flying 'alien creature', who taught him his trade, broke his heart and left, yet he must've known that she was on a different level to him. Maybe he saw her again one day, when he was an old Elf, and to his surprise found that she was still young and beautiful?

I hope you've enjoyed this in-depth look at the Völund story. I believe that it is what the movies call a 'smoking gun'. A piece of evidence that is practically irrefutable.
Many will still say no, it's just a fairytale, but I can't see it that way. Two solid, text-based pieces of detailed evidence, full of anachronistic technical (and physiological) data, and one outrageous 3D piece of artwork, clearly illustrating a fully anachronistic object, an obviously jet powered flying machine. Anyone who knows anything about flight, and can put aside disbelief and open their mind, looking closely and thoughtfully at the evidence, should be able to say that perhaps we are very wrong about the progress of technology in human history.
In fact I would go so far as to say that this is as close to proof as we could hope to find, (aside from actually digging up an ancient flying machine). The stories and the artifact point to either unknown human civilisations, as advanced or more advanced than we are now, or to extraterrestrial civilisations, based here for a very long time, who gifted some of our ancestors with high technological understanding.

The next question we could ask is, are there other such flying stories in the corpus of old Norse history?
The answer is yes indeed! There is in fact a plethora!

If we go back into Gylfaginning, from the Prose Edda, we come to a very interesting little story about the beautiful goddesses of the Aesir people.

As you will remember, the word 'Aesir' refers to the great family of 'Powerful Ones' from Old Asgard and it's surrounds.

A male 'Powerful One' is called an Áss, (a somewhat unfortunate spelling in English, but pronounced 'Owss'). This word is still incredibly common in Scandinavia, found in compound place names all over.

A female 'Powerful One' is called an Ásynjur (sounds like 'oww sinyure').

In Ch 35 of Gylfaginning (The Prose Edda), Gangleri (aka Gylfi) asks 'who are the Ásynjur?' 'Harr', (High)/Odin), reels off a very informative list of fourteen of these goddesses, and then tells us that there are other goddesses who are the mysterious Valkyries, (just like our three beautiful alien creatures we met earlier in the chapter).

It is the fourteenth Ásynjur, Gná, (sounds like 'ga now'),who is of great interest here.

This is my translation-

'Fourteenth is Gná, she is sent by (the Ásynjur) Frigg, into many homeworlds on her missions. She has a 'horse' that runs through the upper sky/outer space and over/under the water, and it is called Hófvarpnir (Hoof striker or Hoof walloper).'

As I have said previously, I consider the word horse not to mean the actual animal, certainly not a magical horse, but a word simply meaning 'a means of transport'. The word that I translate as 'upper sky and outer space' is 'lopt', and the word I translate as over/under the water is 'lög', which literally means 'lake'.

What is being described here is what we would now call both a UAP and a USO, an unidentified craft that can travel through the air **and** underwater.

A transmedium craft!

The story gets even better, as here we have one of the very earliest recorded UAP mass sighting accounts.

'There was one time as she rode, that some Vanir, (those high tech rivals and then partners of the Aesir, probably from the Lake Van area in Ancient Armenia), saw her riding in the sky.

'One of them said:

"What there flies, what there travels, on it's way through the upper sky?"

(An interesting alternative translation, from 'Gods of the North' by Brian Branston - reads - "Hey! What flew there? What fizzed away clearing the tops of the clouds".)

She answers:

"I do not fly, though I do travel,
I make my way through the upper sky
on Hófvarpnir, whom Hamskerpir
sired with Garðrofa".

(Once again, Brian Branston translates this verse – 'I'm not flying, though I fizz away, clearing the tops of the clouds'.)

I like that word 'fizz', because it really expresses something of the sound of a speeding jet, high up in the sky, driven by fast expelled gas. Pretty much what a jet is.)

Odin completes his explanation to Gylfi -

'The name Gná comes from the word 'gnæfa', meaning 'to tower/rise high', to 'travel high up'. The people on the ground seem to be asking each other a natural question, just as modern

people do when they see an unidentified flying object. "What the heck is that up there zooming above the clouds?".
Next thing Gná is speaking directly to them, telling them not to worry, because 'it's only me flying in my means of transport'.
How did she hear them? And why did she bother coming down to speak to them?
Maybe, as with so many others of these ancient stories, she had paranormal gifts and heard their thoughts. She realised that they were of the Vanir, the Aesir's new best friends, so she 'fizzed' down and landed 'VTOL' (vertical takeoff and landing) style, near them. We can just imagine her, a very beautiful young woman in a flight suit, taking off her helmet and walking towards the Vanir with a smile.
Maybe she gives them a close look over her aircraft. Maybe she even takes them for a joyride, who knows!

The names of the 'horse's' are very telling.
Gná's aircraft is named 'Hófvarpnir', meaning 'Hoof Striker', which definitely sounds like a fighter aircraft which strikes with its forward facing weapons.
The craft's father, (the previous model of aircraft that it was based upon), is 'Hamskerpir', which means 'Sharp Shaped'. This was a bit of a translation win for me, because most texts said the word was untranslatable. Because of that initial word, 'ham', which we have encountered many times before, I thought that this must mean shape, and then I took a guess at 'skerpir' (because a lot of words with 'sk' at the start in Old Norse are often spelled as 'sh' in English e.g skip is ship, skirt is shirt, etc.).
So 'skerpir' could possibly be 'sharp', thus 'sharp shape'.
I double checked this by email with Professor Jakobsson, and he concurred that this was a reasonable translation.

When I was in the Museum Library of the University of Lund, looking at the Völund broach, there was quite a collection of bird-like artefacts, many having sharp shaped artificial looking wings, which suggested some kind of stylized fighter plane with swing wings.
The 'mother horse' of 'Hofvarpnir', was called 'Garðrofa', which surprisingly means 'fortress destroyer'! Another perfect fighter bomber name!

This story of Gná not only backs up my thesis, (that there was a LOT of high-tech flying going on in the ancient North and in Asia Minor), but it is a charming and human story. For this sophisticated and very powerful lady to drop down from 'above the clouds', and explain who she is, and show off her craft up close to these interested, (and perhaps terrified), Vanir people on the ground, is strangely modern and realistic.

The next ancient flying story we look at stars the one, the only Loki, the popular yet infamous character from the Marvel films.
The story is told to that Jötun Wizard and home brewer, Aegir, at the very start of Skaldskaparmal (The Prose Edda).
Three Aesir - Odin, Loki and Haenir - have set out on a long mission, apparently walking over mountains, and through wild places, and find themselves running out of supplies. They come across a herd of oxen, and kill one of them for food, but for some reason it just won't cook. They hear a voice from up above them in a large tree, and when they look up, they see that it is an eagle, and as it says in the story, 'not a little one'.

The eagle bargains with them for some of the ox, saying that he will allow it to cook if they share it. He is the one disrupting the cooking process, but the three Aesir reluctantly say yes. The cooking begins and then the eagle swoops down and rips off a very large chunk of cooked ox, and flies away with it. Loki gets very angry and strikes the eagle with a pole that he has got from somewhere, and the pole weirdly sticks to the eagle.

The eagle flies low and fast, and Loki gets dragged through trees and over rocks and stones. He's not having a good time, but he finds that he can't let go of the pole. When they are out of earshot of the others, the eagle, who turns out to be the giant Thiazi, makes a deal with him in return for letting him go.

Loki must trick the Ásynjur woman, Idunn, (Íðunn), into coming outside of Old Asgard into a nearby forest, where the Jötun (giant) will be waiting to kidnap her.

She is an extremely important person to the Aesir, as she is the one who provides them with what I call their 'immortality therapy', her mysterious 'apples'.

Loki goes ahead with this cowardly plan, and the giant takes Idunn back to his fortress stronghold. Without her daily therapy the long living Aesir soon start to turn into grey headed, grey bearded old people, with creaky backs and bad knees.

(This in itself is very powerful evidence of ancient medical high tech. 'Gods' do not get old!)

The Aesir are not impressed, and demand to know who last saw Idunn.

Loki is quickly found out, captured, and the now cranky and rapidly aging 'gods' threaten him with torture and death, unless he tells them what's going on. Loki becomes very afraid, confesses his cowardly crime, and agrees to go after the giant and bring Idunn back.

To do this he needs to borrow a flying craft, as Jötunheim is a long way off.

He asks 'ef Freyja vill ljá honum valshams, er hon á' (if Freyja will loan him a Hawk Shape, that she has).

So once again we are hearing about the same type of flying craft that we have previously encountered, flown by the beautiful 'young alien creatures', the Swan Shape crafts.
Shape's named after birds.
Off Loki flies, grabs the goddess, (and her 'apples'), from Thiazi's (Þjazi's) fortress, and puts her in a nut shaped pod on the side of the craft (an emergency pod?).
They take off from the fortress and head for home at full throttle.
Unfortunately, the giant has just come in from doing his daily exercise, rowing in the sea, and finds Idunn gone. He jumps into his own, larger aircraft, his 'arnarhamr', (Eagle Shape), and 'flys after Loki and **'dró arnsúg í flugnum'**.
This is an amazing detail!
It literally translates as 'drew eagle-suction in flight'.
The Old Norse word 'arnsúg', (eagle suck), is very interesting. It can mean the 'rushing sucking wind caused by the flight of an eagle', describing a very powerful suction and vortices left behind an eagle's rapid flight.
One translator writes that 'he (Loki) caused a storm wind by his flight'. It could even be an attempt to describe the shocking crash of a sonic boom, as a jet aircraft breaks the sound barrier.
I thinks it's a pretty good description of the flight of a roaring full throttle jet fighter.

Loki and Idunn had a reasonable head start, but it seems that Eagle Shapes are bigger and faster than Hawk Shapes, as in the real world. Loki is going as fast as he can in his smaller Hawk Shape, but he has the added weight of Idunn, and the drag caused by the emergency rescue 'nut' pod she is in.

His sensors are telling him that the Jötun is catching up behind him very fast.

It doesn't say so in the text, but maybe some form of air to air weaponry is also being fired at him. The Aesir see this situation on their own scopes, and we are told that they go down 'under Asgard' and 'fire up wood shavings'.

(This imagery of going 'under Asgard' fits perfectly with my earlier conjecture, that the 'herbergi', the army mountain sanctuary, is under Asgard, and that's where the Aesir have their anti-aircraft defenses set up).

The Hawk Shape screams down out of the sky, landing VTOL beside the inner wall of Asgard, (like the 80's Hawker Harrier jump jets of the RAF, and the US Marines).

Thiazi and his Eagle Shape craft overshoot the target, and the Aesir let rip with their 'wood shavings', (anti aircraft defences, probably giant ray gun affairs).

The Eagle Shape bursts into flames, spinning and crash landing within the walls of Asgard. The enraged Aesir charge in, wrathfully running, (slowly), on their golden walking frames, and finish off poor old Thiazi. We are told that this killing was greatly renowned, (though I suspect that they left out the walking frame part).

Next stop, Idunn's therapeutics, and the 'gods' are back to being frisky kids again.

Yet another story tells us about a larger and even more versatile craft.

The Aesir leader, Freyr, (a male, not to be confused with Freyja, the so called 'love goddess), had a marvellous flying machine given to him by Brokk, one of two great Dwarven Master craftsmen, (who Loki had set in a manufacturing competition with each other).

This machine is described as a huge boar, (a male pig), called Gullinbursti, (Golden Bristles), which pulled a great flying chariot. Freyr drove Gullinbursti to the funeral of Odin's son, Baldr (who was so beloved of all creatures that even a great company of Frost giants (Hrimþursa's) and Mountain Giants (Bergrísar) turned up to attend it).

Brokk, running through the flying boar operating instructions, told Freyr that Gullinbursti 'could run through the upper sky/outer space (lopt), and underwater (lög), continuously through night and day, faster than any horse (mode of transportation), and it never became so dark at night, or in the murky homeworld ('myrkheimum'), that there was not ample light wherever it went.
Light shone from its bristles."
Can anyone say UAP / USO?!
(For more on USO's - Unidentified Submerged Objects - being observed in the modern era, check out the amazing interviews with retired Rear Admiral (United States Navy), and oceanographer, Timothy Gallaudet, and the recent book 'Over the Horizon - a Sailor's Voyage into the Unknown', by Ed William).

Fascinatingly, that word 'lög', lake/water, is also a very archaic, (pre-Viking Age), word for…wait for it…'bath water'!
Have you ever seen bath water after three or four dirty kids have been in it?
Very murky!
Check out the word that Brokk used - 'myrkheimum' - you can see the English words here - the Murky Home (homeworld).
This is literally telling us that the Gullinbursti craft not only skims along just below the surface of the water, but that it goes deep, deep down, into the murky depths.

When you think about this concept - the Murky Homeworld, we are suddenly presented with the possibility that there is a whole hidden society, deep down in the murky depths.
If you follow the UAP / UFO subject at all, you will know that many researchers now consider that the obvious place for the longterm visitors to make their bases would be down deep under the sea, a place where humans very rarely go.
UFO lore contains so many stories about objects appearing from and travelling under water. In fact, the 'best UFO photo ever taken', a great favourite of mine, is an image accidentally captured by a government mapping aircraft in Costa Rica in 1972.
It shows, in crystal clear detail, a huge (120 – 200 feet across) circular (sunwheel?) craft either emerging, or entering, a deep lake in that South American country.
It appears that these craft flashing through our skies are just as happy racing through deep water!

Let's have a look at the original verses shall we?

En Frey gaf hann göltinn ok sagði, (But Freyr he gave the boar and said,) *at hann mátti renna lopt ok lög, nótt ok dag*, (that he might run through sky/outer space and dark water, night and day,) *meira en hverr hestr*, (faster than any horse/means of transport) *ok aldri varð svá myrkt af nótt eða í myrkheimum*, (and nowhere was so murky/dark, even in the night or in the murky worlds) *at eigi væri ærit ljós þar, er hann fór*, (when no light was there, where he travelled,) *Svá lýsti af burstinni* (but that light shone from it´s bristles).

This 'boar' seems to represent a large craft, perhaps somewhat boar shaped in its design, (taller than it is wide, more solid at the forward end, hump backed?), that glows very brightly, moves extremely fast

high in the sky or through space, as well as impossibly fast through the water and deep down underwater.
It has no problem navigating through those deep darknesses, because of its powerful lights, (and onboard navigational technology?).
Wouldn't you agree that this passage has all the hallmarks of a competent, pre-modern attempt to describe a glowing, transmedium machine.

Carrying on with this underwater theme, let's rewind back to the story of Velent/Völund, from that second saga version, Thidrek of Bern's Saga, to before he had the misfortune of meeting the very unpleasant King and his Queen.

Here's the translation.
'Velent now travelled as far as he could for three days. Then he came to a great river. It was called Visara. But he could not get across the river. There was a great forest beside the river, and there he stayed for a while on account of bad weather, and not far from there was the sea. Velent made preparations. He walked along the riverbank and saw where a great tree stood, and he felled it to the ground. Then he split the tree apart and hollowed it out inside. In the narrower part, where the branches had grown, he placed his tools and his belongings, and in the thicker part of the tree he put his provisions and drink, and he himself went inside and sealed it so tightly and securely that nothing of any kind could harm him.
Over the windows which were in the tree, he placed glass, and it was so arranged that he could remove it whenever he wished. And when the glass was in place, no more water entered than would have through a whole, unbroken tree.
Now the tree-trunk lay beside the river, and inside it was Velent, with all his belongings and tools. And he hid himself in the

hollowed log until the trunk drifted out into the river. The trunk was carried into the sea, and then out into the open ocean, and it drifted for eighteen days before at last coming ashore.'

Now what sort of thing seems to be being described here?
I'll give you a second.
Did anyone put up their hand and say 'submarine'?
If you did, you can go to the top of the class!
I have to admit that I have just come across this story whilst researching for this chapter. I've put the sentences about the glass in bold, because I think they are mind-boggling. A glass canopy that makes the log watertight! Velent is in there for 18 days with all his supplies, and his tools!
If we're being realistic, he would need a source of air, food and water supplies, and somewhere to sleep. Why does it need to be watertight? How rare was glass back then? Why didn't he just make a big log canoe?

Like you, I don't think this is a log that we are talking about here. It seems that, as he later built himself a jet powered flying machine, Velent/Völund just built a mini-submarine!
Let's listen to what the saga says regarding how the evil King and his men first come across him, after the 18 days that he travels (on top of, or under the water?).

'There was a king named Niðungr. He ruled over Jutland, in the region called Þjóði.
And one day, the king's men were rowing on the sea, casting a dragnet close to shore to catch green fish for the king's table. And they cast their nets and drew them to land, and the net became so heavy that they could scarcely pull it ashore.

Now they saw that a great and wondrous tree-trunk had become entangled in the net. They hauled the trunk to land and examined it closely to see what sort of tree it might be. They found the wood was most strangely and skillfully carved, and so they supposed it must be a treasure-chest of some kind, so heavy and well-fashioned was it.

They sent a man to the king and asked him to come and see this marvel.

And when the king arrived and saw the trunk, he ordered them to open it and discover what might be inside. But when they began to hew into it, Velent, hearing what they were doing, called out to them and bade them stop, saying that there was a man inside the trunk.

And when they heard the voice, they thought it must be the devil himself within the tree, and they were sore afraid, each one fleeing to his own place.

Then Velent opened the trunk and stepped forth before the king, saying, "My lord, I am a man—not a troll—and I beg you earnestly to grant me peace: peace for my life and for my possessions."

The king saw that this was a fair man and no rogue, though he had come there in a most wondrous fashion. So he granted him peace and allowed him to keep all his belongings. Now Velent took his tools and his treasure and hid them secretly in the ground, along with the trunk.'

Now in Scandinavia back then there were trees everywhere, (as there still are today).

So for the warriors to 'scarcely imagine what kind of tree that was', and to think that it was worth requesting the King to come and see it, was significant.

They describe the 'tree' as being carved 'wondrously well', though the creation story doesn't tell us anything about Velent carving the outside of it. Maybe it had rounded ends and panels and rivets, which might have been conceived of as being carved?
The King's men consider it unusually heavy and 'well made', which doesn't sound like a tree does it?

It strikes me that a large submarine craft, perhaps dark brown in colour, could only be understood by these people as a huge log. Trees and logs often drifted in from the sea, and there was no other way to conceive of such a structure.
The fact that we are told that Velent set waterproof glass over the 'window set in the tree' sounds very much like modern manufacturing and design. Maybe there was a turret where the glass observation window was. Who knows, maybe there was even a space for a flying machine on the deck!
There is a lot more to this story than meets the eye. Randomly floating around in the sea in this object for 18 days is rather odd. That's a long time and would've required a lot of supplies and freshwater. Why would a person who could build such a thing not just cross the river?
It really would make more sense if this was actually an ancient submarine, with some form of propulsion, piloted by an amazing Elf engineer who created it to travel a very long way, undetected by people and ships.
Maybe one day we will discover more information, or even a broach shaped like a submarine!

We will leave Velent/Völund and his submarine there on the beach, surrounded by the awestruck Swedes, and finish off this chapter with a look at some really huge flying craft, described in the Eddas and Sagas, craft that could well be those enormous sunwheels that we looked at earlier, carrying the Aesir on their invasion and takeover of the North.

For starters, there is one, owned by Freyr, (the owner of the multi-medium travelling Golden Boar), which always strikes people as pretty cool.
Its name was Skidbladnir (Skiðblaðnir), and even the Aesir thought that it was the coolest ship.
This is what High tells Gylfi -
'So is it here said, in the Aesir's own words:
Ash Yggdrasil,
it is the highest / most renowned of trees,
but Skidbladnir ship of ships,
Odin Ása (god of gods)
but Sleipnir divine / exceptional horses (horse of horses)
Bifrost bridges (bridge of bridges)
but Bragi Skalds (Old Norse court poets) (skald of skalds)
Hábrok hawk of hawks
but Garmr hound of hounds!'

You well might ask why this ship, Skidbladnir, is more special than others?
Let's listen to the exchange between the Wizard King of Sweden and the one eyed Chieftain of the Aesir -

'Then Gangleri said: "What is there to say about Skíðblaðnir, that it is the best ship?
Is there no great ship the same as it?"
High said: "Skíðblaðnir is the best of ships and with most skill created, but Naglfar is the largest ship; that one belongs to Múspell. Some dwarves, the sons of Ívaldi, made Skíðblaðnir and gave the ship to Freyr. It is so large that all the Æsir may sail on it, with

weapons and war-gear, and it generates a favorable wind as soon as the sail is raised, no matter where it is to go. But when it is not to sail upon the sea, it is made with such great craftsmanship, and out of so many parts, that it may be folded up like cloth and carried in a pouch."

Then Gangleri said: "Skíðblaðnir is a good ship, but there must have been an almighty amount of 'great knowledge' involved in its making...'"

The craftsmen who made this incredible ship were 'black dwarves', called the 'Son's of Ivaldi', and they were something like the competing aerospace corporation to Brokk and his brother (also 'black dwarves').

(The Old Norse word I have translated as 'great knowledge' above is fjölkynngi, often mistranslated as 'sorcery' or 'witchcraft', and sometimes as 'magic', by later Christian influenced translators. As once famously stated by science fiction writer Arthur C Clarke, in his Third Law - 'Any sufficiently advanced technology is indistinguishable from magic'.

This wonderful ship is obviously huge, because all the Aesir together add up to a lot of people, if we include all their very large extended families.

Its ability to always generate a 'favourable wind' really suggests something like a motor, something like the wind created by jets, rockets or some more advanced arcane technology. Perhaps something like the anti-gravity technology that we imagine powers the superb and incredible craft, seen in our skies for a hundred years, (and for thousands of years before that).

The big question is, how could a craft this large be folded up, and put in one's pouch?

Believe it or not, I have put a fair bit of time into thinking about this.

How could even very high technology account for such a thing?

The only possibility I can come up with is this, that the object folded like a cloth, that Freyr carried in his pocket, was an advanced nanotechnology printing device, something that could literally 3D print this particular ship out of an easily accessible raw material. Something like silica sand, which is an extremely common beach sand that can readily be converted to ceramics, glass and other useful products, such as, I don't know...great glowing star ships?

Perhaps this technology could also devolve the ship, if the owner needed to do such a thing, leaving behind once again just a pile of sand?

Or it could be just magic!

And now, finally, we come to The Mighty Thor!

We read, (once again in Gylfaginning, in the Prose Edda), that Gylfi/Gangleri asks of Odin and his two identical brothers - "What are the names of the other Æsir, and what do they do? Or what great deeds have they accomplished?"

High (Hárr/Odin) said: "Thor is the foremost among them. He is called Ása-Thor (Thor of the Aesir) or Öku-Thor ('Driving' Thor). He is the strongest of all the gods and men. He has a realm called Thrudvangar, and his hall is named Bilskirnir. In that hall, there are five hundred and forty rooms. It is the largest house known to men'.

This huge 'hall', Bilskirnir, would appear to be located up high in Old Asgard, in that area at the end of Yggdrasil, somewhere near the great space station Himinbjorg (Sky/Outer Space mountain), owned by the watchman Heimdall.

Thor's great hall orbits the Earth in an energy/power field, which is the translation of Thrudvangar!

This energy or power could be electrical, (fitting for the God of Thunder and Lightning), or it could be some other form of power that we are unaware of.
Perhaps this was a protective field shielding Bilskirnir against attacks from his sworn enemies, the Giants (Shields up Mr Sulu!). Perhaps it was some kind of cosmic charging station for all the ships of the Aesir?
What I find very interesting about the description is that 540 rooms, to us, is not all that unusual, say in a large hotel complex, but in the ancient times this was an extraordinary number. What this really points to is not only the very large size of this craft, but also the number of crew involved. This is a very serious mothership. We are not given any description of light associated with Thor's craft, but it seems to be a given that it would've been very bright by Bronze Age Earth standards. Especially when you live in a power field!

The most famous hall of all, of course, is Valhalla, meaning literally the 'Hall of the Valiant (slain)'. This is Odin's great ship, and interestingly, it too appears to have 540 rooms as does Thor's 'Bilskirnir', as we learn from this conversation between Gangleri (Wizard King Gylfi) and Odin himself:
'Gangleri said:
"These are strange tidings that you tell. A tremendously large house Valhalla must be! Overcrowded must it often be at the doors." Hárr answered:
"Why ask you not this, how many doors are in the hall or how large? If you hear it said, then you will say, that it is strange indeed that none are hindered from going in and out if they will. But that can truly be said that it is no more difficult to arrange space inside it than to enter it. You may hear it in Grímnismál:

'Five hundred and forty doors
I believe Valhalla has.
Eight hundred Einherjar
Will race out at once from each door
When they fare to fight the wolf.'"

We learn a number of things here. We are encountering a very advanced type of craft indeed. According to this account, there is never any trouble accommodating any sized group of people within. It's as if the whole of the interior can morph and readjust itself, depending on how many come in, so that no one ever feels cramped. Eight hundred Einherjar, (Odin's elite fighting force, gathered in preparation for Ragnarök, the 'Judgement of the Ruling Ones/the Powerful Ones/ the Elohim'), can exit simultaneously through each of the 540 doors, as they charge into battle.
That's 432,000 men all charging out of the great ship at once! These Einherjar are composed of all the heroic slain warriors, picked out from fights and battlefields over the ages by the Valkyries, and brought to Valhalla.
(Einherjar literally means 'One Man Army'!)

Valhalla is described by Gylfi, when he first arrives up in Asgard, as being so high that he can't see over it, and we learned that the roof appears to be covered in golden shields.
Just imagine this vast metallic star cruiser landing in Sweden on that flat topped mountain base beside Lake Vänern called Valhalla (Halleberg)!
I find it quite telling that so many of these great shining Aesir 'Halls', out in space, are described as being metallic. This really drives home the point that these are not mystical timber and thatched roofed magical palaces.

The great lady Freyja, not to be left out, has her own great hall. This is literally a 'mother' ship, considering that she is the great love goddess, and mother figure symbol. Even today in Iceland, a housewife is called a Húsfreyja - the love goddess of the house. (As an aside, the beautiful Gefjun/Freyja could quite possibly have been there whilst Gangleri/Gylfi was visiting Old Asgard and being questioned, asking questions, and being shown around. Wouldn't that be heartbreaking for a young man, hopelessly in love, if she perhaps treated him imperiously? Then again, maybe the impossibly beautiful lady had some mercy on him, for old times' sake?

Freyja is sometimes called 'The Lady of the Vanir', and of course we remember her intimate connection with the great Swedish lake Vanërn. It's really not hard to understand why Gylfi fell for her so hard, as it says in Gylfaginning that Freya was the most beautiful of all the goddesses, and that she had a hall up above the sky, (himni), called Fólkvangr, which means 'Field of Warriors'.
We learn that 'whenever she rides to battle, then has she half the valiant slain and Odin has the other half'.
It would seem that she is the Commander of the Valkyries, and as I suspected, regarding those 'young alien creatures' who married Völund and his brothers, Valkyries appear to be Aesir as well.
The fact that Fólkvangr is referred to both as a field, and as a hall, speaks of its massive size, like the other two that we just looked at. Odin´s ship Vallhalla, and Thor´s Bilskirnir, both having 540 rooms and doors, and some very advanced technology that fluidly creates enough space within, makes me suspect that Freyja's Fólvangr quite likely was the same.
Perhaps they were three of the same type of ship, like a brand of massive 540 room interstellar spacecraft, manufactured somewhere offworld. Maybe in one of the exotic homeworlds we

visited earlier. Freyja has another hall named Sessrumnir, said to be 'large and beautiful'.
Guess what it´s name means?
'Many seats'!
Sessrumnir is also catalogued as a ship in Snorri's great list in Skaldskaparmal.
So there's no doubt that this is a very large flying passenger craft, (not just a grounded hall), and if it's anything like Odin's craft, then it could be accommodating up to half a million people. Really sounds like one of those vast space arks, doesn't it, (think of the final scenes in the film 'Interstellar').

I would like to add something very important at this juncture, something which I did mention earlier in the book, and that is - despite my obvious and dedicated retelling of these stories, seen through the naturalistic high-tech paleocontact lens, I do not mean to disparage the more spiritual interpretations of all these stories. It might seem like a contradiction, but I personally think that the truth is a mixture of both these aspects. There's something extremely strange and mysterious going on here, a subject which I will deal with at much greater length in my next book, 'Viking Superpowers - Way of Midgard'.
Suffice it to say that I suspect that our reality is not quite as concrete as we would like to think.

So to bring this extremely interesting chapter to an end, (I hope that's how you have experienced it), I have one more tale of a very large 'hall', a great mothership, based up there in the sky. This one has a special meaning for me, as it connects with something that happened to me in Iceland, when I visited on my Viking Superpowers Research Tour in 2024.

I had been asked by my Icelandic friend, Simmi Valgeirsson, if I could help with creating a book cover and some inked maps of Iceland and Scandinavia, for a book that he had been helping research. The book is called 'Rescuing Árni', by author Stephany Evans Steggall, the riveting true story of one of the first Icelanders to come to Australia, Árni Olafsson Thorlacius.
Árni became the rescuer of the only survivor of the terrible 1857 shipwreck of the 'The Dunbar', in which 122 people perished, off the cliffs of Sydney, Australia.

It turns out that the President of Iceland at the time that I visited, Guðni Thorlacius Jóhannesson, was related to Árni!
He had heard that I was visiting Iceland, and had seen the book cover and maps I created, and sent me an invitation to visit him at the official Presidential residence, Bessastaðir, at Álftanes near Reykjavík.
So you might be wondering what this has to do with this last great shining mothership?

Well, let's have a look at what is written in the Prose Edda - 'Forseti is the son of Baldr and Nanna Nepsdóttir. He owns a hall in the sky/outer space, which is called Glitnir. And all who come to him with legal disputes leave at peace. That is the best court among gods and men. Thus it is said here:

'Glitnir, is called a hall,
It is held up by gold
And also roofed with silver.
There Forseti
Dwells most of the day
And puts to sleep all disputes.'

Forseti in Old Norse means 'the fore seater, the front seater'. Literally the person who pilots the ship or the tribe or the nation. The President of Iceland is called to this day - Herra Forseti, 'Mr President'!
I think that the original Aesir man Forseti is essentially a pilot, the front seater, (which is what fighter pilots call the pilot of a two-seat fighter plane, who sits up front).
He is also obviously a great lawyer, which is a good background for a President!

I like to think that he was the chief pilot of the Aesir, under Odin's command, flying special missions, training young pilots, and overseeing all important aviation and spaceflight matters in Old Asgard.
So let's now 'zoom climb' to our final chapter, once again a story involving flying, and I think you will agree, it's the most amazing of all these amazing stories!

THE SMOKING GUN

The Mirriam Webster online dictionary defines 'smoking gun' as - **'something that serves as conclusive evidence or proof (as of a crime or scientific theory).'**
My 'scientific theory', (though some crime is definitely involved), is that the stories (including poetry), preserved in Old Norse manuscripts from Iceland, and in the pictographic rock carvings and three dimensional artifacts reaching back to the Bronze Age, contain carefully preserved accounts of visitation and dominance of the human race, by technologically advanced humanoid beings, either extraterrestrial or cryptoterrestrial, as well as serious accounts of paranormal human and humanoid superpowers.

Having reached this final chapter, I hope that you feel the same way as I do, that there is a heck of a lot of very strong evidence backing this theory.
Regarding smoking guns, you might even say there are potentially several, such as anachronistic artifacts like the Völund 'jet powered flying suit' broach from Uppsala, backed up by not one, but two extraordinary ancient descriptive sagas.
There is the flight-testing near fatal G-force accident, describing incredibly modern aeronautical experiences and knowledge,
And not forgetting a surprisingly realistic description of a submarine.
Much of what I consider strong evidence, however, is really still a matter of whether one can stretch their imagination outside the

conventional interpretations, and believe some, or all, of my literal translations of these old stories.

My sincere hope also is that I might have helped change some minds about the credibility of the great Icelandic Chieftain and historian Snorri Sturluson, who, (I believe), has been falsely maligned for generations, whilst at the same time being absolutely irreplaceable in the study of the great stories of the North.
The truth is, I have only revealed a fraction of my discoveries in this field so far, and there's a lot more to come. The study of paleocontact and the paranormal in the Viking Age, and reaching back all the way to the Stone Age, is still a relatively new field, which my friend Col. John.B.Alexander calls 'a road less travelled'. Exciting times if what Morpheus says is right and all!

So…what is this particular 'smoking gun' that I wish to present before you today?

As so often happens in life, the simple things discovered at the start of a quest can end up being the most significant.
Back on the 12th of December 1985, I ducked into a quaint little bookshop, literally half a mile down the road from my parents house in Brisbane, Queensland, Australia.
The shop was called 'The Booksmith', and it was owned by a classic English gentleman, who I recall wearing a Tweed coat, sporting a beard and glasses, and possibly smoking a pipe. There was definitely something of J.R.R Tolkein, (or was it Gandalf), about him.
His shop was stocked wall to wall with books of all kinds, and he was one of those geniuses who seemed to remember every single one in detail. I had but to ask, and he would go and find me a book or two about whatever arcane subject I mentioned.

We both shared a passion for Medieval and Dark Ages history, and on this particular day, as I walked in, he jumped up and said something along the lines of "David, I'm so glad you dropped in, I've got just the book for you".

It was a hardback edition, complete with dust cover, of 'The Mound People – Danish Bronze-Age Man Preserved', by (Professor) PV Glob, first published in 1970.

It was the follow up book to Professor Glob's famous study, 'The Bog People', (which I had also bought there), showcasing the most incredibly well-preserved bodies found in Danish bogs.

Those bodies were from approximately the time of Christ.

The Mound People reached back another one to two thousand years, to the Bronze Age of Scandinavia, which we have been visiting throughout this book.

I found 'The Mound People' to be a revelation, having hitherto mainly focused my studies on the Viking Age. I learnt that the peoples of Scandinavia in the Bronze Age possessed excellent ocean-going ships, had established regular trade routes all the way down to Greece, and imported all sorts of exotic goods, including glassware, wine and classically designed objects.

Their aristocracy had been buried in large mounds, in well-sealed oak coffins, and the preservation of their 3000-year-old clothes within the coffins was astounding.

Two women's outfits really stood out. One was found at Borum Eshøj, a set of clothes belonging to an elderly lady, consisting of a short-sleeved shirt and a long pleated dress, with a belt whose ends suggested flowers. She also had worn quite an elaborate open weave hair net.

The second burial was of a young girl between 18 and 20 years old.

She had been blond and slender and undoubtedly an aristocrat.
Her costume, however, caused an attack of the vapours when it was revealed in 1929.
Unlike the elder lady's modest outfit, this fair young maiden‘s outfit would not be out of place at a modern beachside resort. It consisted of a top, very similar to the elder ladies, and a little hair tie, but then it was revealed that she had a bare midriff, and, very low on her hips a see-through miniskirt, with a band around the waist and one at the lower hem.
The two bands were connected by many fine corded strands.
She wore nothing beneath the skirt, and about her waist was tied a very mysterious ornament.

This was a bronze disc, approx. 6 inches wide, patterned with elaborate patterns of incised and joined spirals in circles, these circles within three other incised circles - a large outer one, one midway, and a small one around a small 'spike' in the centre of the disc.
I have always found it a beautiful but strange object, especially because of the spike in the middle. It is almost as if it were a physical barrier, a sign that this girl was off-limits, that she was the property of someone powerful.

Now what I'm about to say is pure conjecture.
I have puzzled over the meaning of this disc for 40 years, it's one of those designs and placements on the body that seems like it must mean something important, rather than just being an ornament or a fashion statement.
Looking at it today as I write, I get the distinct feeling that this disc is somehow connected to the sun symbols, the sun wheels, to the Sky People. Looking closely at its inscribed designs, I am suddenly

put in mind of another wonderful artefact in Professor Glob's book.

It is from page 102, and it is titled 'the sun drawn by the sacred horse from Trundholm', and it has always greatly appealed to me. This wonderful object was one of the first things I made a beeline for when I visited the National Museum in Copenhagen. It has six wheels, with a horse at the front on four, and then a large Sunwheel being drawn behind it, held up by the other two wheels. One side of the Sunwheel still has its gold leaf mostly intact, inlaid over the top of the engraved metal. The swirling designs within circles is almost exactly the same as the designs on the small disc worn around the girls waist.

Another thing that strikes me about these two designs is that they are very similar to the carved circle I found on the 3000-year-old stone in Sweden, at Hagbards Galge, an area that has been famously associated with crop circles and sightings of anomalous craft.

So I am wondering whether this young woman could have been one of those beautiful young 'Earth Mothers', married off to the young sons of Odin, those Aesir who appeared from the sky in their great Sunwheels? Or could she have perhaps been destined for such a marriage, but sadly died of illness or accident before that could happen?

We shall never know, but I must admit this whole story makes more and more sense to me. It seems that the art and artefacts of the Scandinavian Bronze Age were absolutely full of such memorials and symbolism, commemorating these very unusual events.

The question I often ask of myself and others is this - if you yourself were to have such an experience, where a great shining ship came down out of the sky and landed in your local park, where

the most extraordinarily beautiful people emerged and talked to you, perhaps took you for a joyride up into the universe, and then brought you back. Do you think that would be the most marvellous thing that ever happened in your life?
Do you suppose you'd ever stop talking about it? Would it not be a major focus of your life ever after?
Imagine if you lived in a culture that simply accepted your word concerning the experience, who even celebrated you for it, as one of the blessed, as one of the chosen ones?

All we've got to do now in our own time is to accept that experiences like these could be possible, and suddenly these ancient mysteries begin to give up their secrets and make a lot more sense.

Which brings me to my 'smoking gun'.

On page 135 of the book 'The Mound People', we find an image of a dark grey stone, roughly lozenge shaped, tapering from one side to the other, with a narrow blunt end.
Professor Glob labels this the Truehøj Farm stone, found in Himmerland in Denmark.
There are two duplicated images on the page, the one at the top is obviously the rock as it was originally carved, and below that is the same rock after having white paint carefully brushed into it's carved areas.
(This practice helps with visualisation of the design, a common practice in archeological circles in Scandinavia).
I mentioned earlier in the book that I consider most of these Bronze Age carvings to be a form of pictographic language, easy enough to interpret if we can detect the underlying story, but open to interpretation if you don't.

Being a classically trained and experienced artist, I have a good eye for detail, and especially for seeing patterns in works that require some imaginative interpretation.
I'm going to apply those skills to the interpretation of this stone, which I believe was created as a direct message to the people of the future.

Us.

It has miraculously travelled across a great gulf of time, bringing a message considered worth the labour of endless hours of chiseling into this very hard stone.
A message telling of something fabulous, unforgettable and worthy of remembrance.
The first thing I see on this side of the rock is a representation of a large ship at it's base, and what looks like a smaller ship above it, apparently up in the sky. Anybody who has looked at the incised rocks of Bronze Age Scandinavia, in Denmark, Sweden and Norway, will recognise these ship shapes.
They all have curving prows and small curving shapes down at the waterline. They generally have a series of straight short marks, sometimes with round heads, representing the crew of the ships. The big ship shape we see on this rock has ten crew marks, which could represent either ten or twenty crew members.

Professor Glob, on Pg 148, writes - (the emphasis on certain phrases and sentences is mine). 'The reason the Bronze Age ship appears on so many bronze objects, almost exclusively razors in Denmark, and in rock-carvings, is that it expresses **a prayer to the powers on high** to protect ships on their dangerous voyages by river and by sea. It was carried as a cult object in processions and offered to the gods as a sacrifice; but to give the sacred processions and sacrificial gifts enduring power they were also carved in stone. The more important anything was in daily life, the greater protective power it had, which is why the ship is to be seen carved in stone on graves - **like for example the one on a small boulder from Truehøj Farm in Himmerland.** However, the ship image has more than one meaning, as is the case with many other rockcarved representations. **Ships may also be regarded, like the Truehøj vessels, as 'boats of Charon' for carrying the dead across the sea of death to another world**. But in whatever way one interprets the thousands of ships dominating the image world of the Bronze Age, they tell us most of all about the class that controlled the metal trade and so ruled Scandinavia.'

I really like that, that the ship image has more than one meaning. That is a big part of what I am about to reveal.
It is also telling that the Professor notes that 'Ships may also be regarded, like the Truehoj **vessels** (plural), as 'boats of Charon' for **carrying the dead across the sea of death to another world.'**
As is the concept that ships carved on objects represent **'a prayer to the powers on high'.**
The Professor is here unequivocally linking these carvings to 'powers on high' from 'another world'. Undoubtedly he is interpreting, as most people tended to do in the past, through that academic lens that see past peoples as simple and religious, superstitiously worshipping 'gods' and fanciful beings that lived in 'heaven'.
Yet he is acknowledging here that this is still all a mystery. We don't know the truth, but from our great distance across time, we can at least tell that there was a serious reverence happening, and a looking to the sun and stars.

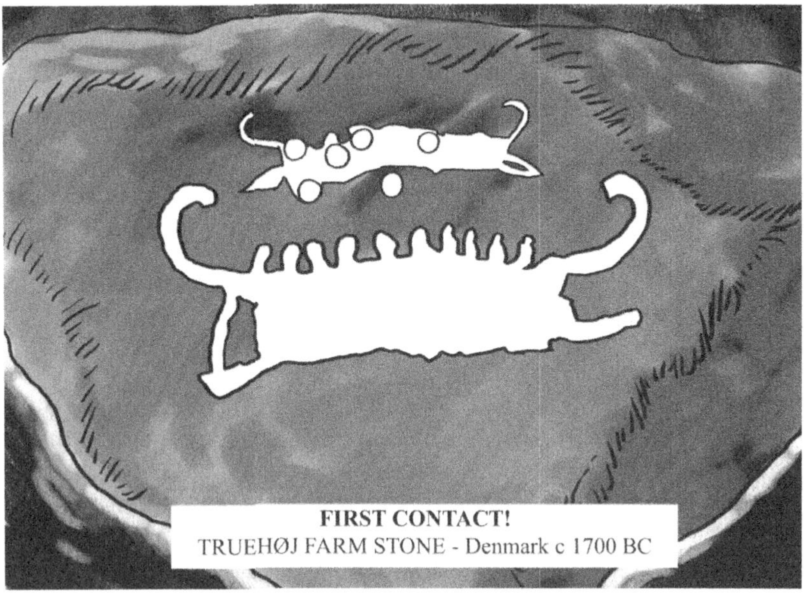

FIRST CONTACT!
TRUEHØJ FARM STONE - Denmark c 1700 BC

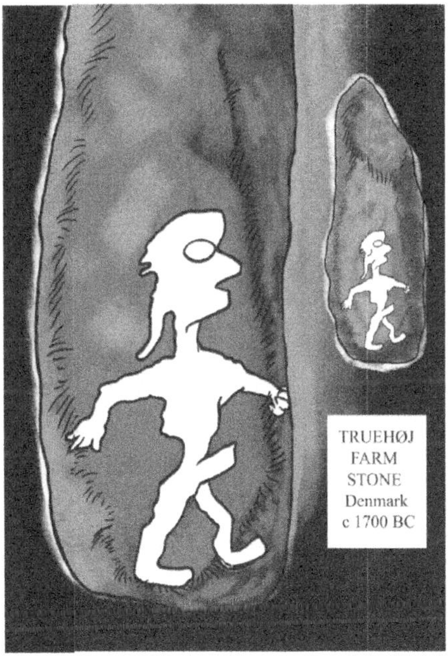

TRUEHØJ
FARM
STONE
Denmark
c 1700 BC

Professor Glob acknowledges that the smaller carved object above the large ship is also a ship, and that the ship could carry people to 'another world'!
When you look closely at this smaller second ship, you see that it has some human ship characteristics, yet at the same time it has a sleeker feel. It's top is rounded, aerodynamic and curved down at the edges. Not unlike, oh, I don't know, perhaps a flying saucer!
The other odd thing about this representation is that it is somewhat pockmarked with small, perfectly round, hemispherical dints. The so called 'cup marks' that we encountered earlier. You will remember my position is that these cup marks, at least sometimes, represent stars, and indeed sometimes perhaps constellations.

So now comes the pictographic interpretation. The ship drawing at the bottom definitely says 'ship', and I believe it is a human ship. The one above it, seemingly at a bit of a distance, above the human ship, is a combination of the word ship, and the word stars.

Starship!

So this side of the message says simply 'we were out sailing on our ship, and in the sky we saw a starship!'.
So now we turn the rock to observe its thin side.
This is an image of what is obviously a male, (because of his erect penis, a pictographic symbol simply saying the word 'male'). What is this male like? He has a large head, a long nose, a prominent chin and a long neck, longer than a normal neck.
His body proportionally is quite small, though you might say his shoulders and chest look almost muscular. He definitely doesn't look like a full-size man, nor does he look like a child.

If I were thinking mythologically, I would say we are looking at one of those dwarves who live under the mountains, and forge incredible golden objects.

If I wanted to think in 'ancient alien paleocontact' mode, (which I do), I would say that he looks somewhat like the grey aliens often experienced in 'alien abductions/close encounters', though from a different species, because of his large nose, large chin, and large tallywhacker.

Thus this second part of the ancient message simply says "we saw a strange little man standing".

Having a background in comic book art as well as in fine art, when I look at this quite excellent and subtle carving, I see a figure stepping out to walk, and there's something about his arms and hands that look to me as if he is beckoning towards himself with his left hand.

So to give a fuller meaning to this pictograph, I would say that it says " We saw a strange little man walking towards us, and beckoning with his left hand, encouraging us to come towards him".

Now we turn to page 137, and once again there are two images of the same rock.

This is where it gets really groovy.

In this image we see, on the left, a little footprint which is rather odd. It has three toes and a long thin tapering heel. Beside it, to the right, is a great big human footprint.

It's what my dad would've called a 'splawfoot'.

Essentially a very broad human footprint, the footprint of somebody who has spent most of their life barefoot on hard ground. Not overly common in civilised countries, but where I come from, a lot of people, myself included, grew up without shoes

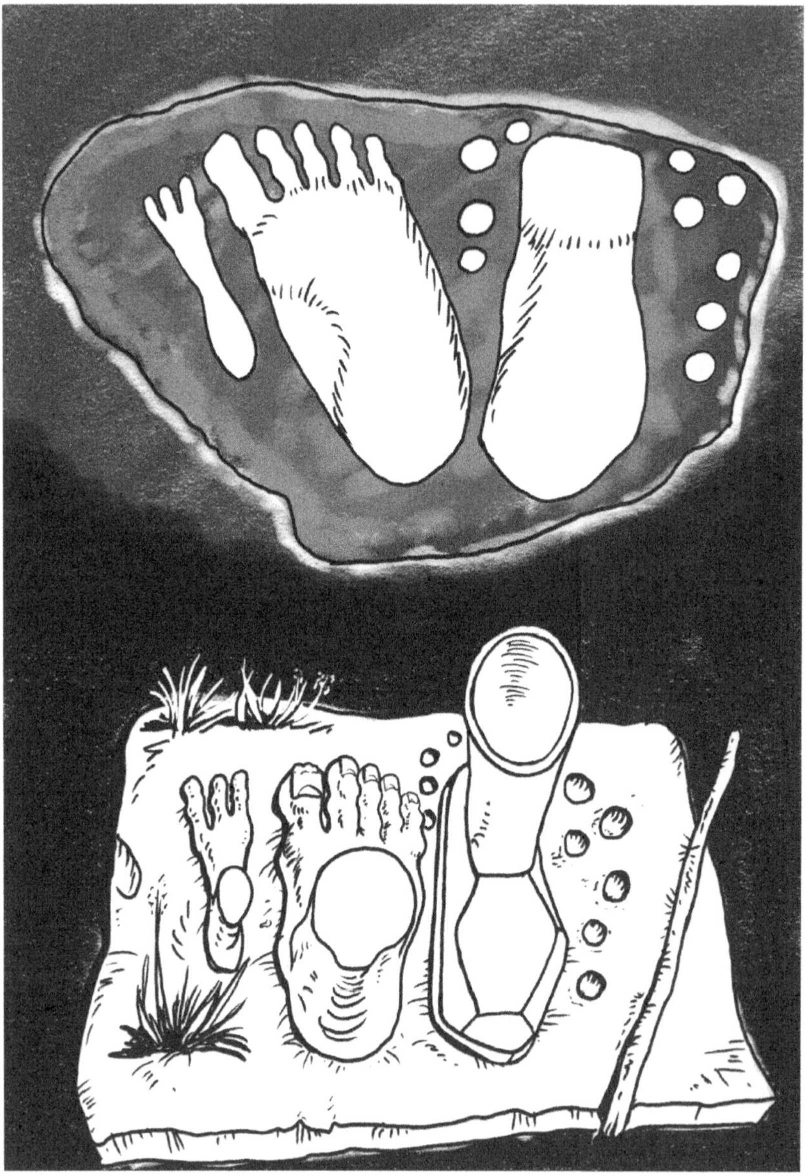

on our feet until we were forced to wear them in our teenage years. So this is the foot of a Bronze Age warrior/sailor/hunter/ farmer. Juxtaposed beside the strange little three toed footprint, it clearly says “this is the little man’s footprint, and I’ve put mine beside it to give you an idea of the size and shape difference”.

Besides these two bare footprints is another shape, one that really seems out of place at first. It’s of a similar size to the big human footprint, but there are no toes indicated, which are very clearly indicated for the barefoot ones. As soon as I looked at the unpainted carving, on the right of the rock, I instantly saw a boot print.

It has a distinct heel at the back, and then it spreads out exactly as a left foot boot print would do. How do I know this? Well a figurative artist like myself constantly draws feet and boots of every kind.

Human feet, and their shoes and boots, are always relatively straight on the inside edge, and they curve out and broaden on the outside edge of the foot or boot. What this tells us is that this boot print is facing towards the man and the little man.

So how do I interpret these prints pictographically?

I believe there’s a really good chance that this carving was based on actual footprints left behind at a meeting of humans, a small dwarf like creature who beckoned them to the meeting, and a space faring being the size of a man, who was wearing heeled boots.

Boots like these were totally unknown to the Bronze Age people of Scandinavia, as they would have been anachronistic even in the Viking Age 3000 years later.

So this side of the message rock is saying “we walked to where the starship had landed, and where the little man was beckoning, and then another being walked out of the starship. He appeared to be a man, with very unusual feet, (and undoubtedly very unusual clothing), and we talked with them both.”

You will understand now why I call this the smoking gun. I can't imagine a clearer story of first contact, written in a language that could be interpreted so many thousand years later, by somebody from a completely different language and time.

And yet there's even more.

When I first started to interpret the mystery of this rock, I noticed that there were a number of those little cup marks to the right of the three different footprints, and I straightaway thought, 'these really look like a group of stars! I wonder if these could be representing an actual constellation?'.

I love looking at the stars, and I have always been greatly interested in spaceflight and astronautics, but I have to admit I've also been mostly ignorant of the patterns of constellations. I just haven't spent any time working at remembering them, except for one which all Australians know, the Southern Cross.

So feeling a little shamefaced, I wrote to Paul Wallis and asked him if he recognized a constellation in this pattern of cup marks. Nothing came immediately to his mind, except that he concurred with me that they definitely look like a constellation of some kind. He mentioned the constellation Cygnus, which plays a part in his new book, but we both couldn't see an obvious connection.

What happened next amazed me. I was browsing online looking for constellation information, and came across a famous Bronze Age artifact called the 'Nebra Disk'.

This fabulous object was discovered in 1999, and I actually remember reading something about it back in that period. It turns out that the disc is from somewhere between 1800 and 1600 BC. The really extraordinary thing is that scholars are sure that this disc represents the sun, the moon, and a star map of the constellation Pleiades.

I excitedly grabbed the Mound People book from my library, and turned back to page 137.

There I saw the same constellation, Pleiades, as plain as day! It looks like people in the Bronze Age had quite a fascination with that constellation.

There is another connection that is even spookier.
Despite the fact that the little grey alien is so entrenched in the minds of most people as the standard inhabitants of UFOs, if you read the lore, you find that there is a vast array of different types of beings encountered, some extremely odd looking to say the least. Probably the least odd are the reported group of visitors called the Nordics.

The Nordics are reported to be a benevolent race of very humanlike advanced beings, looking like some kind of Swedish cliche, very beautiful, blue or green eyed, tall and with long blonde or white hair.
It appears that people who have met these beings are always informed telepathically that they come from the Pleiades constellation!

So to conclude this chapter, and to metaphorically blow the smoke from the barrel of my smoking gun, I will imaginatively retell this 3000 year old pictographic story as I interpret it.
"We were out with all the crew sailing in our warship one day. We saw something in the sky, very bright. It reminded us of a ship as it sailed along, yet it seemed to be made of metal rather than timber. We were awestruck and brought our ship to a stop.

This flying ship silently came down and landed on the shore opposite us.
A door opened in the side of the flying ship, and a strange little man stepped out. He walked towards us, and we saw that he

seemed to be beckoning, urging us to come to him. He was very small yet sturdy. He was wearing clothes, but we could tell he was a male. His head was much larger than his little body, and he had a strange long nose and a big chin.
Although we were all very afraid, as warriors we were not about to show it, so we rowed our ship to the bank. We stepped off our ship, and as we did we saw a man, who looked somewhat like us, step out of the strange and extremely brightly lit doorway of this flying ship.

He walked towards us, and as he approached, we saw that he was tall, a bit taller than we were, and on his body he wore clothes. The cloth however was so finely woven that it looked as if it was perhaps the skin of a fish. His feet seemed as if they were carved out of wood, yet they had that same fish skin quality as his clothes. Strangely, we could hear him talking to us, yet his lips didn't move. He explained that he and his people were moving into our country soon, but that if we would make pacts of peace together, we would greatly benefit from their guidance and skills, and we would give our children to each other in marriage.
He told us that his people were not originally from the Earth, but that they had come a very long way from the stars. He said that his ship was a star ship, that could sail far above the Earth, even back to where he had come from amongst the stars.
He drew a constellation of stars on the ground, and we were aware of this pattern.
We spoke of many things, and we believe now that some strange things happened to us then, that we can't quite remember.

The two beings re-entered their ship, the bright door closed, and the ship silently floated up into the sky, and then went straight up

like a streak of lightning. Of course we were excited, and keen to tell our families, and our people, what had happened.
I am an artist of the people, a craftsman who makes objects from bronze and gold, and I sometimes carve very important stories on our sacred rock places.
When the two beings left, I saw their footprints in the clay of the riverbank, and I cut that piece out and preserved it. I have copied those prints carefully in this carving, and you will see that the little man had been barefoot, and that his feet were very strange, almost like a bird, with only three toes and a long thin heel.
I have carved my own footprint so that you can see the difference in our size, and I have carved the strange footprint of the tall man beside mine, so that you can see that he was facing me. As I was talking to the tall man, the little man stood beside me and watched. He seemed to be of a very different race, but he was working with the tall man as an equal. We saw no other crew on their starship. I have carved our story on this rock, so that our children and our children's children will remember this wondrous encounter. We send you our greetings, children of the future, and hope that one day you will know more about who these people are who visited us from the sky".

I too send my greetings and look forward to the next time we meet!

David Lovegrove.

Made in the USA
Las Vegas, NV
07 February 2026

41207243R00173